Valleys of Song

Valleys of Song

Music and Society
in Wales
1840–1914

&

GARETH WILLIAMS

UNIVERSITY OF WALES PRESS
CARDIFF
1998

Contents

Illustrations

Preface

వు

It is a privilege as well as an obligation to record the several debts I have incurred in writing this book. Professor Hywel Teifi Edwards and Dr Rhidian Griffiths read the typescript in its entirety, and time and again they rescued me from elementary and embarrassing gaffes, some of which I fear may still have eluded even their vigilant and authoritative scrutiny. Among the many others whose contributions ranged from reading specific chapters to sustaining me with encouragement and references I particularly thank: Asa Briggs, Andy Croll, Lyn Davies, Trevor Herbert, Jeff Hill, Richard Holt, Ieuan Gwynedd Jones, Peter Lambert, Pierre Lanfranchi, Tony Mason, Paul O'Leary, Roger Price, Ken Richards, Michael Roberts, Dave Russell, Dai Smith, Eugen Weber and Chris Williams.

I am grateful to my departmental colleagues for lightening my teaching load and allowing me two clear semesters of study leave for research and writing; the expenses incurred thereby were defrayed by bursaries from the University of Wales Aberystwyth David Hughes Parry and Senate Research Funds. I have good reason to thank too the staff of several libraries, especially Huw Walters and other friends at the National Library of Wales, Elizabeth Bennett of the South Wales Miners' Library, Emma Lile at the Museum of Welsh Life, Cardiff, and Alun Prescott of Aberdare Central Library's reference department. Like all historians I have been dependent on the work of others who can only inadequately be acknowledged in the footnotes and bibliography; in addition to those already mentioned, Dulais Rhys, John Hugh Thomas, Huw Williams and Christopher Wiltshire will recognize the fruits of their own researches in the present work, and must likewise be absolved from any responsibility for the interpretation I have put on them.

At the University of Wales Press I was exceedingly fortunate in the erudition of my watchful copy-editor Henry Maas, and in the professional expertise and good advice of Ceinwen Jones and Liz Powell. That I was able to submit a readable typescript at all is due entirely to the word-processing skills of Dorothy Evans whose unfailing good humour and calm efficiency in producing endless drafts, emendations and revisions exhausts my superlatives but not my enormous gratitude to her and her family.

My final debts are even more difficult to quantify. In a profound sense they defy adequate record and repayment. Mary did not create a database or compile the index, but without her love and support the book would never have been written. The dedication is to the memory of Enid and Emlyn Williams, amateur musicians born into the social and cultural environment described in these pages, and shining examples of it.

G.W.W.
September 1998

Acknowledgements

శు

The author and publishers gratefully acknowledge the following sources for permission to reproduce illustrations in this volume:

University of Wales Swansea Library, South Wales Coalfield Collection: p.187

The National Library of Wales for illustrations from Frederic Griffith, *Notable Welsh Musicians of Today* (London, 1896): pp. 41, 92, 124, 158

The National Library of Wales: pp. 71, 165

The Western Mail: p. 184

Treorchy Library, Rhondda Cynon Taff County Borough: p. 127; and with Mr C. Batstone: pp.131, 139

Aberdare Library, Rhondda Cynon Taff County Borough: pp. 43, 55

Merthyr Tydfil County Borough Council Library Service: pp. 69, 107

Introduction

ɞ

An English visitor to the National Eisteddfod at Merthyr Tydfil in 1881 noted how interest

> culminated in the choral competitions . . . On the last day . . . six choirs entered, having an aggregate of one thousand four hundred and fifty-six voices . . . Ten thousand people passed through the turnstiles of the park, and six-hundred pounds was taken in admissions . . . It took three hours to hear these six choirs sing. During all this time the vast audience remained standing, packed with a dense pressure, suffering evidently the greatest physical discomfort; yet orderly, eager, electrical . . . Here were the common people themselves, crowding to no brutal sport, not even to clap-trap or flimsy entertainment, but to genuine art. It was just the consummation for which social reformers sigh . . . [1]

The crowds followed the choirs because in the second half of the nineteenth century towns and villages in many parts of Wales, in the populous industrial valleys of the south in particular, were the sites of a range of musical – instrumental, orchestral, above all else choral – activity quite remarkable in its intensity. It galvanized communities, mobilized armies of supporters and inflamed local passions to a white heat. One of its crucibles, clearly, was Merthyr, where the writer Glyn Jones was born in 1905 and on whom its fervent choralism left an ineradicable impression, so that when in the 1930s he attended the Three Valleys Festival at Mountain Ash, he could still be moved by the massed voices:

> Their first song, soft and sand-flow smooth – my blood
> Broke into antish uproar, my tight throat locked
> Hearing that black-and-white-sexed fanshaped choir-
> Keyboard keening the sweet Handelian act.[2]

In pre-1914 Wales, 'Handelian acts' were not always so sweet, and could often inspire behaviour that was the despair of social reformers. 'Thousands crowded into the pavilion and excitement ran high', reported the *Musical Times*'s correspondent at the National Eisteddfod held at Newport in 1897, 'for next after a football match Welshmen enjoy a choral fight'.[3] An estimated fourteen thousand were present for that particular encounter, and as it turned out they would witness one of the choral upsets of the decade as 'the great fighting choir of Merthyr', the Philharmonic conducted by the inflammable Dan Davies, was defeated by pretenders from Abersychan and Pontypool in a sulphurous atmosphere of bitterness, threats and violent controversy that transfixed not only the Welsh press but the London papers too.[4]

These rivalries – far removed from their roots in Nonconformity and temperance – whose propensity for mayhem has no equivalent even in the working-class musical bastions of Yorkshire and Lancashire,[5] not only aroused the passions of those directly involved, but electrified their audiences as well, massive crowds like the fifteen thousand straining, with the sixty reporters present, to catch every note of the main choral competition at Merthyr in 1901. It was only then that the immense audiences at these gladiatorial eisteddfod contests came to be exceeded by the crowds at the sporting events they so much resembled: the twenty thousand packed into the pavilion in Swansea in 1891 far outnumbered the eight thousand spectators at the rugby international at Newport earlier in the year; and while there were fifteen thousand at the Cardiff Arms Park to watch Wales beat England in January 1893, there were twenty thousand at Pontypridd in August to hear John Price's Rhymney choir defeat five others, each numbering between a hundred and fifty and two hundred voices.

The test pieces on that occasion were compositions by Edward Stephen ('Tanymarian'), Cherubini and Mendelssohn, whose dramatic choruses were particularly savoured by Welsh choristers and audiences. His oratorio *St Paul*, which had to be prepared in its entirety for the choral competition at the Llanelli National Eisteddfod in 1903, was sufficiently well known to the twenty thousand present that large sections of the 'enormous, unruly crowd' accompanied the eight competing choirs in a kind of collective sing-along, even as the familiar choruses were being performed. Earlier, the 'huge, noisy audience' had smoked and shouted uncouth remarks during the speech by the bishop of St David's until the harassed prelate was forced to draw his remarks to a premature close.[6] There was gambling ('Six to one on Llanelli' were the odds shouted at Aberdare in 1885) and fighting among supporters on the rear benches at the Swansea National in 1891.[7] At the local level – for the National event was merely the apex of a broad-based infrastructure of chapel, village, town and regional eisteddfodau – mob law, occasionally requiring police intervention, was the rule rather than the exception in the cauldron that was competitive choralism in Wales from 1880 to the First World War. And running through it all, engulfing singers and spectators, rippling and eddying out to the furthest corners of their communities, was music that ennobled and elevated even as it enthralled and excited.

This ardent choralism intrigued onlookers. The representative of the *Musical Herald* who in 1911 was staggered to discover that there were sixty-nine choral entries at that year's Carmarthen National Eisteddfod, compared with the mere seven when the festival had last been held there in 1867, was forced to declare that 'Wales has become one of the great choral nations of the earth'.[8] What John Graham, the special correspondent of the *Musical Herald*, rightly characterized as 'the sudden rise of Welsh choralism'[9] intrigued the Welsh themselves, and it became a focus for national debate, discussion, criticism and, often, condemnation.

Curiously it was a phenomenon which, with very few exceptions,[10] has intrigued Welsh historians rather less. While many facets of the political, religious, economic and social history of nineteenth- and twentieth-century Wales have in recent years attracted scholarly attention, the role of music-making as a prominent constituent of local consciousness and significant shaper of national identity remains relatively unexplored.

There have been valuable studies of specific aspects of Welsh music, such as those by Osian Ellis on the history of the harp and Hywel Teifi Edwards on the mid-Victorian eisteddfod, by David Allsobrook on the Council of Welsh Music under Sir Henry Walford Davies and by Trevor Herbert on brass bands. Our knowledge of Welsh folk-song has been extended by the researches of Roy Saer, Daniel Huws, Meredydd Evans and Phyllis Kinney, and I am deeply conscious of my indebtedness to the contributions to the history of Welsh music publishing and hymnody by Huw Williams and Rhidian Griffiths. We sorely need more studies of music in the localities, like those of John Hugh Thomas for Swansea, the late John Haydn Davies for the Rhondda, Lyn Davies and Rhianydd Morgan for the Aman Valley, and Andy Croll's fine doctoral dissertation on 'civilising the urban' in late-nineteenth-century Merthyr, which we must devoutly hope will see early publication in order that the dominant seventh chord that is David Morgans's survey of the *Music and Musicians of Merthyr and District* (1922) may be brought to a fittingly splendid resolution.[11]

The structure of this book is roughly as follows. Chapters 1, 4 and 8 assess the contributions as composers, critics, enablers and reformers of Brinley Richards, John Thomas ('Pencerdd Gwalia'), Joseph Parry, D. Emlyn Evans and David Jenkins. Chapter 2 examines the seminal influence of the temperance and tonic sol-fa movements, the emergence of the *cymanfa ganu* and the drive to establish musical literacy and a reformed hymnody, a programme fuelled by the inexhaustible energies of the Revd John Roberts ('Ieuan Gwyllt'). Chapter 7 looks at the perceived crisis which afflicted and eventually redirected Welsh choralism at the beginning of the twentieth century, while chapter 9 examines the rougher side of the competitive urge before proceeding to a consideration of the resonance and repertoire of that emblematic Welsh musical institution, the male choir.

These developments are located in a specific context in core chapters 3, 4, 5 and 6 where, taking my cue from Professor Gwyn Jones who 'would put nothing past those impassioned music-masters who control the ocean-swells and avalanches of three-valley chapel *Messiahs*',[12] I offer a more detailed depiction of the emergence and growth of choral singing in the tumultuous, historically central iron- and coal-producing communities of Merthyr, Aberdare and the Rhondda.

I look, occasionally, elsewhere: eastwards to Rhymney, Tredegar and Ebbw Vale, west to the Swansea Valley, and, too infrequently I fear, to mid and north Wales. The remarkable musical activity that once energized Builth Wells and Llanidloes, and the rich choral nurseries of industrial north-east and north-west Wales deserve further study in their own right. I venture as far afield as the Crystal Palace with Caradog's South Wales Choral Union and to Chicago with Tom Stephens's Rhondda Gleemen. I am well aware that Madam Clara Novello Davies's Welsh Ladies' Choir won in Chicago, too, in 1893, as they did at the Paris Exhibition in 1900; though probably not sufficiently aware for critics of my 'brazen intellectual male bias'.[13] Nevertheless, it is a matter of historical fact that the male choir attained, and has retained, a higher profile in Wales than anywhere else in these islands. I will be engaging, implicitly rather than explicitly, with issues that have featured prominently in the recent discourse of professional historians, but I confess to being less interested in the construction of specific gender identities than in the more general process of cultural production, one in which performers and publics are partners rather than providers and recipients.

My primary aim has been to recover, in all its rich profusion, some of the enormous musical vitality of these south Wales valleys, from oratorio to amateur opera, from drum-and-fife bands to working-class orchestras, from temperance anthems to the palace of varieties. The real challenge, when 'studies of phenomena that are by definition popular tend to be expressed in terms that even highly-educated non-specialists have great difficulty in following',[14] is to satisfy the academic rigour of the research councils without sounding too ridiculous in the ranks of the Treorchy Male Choir or the Cwmaman Institute Amateur Operatic Society. What follows, therefore, is not a deconstruction of the Revd Eli Jenkins's polly-gartered 'Praise the Lord! we are a musical nation', but an attempt to answer the question posed by another of *Milk Wood*'s voices, 'How's the tenors in Dowlais?'[15]

This is their story.

1

Songs of Wales

৩০

1. The Land of Harp and Feathers

'A few years ago', remarked the music journal *Y Gerddorfa* (The Music Place) in 1873, 'there were very few choirs [in Wales] from Holyhead to Cardiff: now they can be counted in their hundreds.'[1] Welsh choralism was a recent and sudden phenomenon, for it can safely be said that in the early nineteenth century Wales was musically in a state of torpor.

The music of the Middle Ages had not been transmitted with the loving care of the poetry, and its legacy was kept alive by harpists – frequently blind, for this affliction was often a qualification for expertise on the harp – who specialized in *penillion* singing and devising variations on popular melodies. The best-known musicians born in Wales in the eighteenth century spent most of their time outside it in fashionable and courtly circles. Typical in both his sightlessness and his aristocratic milieu was John Parry ('Parry Ddall': Blind Parry) of Ruabon who gave concerts in London, the university cities and Dublin, was patronized by Wales's greatest landowner Sir Watkin Williams Wynne, played to Handel and inspired Thomas Gray to write 'The Bard'. 'Mr Parry', wrote Gray in a letter of 1757, 'has been here and scratched out such ravishing blind harmony and tunes of a thousand years old . . . enough to choak you.'[2]

Parry was one of the three harpists primarily responsible for the task of collecting and publishing Welsh melodies that began in the eighteenth century. It was again symptomatic of the poverty of resources within Wales that each collection was published outside it. To Blind Parry's own *Antient British Music* (1742, with a second, important, edition in 1793) and *British Harmony* (1781), published a year before his death, ought to be added two others, Edward Jones's ('Bardd y Brenin', The King's Poet), *Musical and Poetical Relics of the Welsh Bards* (1784) and *The Bardic Museum* (1802). Jones was as much an antiquarian as a musician and became harpist to the Prince of Wales, later George IV, in 1788; a sworn enemy of Iolo

Morganwg, he was a link with the later eisteddfod movement by virtue of his presence at the historic – if unhistorical – Gorsedd held by Iolo on Primrose Hill in 1792 and incorporated into the eisteddfod's pageantry from 1858. The other collector was another John Parry ('Bardd Alaw', 1776–1851) who modulated from the harp to playing in a militia band, became musical director of the Vauxhall Gardens concerts in London, wrote music for plays at Drury Lane, and published collections of tunes for military bands (1807) and for combinations of harp or piano, flute and cello (1805), *Welsh Melodies,* which went through three editions between 1822 and 1829, and *The Welsh Harper* in two volumes, 1839 and 1848, essentially a reprint of Jones's *Bardic Relics* with some of his own additions. And sometime in the early nineteenth century, thanks probably to Bardd Alaw, the art of *penillion* singing to the harp – the superimposing of a sung descant above a constantly repeated melody on the accompanying instrument – was concocted in its recognizably modern form; by the time Owain Alaw's *Gems of Welsh Melody* was published in 1860, what was essentially an unsophisticated, even artless, activity was believed to be 'of the hoariest antiquity', though its transformation into something more elaborate and uniquely Welsh was a recent and self-conscious innovation, a classic instance of 'the invention of tradition'.[3]

More prolific, and chronologically and substantively a stronger link with the musical ferment of the second half of the nineteenth century in Wales was John Thomas ('Pencerdd Gwalia', 1826–1913), who was born in Bridgend and won a triple harp at twelve years of age at the Abergavenny eisteddfod in 1838. His music was drawn to the attention of Byron's daughter, Ada, Lady Lovelace, who sent him to the Royal Academy of Music where he spent six years learning harmony from Beethoven's pupil Cipriani Potter, and studying the harp with J. B. Chatterton. During the 1850s he toured Europe from France to Russia, and met Rossini and Meyerbeer. No one, remarked his obituarist, can have played before more crowned heads than John Thomas, implying with some justification that it is difficult to see what else he needed to do to have been knighted, given his accomplishments and celebrity in high places. He became harpist to Queen Victoria and professor of the harp at the Royal Academy in 1872, the year in which, a sign of the times in his native land, he established the London Welsh Choral Union. He worked extensively for musical and other publications, notably the *Musical Times,* *Seren Gomer* and *Myvyrian Archaeology,* and composed prolifically, his more substantial works including a harp concerto, several symphonies and overtures, vocal music in various forms from operas to cantatas, two

of which *Llewelyn* and *The Bride of Neath Valley* were first performed at
the Swansea (1863) and Chester (1866) eisteddfodau.[4] His four volumes
of Welsh melodies (1862–74) began life as a two-volume collection of
Songs of Wales in 1862, but this never attained the popularity of the single
volume of the same name published in 1873 by Brinley Richards which
would become as common in Welsh homes as the Bible up to the First
World War, and secure for the Christian name Brinley a popularity to
equal that of Handel and Haydn.[5]

A tall, pale, thin man with a small head, a high forehead and large dark
eyes, Brinley Richards (1817–85) was the best-known Welsh musician of
the nineteenth century, after Joseph Parry. Born in Carmarthen and
intended for a career in medicine, it was the award by Bardd Alaw at an
eisteddfod at Cardiff Castle in 1834 of a prize for a set of variations on
the Welsh Melody 'Llwyn Onn' (The Ash Grove) that deflected him from
the medical direction. The duke of Newcastle came forward to provide
the patronage necessary, as John Thomas had discovered, to pursue a
career at the Royal Academy of Music, and future sponsors would
include the earl of Westmorland, who in 1823 had founded it, and the
countess of Beauchamp. With such encouragement and finance he went
to Paris, where he took piano lessons from Chopin, cultivated the
friendship of César Franck and returned to the RAM and to recognition
as one of the finest pianists of his generation. He arranged the
compositions of the masters for piano in three volumes and wrote some
ornate pieces of his own, one of them dedicated to Chopin, including a
piano concerto. But his fame rests partly on the song 'God Bless the
Prince of Wales', to words of 'Ceiriog' (John Ceiriog Hughes) at his most
sycophantic, written for the wedding of the heir apparent in 1863, and
even more on his *Songs of Wales* for solo voice and piano, published ten
years later in the enthusiastic wake of the triumph at the Crystal Palace
of the South Wales Choral Union, a success which induced him 'to offer
the present work as the best proof of the musical genius of my country'.[6]

Between them, Brinley and the Pencerdd had the Welsh musical world
stitched up. As rector, later archdeacon, John Griffiths demanded in
1867, England should really thank the Welsh for giving her such inspired
artists: 'We have produced the finest pianist in London if not the world –
Brinley Richards. Who sweeps the strings of the harp like Pencerdd
Gwalia . . . whose sweet tones . . . go down and grapple with the deepest
feelings of the human heart?'[7]

Whether through innate modesty, or a great deal to be modest about,
Brinley Richards never wrote anything that could remotely be described as

abstruse; he eschewed even the mildest chromaticism in favour of element-ary diatonic sweetness. The arrangements in *Songs of Wales*, intentionally 'very simple and designed for the average solo pianist' are at times attenu-ated to the point of emaciation, deliberately resisting the arpeggios and ornaments of which he was capable as a virtuoso pianist. His Welsh credentials looked bare too, having trodden too well the familiar path of the almost denationalized London Welshman. He confessed to the English critic Joseph Bennett 'how much I have lost, and how very little I have gained, by my connection (with) and effort on behalf of Welsh (eisteddfod) meetings. I owe Wales little beyond my birth, for everything I have obtained in my professional life I owe to England alone.'[8]

Yet this Anglican, middle-class, non-Welsh-speaking social climber was not indifferent to Welsh musical fortunes and careers, and his finger can be found in most of the musical pies of the time. He was one of the first to identify the compositional ability of Joseph Parry, and he sought to promote it; he was warmly in favour of the new University College at Aberystwyth; he adjudicated at the Crystal Palace meetings in 1872 (allegedly shouting 'Listen to the band' as the choir conducted by Griffith Rhys Jones ('Caradog') went out of tune), and was ever support-ive of emerging Welsh talent, whether students in London like the tenor Ben Davies, or the ten-year-old David (Vaughan) Thomas, to whom Brinley awarded the prize for playing the harmonium at the last National Eisteddfod he attended in 1883.[9] A frequent visitor to Wales as an adjudicator, his knowledge of Welsh music was nevertheless minimal, and, to a forthright and informed critic like D. Emlyn Evans who was well read in his country's musical literature, Brinley's much-touted and frequent lectures on Welsh music were little more than a farrago of ill-informed and half-baked notions derived from second hand.[10]

Even so, Brinley could not fail to be struck by the transformation of Welsh musical life during his lifetime and by the strides being made in choral singing. He claimed there had been no Welsh choirs at all at the Beaumaris eisteddfod of 1832, where the only vocalists were harp singers. If there was any recognizable Welsh music it was mostly harp music, and the harpists were in London. One of Brinley Richards's enduring accomplishments was to oversee this shift from a harp and *penillion* culture, artificially constructed for the delectation of metro-politan sophisticates, to a democratic popular choral culture rooted in the lives of ordinary people; and though he contributed nothing to the burgeoning Welsh choral repertoire, he was instrumental in promoting the idea of the evening concert of vocal and orchestral music.

The forum for achieving this was the eisteddfod. But only over the dead body of the Revd John Roberts ('Ieuan Gwyllt'), a commanding figure in the religious, musical and literary life of mid-nineteenth-century Wales who viewed both Pencerdd Gwalia and Brinley Richards as dangerous purveyors of dissolute European ideas, Italianate in the case of the former, while Brinley was irredeemably French. Gwyllt considered it futile to look to them for genuinely Welsh compositions, for their musical and social conditioning wholly prevented them from capturing in their work the peculiar melancholy of the Welsh; it was to Noncon-formity, temperance and the *cymanfa ganu* (hymn-singing festival) that he preferred to attribute the improved health of Welsh music, to the moral and musical education and social and organizational discipline of the chapel, not the competitive, mercenary eisteddfod.[11]

Chapel and eisteddfod were the key institutions in the Welsh musical renaissance from the 1860s, but of the several developments constitutive of that effervescence – a concert tradition, the rise of glees, cantatas and dramatic oratorios as forms of composition and performance, the (slower) growth of instrumental music – none was intrinsically Welsh, any more than the triple harp which originated in sixteenth-century Italy and which Brinley Richards, with the support of the Celtophile Lady Llanover, sought unavailingly to promote as the traditional native 'Welsh' harp against the European orchestral pedal harp favoured by the Pencerdd.[12] The 'land of song' would rest on the two pillars of Noncon-formity and industrialization, but the Welsh became a singing people no less as a result of influences emanating from England and Europe, the salon culture of the middle class and their more mundane concern to extend forms of rational recreation to the lower orders.

Cantata is an Italian word of Latin origin, and a musical form most fruitfully explored by the Germans Buxtehude, Bach and Telemann. A cantata culture established a firm foothold in Wales in the 1860s through the medium of the National Eisteddfod. It was launched by Owain Alaw's royalist *Tywysog Cymru* (The Prince of Wales, 1862) with an unctuous libretto by Ceiriog, and by Pencerdd Gwalia's *Llewelyn* (1863). Written for the Swansea National Eisteddfod of 1863, its première collapsed in chaos when one of the pillars supporting the gallery in the pavilion broke, others cracked, and the crowd panicked. It received its first performance the following June in St James's Hall, London, with a choir from the Royal Academy of Music under Henry Leslie and a sixty-strong orchestra from the Royal Italian Opera, a performance which impressed even metropolitan critics generally disposed to dismiss all things Welsh with amused contempt. It cost a guinea to buy, however, and as *Y Cerddor Cymreig* (edited by Ieuan Gwyllt) protested to the composer, it was 'too dear, my friend, for the colliers, miners, quarrymen, craftsmen and labourers of Wild Wales'.[13]

This was followed by a cluster of compositions like Owain Alaw's *Gŵyl Gwalia*, J. D. Jones's *Llys Arthur* (Arthur's Court), Edward Lawrence of Merthyr's *Siege of Harlech*, premièred at Llandudno in 1864, and most popular of all, another of Pencerdd Gwalia's products, *The Bride of Neath Valley* (Chester, 1866) and Eos Bradwen's *Owain Glyndwr* (Rhyl, 1870). These were all works based on Welsh melodies, a habit that Joseph Parry would find difficult to shake off, complemented by the fresher compositions of a new generation of Welsh composers who found a facility for churning out glees, part-songs, duets, quartets and anthems with exhausting frequency. Joseph Parry picked up twenty prizes with compositions of this kind at the National Eisteddfod between 1861 and 1866 (doubtless more, had his entries in 1865 not been lost between Pennsylvania and Aberystwyth), and he was only the tip of an iceberg consisting of W. T. Rees ('Alaw Ddu'), D. W. Lewis, D. Emlyn Evans, Gwilym Gwent and John Thomas, Llanwrtyd. The popular but at least original song-writers R. S. Hughes, William Davies, D. Pughe Evans and John Henry had yet to arrive – no prize was offered for a Welsh song between 1860 and 1868 – to alleviate the pressure on the constant use of the patriotic melodies and folk-songs with which Wales, it appeared, was extraordinarily well endowed.

The publication of traditional Welsh airs, which had its origins in the eighteenth-century collections of Blind Parry and Edward Jones, and, later, of Bardd Alaw, entered a new phase in 1844 with the publication of Maria Jane Williams's prize-winning (Abergavenny, 1837) *Ancient National Airs of Gwent and Morganwg* (Glamorgan), a copy of which was presented to a graciously mystified Queen Victoria. *The Cambrian Minstrel* (1845) by John Thomas ('Ieuan Ddu') and Bardd Alaw's *Welsh Harper* (1848) provided the platform for a significant popularization in the 1860s, a staging that conceals decades of Welsh melodic self-consciousness; the collections of Owain Alaw and Pencerdd Gwalia can now be seen as harbingers of Brinley Richards's historic volume of 1873.

Self-conscious but not yet self-confident; and as always, an English or at least metropolitan approval was sought first. In 1862 the Pencerdd presented a concert at St James's Hall where he deployed a choir of 420 harps to perform his own arrangements of Welsh airs like 'Ar Hyd y Nos', 'Men of Harlech' and 'Hob-y-Deri-Dando'. With Edith Wynne as soloist and Sir Julius Benedict conducting, this logistical feat was repeated on several capital occasions in the course of the next two years.[14] The popularity of these melodies in London legitimized and reinforced their appeal at home, leading Brinley Richards to assert that Welsh airs were among the world's best, and the poet 'Talhaiarn', who had already seen off Ieuan Gwyllt's protestations that 'Hob-y-Deri-Dando' was immoral, to proclaim that the 'Marseillaise' paled alongside 'Men of Harlech'.[15] These airs, the more rousing set to ballads recounting heroic events in Welsh history, soon made their eisteddfod appearance as test pieces and as concert items for popular soloists of the day like Edith Wynne, Lewis Thomas, Llew Llwyfo, Robert Rees ('Eos Morlais') of Dowlais and, from the same musical nursery, the young Megan Watts, whose repertoire on her 1865 tour of Wales, arranged by her trustees to finance her further musical education, included a good deal of Handel ('I Know that my Redeemer Liveth', 'Oh had I Jubal's Lyre', 'From Mighty Kings', etc.), Haydn and Rossini, judiciously admixed with Pencerdd Gwalia's 'Llewelyn and Gelert', that princely saga about one man and his dog, as well as songs by Owain Alaw and other Welsh airs.[16]

Within the next few years London audiences would encounter a new kind of Welsh musical experience, in the robust form of the South Wales Choral Union conducted by a self-educated blacksmith turned publican, whose triumph at the Crystal Palace accelerated the cultural drift already under way in eisteddfodau from literary competition to the more accessible, involving, exciting and democratic choral concerts.[17] It was the developments of the 1860s that laid the foundations of that choral leap forward exemplified by the appearance of the first journal devoted to musical affairs to last more than a year (until 1873),[18] *Y Cerddor Cymreig*. It was launched in Merthyr Tydfil in March 1861, and its first print run of 4,000 briskly sold out.[19] Its first number ran items on the history of music, principles of harmony, the musical press and biographies, soon to be followed by a glossary of Welsh terms on vocalization: thus, for instance the larynx, *y brefant*; the glottis, *y beudeg*; and the epiglottis, *yr arfeudeg*.[20] It reported on the Three Choirs Festival and the London scene, thereby acquainting Welsh readers with the Sacred Harmonic Society's programme of masses by Haydn and Beethoven, and the Mozart *Requiem*. They were also introduced, perhaps for the first time in most cases, to the world of professional opera, and heard of Meyerbeer's *Le Prophète*, Donizetti's *La Favorita* and Verdi's *Rigoletto*.

It was clear too, from the *Cerddor Cymreig*, that there was already significant choral activity in Wales itself. At Easter 1861 the 140 members of the Swansea Choral Society which drew on choristers from Pontardawe to Llanelli gave their first concert under Dr Evan Davies, who in December conducted Haydn's *The Creation* in Aberdare, Merthyr and Cardiff as well as Swansea, and in 1864 headed up the Swansea Festival, at which he conducted *Messiah*. In April 1861 the Gwent Music Society of Rhymney gave their sixteenth annual concert of glees, choruses and part-songs. At Whitsun that year two Aberdare choirs competed at Pontypridd for a prize of £8, won by the choir conducted by Caradog, who went on to share the prize at the Aberdare National Eisteddfod some weeks later with the Dowlais Temperance Choir, with 'Thanks be to God' from Mendelssohn's *Elijah*.[21] The musical topography of what Caradog in 1878 would call 'the land of song'[22] could already be discerned.

In numerical terms it was an unsteady but accelerating growth. Only one choir appeared at the Aberystwyth eisteddfod in 1865, but in 1873 there were six entries for the chief choral competition in Mold, and at Newport in 1897 fifteen mixed and ten male choirs. There were seven choirs in all competing at the Carmarthen National Eisteddfod of 1867; when it was next held there, in 1911, there were sixty-nine. Put another way, there was no Welsh representation among the choirs competing at the 1867 Paris Exhibition, but there were two male choirs and a ladies' choir from Wales at the Paris Exhibition of 1900, as there had also been at the Chicago World's Fair in 1893.[23] Solo singers followed the same trajectory: at Aberdare in 1861 there were four entries each for the soprano and tenor competitions, singing arias by Verdi in each case: at the 1891 Swansea National there were thirty-three sopranos and fifty-three tenors, as well as seventy-two baritones, seventy-one basses, and twenty-four contraltos. And at Swansea's evening concerts John Ambrose Lloyd's 'sacred cantata' *Gweddi Habacuc*, the winning composition at the 1851 Porthmadog eisteddfod, was performed.

These competitions and performances testify to a musical scene that was already active, particularly in the populous older industrial districts of Merthyr, Rhymney, Aberdare and the Swansea Valley where choral unions were by 1860 already well established. The reformed eisteddfod and the imported concert tradition provided the institutional framework for the expression of a wider musical talent than that permitted by the chapels. To Ieuan Gwyllt Nonconformity and temperance were the engines of musical education and growth, and he was disposed to castigate stage rhetoric about Wales and its language by people who knew neither; the nation's culture, he firmly believed, was the product and property of people whose names and faces were never heard or seen on the eisteddfod platform.[24] As an assessment, albeit a cantankerous one, it was not far wrong. The moral imperatives and social networks of Nonconformity and temperance were the seedbeds of the choral tradition, with Swansea, Aberdare and Merthyr the focus of striking activity from the middle of the nineteenth century onwards.[25] In these places a mature musical life was already in existence, in Aberdare from the 1850s and in Swansea even earlier.

2. Swansea Sounds

Since the late eighteenth century Swansea had enjoyed a thriving associational life linked to the gentry 'season' which attracted actors and musicians from the west of England. In 1805 a catch club was established for singing rounds and glees, and in 1817 the people of Swansea may have been the first to hear a symphony performed in Wales when a concert of vocal and instrumental music at the town hall included Haydn's 'Surprise' Symphony. Swansea acquired its own orchestra in the 1820s, the Harmonic Society, though it is unlikely to have been composed of local residents since until the end of the nineteenth century leading instrumentalists came from the west of England to accompany at festivals, concerts and the National Eisteddfod. In like manner a London company gave Swansea its first taste of opera in the 1820s with *Der Freischütz* which had received its first performance in Berlin only in 1821.[26]

The demand for large-scale music-making led to Swansea, a thriving metallurgical centre whose population had risen from 19,000 in 1841 to over 51,000 twenty years later, equipping itself with a variety of recreational amenities like the Assembly Rooms built in St Helens Road in 1863, the 2,500-capacity Music Hall the following year, renamed the Albert Hall in 1881, and the Drill Hall. By the 1880s, with the addition of the Theatre Royal, and the 'New Theatre and Star Opera House' in Wind Street, Swansea had several concert venues for the visits of touring English opera companies, familiar from the 1840s when *La Sonnambula* and other operas had received a less than enthusiastic reception. *Acis and Galatea* and *Il Trovatore* were among the English Opera Company's six performances at Swansea in 1857, and by 1880 the discerning gentry and bourgeois residents of a town that had 'the most vital musical culture in Wales' could enjoy touring productions of *Don Giovanni, Lucia di*

Lammermoor, Martha, Lucrezia Borgia, La Traviata, Il Trovatore and *Fra Diavolo*.[27] String and wind chamber groups became a feature of Swansea's musical life at this time, antedating the chamber concerts held in Cardiff in 1885–6 that are claimed to be the first of their kind in Wales. 'To study classical music for its own sake and perform necessarily in public for the advancement of music' was the motive behind the foundation in 1881 of the Orchestral Society which in 1889 became the Swansea Music Society.

The diversity of Swansea's musical life in the 1880s is illustrated by the differing career paths of its three leading musical lights. W. F. Hulley (1853–1929) left his native Yarmouth in 1873 to become music director of Swansea's Star Opera House. A civic-minded and versatile musician – violinist, conductor, composer and impresario – he presented popular concerts at the Drill Hall at reasonable prices and introduced classical items like a Haydn symphony as well as the tenor Eos Morlais into the proceedings. In 1875 he was appointed organist and precentor at St David's Roman Catholic Church where he presented Weber's Mass in G as part of the morning service and formed the Swansea Amateur Operatic Company in 1878 which began performing the Savoy operas almost as soon as they appeared in London and for which he composed operas with a maritime setting, like *The Coastguard, or The Last Cruise of the 'Vampire'* (1884). Hulley was sufficiently thought of by Adelina Patti to be invited to produce *La Traviata* for the opening of Craig-y-nos conducted by Arditi and performed by an all-star cast from Europe and New York. Hulley also became well known outside Swansea for providing orchestras to accompany in concerts throughout south Wales.[28]

W. T. Samuel (1852–1917) was more representative of the indigenous chapel and eisteddfod culture. Born, like Brinley Richards, in Carmarthen, an ardent organist from his teens and a student for a brief period under Joseph Parry at Aberystwyth, he moved to Swansea in 1880 to become organist and precentor at Mount Pleasant Baptist Chapel where the tonic sol-fa class was already a hundred strong, and Samuel soon established more, one class in Ben Evans's shop numbering 150. Founder-secretary of the South Wales Tonic Sol-fa Conference, composer (his temperance chorus for children, 'Storm the Fort of Sin', 1876, had sold over 30,000 copies by 1891), examiner, adjudicator, conductor and choirmaster, Samuel was hailed by the main sol-fa organ, *The Musical Herald*, as 'the major of the South Wales division of sol-faists', a description well suited to the militant pentecostalism of the editor of a Welsh version of Sankey's *Sacred Songs and Solos*. He was the first Welsh tonic-solfaist to become a professional musician and, ominously, was 'never happier than when giving his oft-repeated lecture on "The Tonic sol-fa system" either in Welsh or English'.[29]

More charismatic than Samuel, and by virtue of his formal qualifications more representative of the professional strain becoming gradually more apparent in Welsh musical life, was the refugee from Aberystwyth Joseph Parry who spent the years from 1881 to 1888 in Swansea, living in Blodwen House, Northampton Terrace where, with the support of the powerful local magnates H. H. Vivian and J. T. D. Llewellyn, he opened the Welsh National College of Music in April 1881 and enrolled a hundred students within the first year. Parry's residence in the town certainly contributed to the 1880s and 1890s being hailed as the high-water mark in Swansea's musical life but it was hardly a musical desert when the Merthyr musician arrived there, for he would have immediately encountered the names of nineteen practitioners and teachers of vocal and instrumental music, invariably with English and often foreign-sounding names that indicate immigrant origins: Board, Lord and Mitchell as well as Benvenuti, Polanski and Fricker, who gave tuition on a small orchestra of instruments, as well as in languages.[30] Nor was the choral achievement unambitious or parochial. As early as 1861 Dr Evan Davies, principal of the Swansea Normal College, had conducted combined town and district choirs in Haydn's *The Seasons*, and in 1876 Silas Evans's Choral Society inaugurated a series of oratorio concerts that within eighteen months included *Messiah*, *Judas Maccabeus*, *The Seasons* and Rossini's *Stabat Mater*.[31]

None of the musicians mentioned so far, however, could command affection or galvanize his community as could William Griffiths ('Ivander', 1830–1910), a native of Aberavon, another metallurgical centre and one of those forgotten areas of intense musical activity in nineteenth-century Wales like Llanidloes and Builth. Brought up in a Presbyterian household and copying out tunes at seven years of age, he became aware from an early age how certain families determined and dominated the music in their chapels, the Wesleyan Robertses, the Anglican Brights and the Baptist Morrises, one of whom in the absence of a piano or harmonium had made a bass-viol from metal sheets which not unsurprisingly produced a 'tinny' sound when used in the service. The Sunday schools of the Aberavon–Maesteg district held an annual singing festival where, Ivander remembered, Maesteg had the best voices and the prettiest girls, while Aberavon had one bass chorister who cleared his throat by vigorously sucking eggs before ascending to the gallery.[32]

In 1850 Ivander moved to Pontardawe, where he became successively accountant and manager of Ynyspenllwch, Clydach, Tinplate Works, and threw himself energetically into the cultural life of the area by teaching and conducting. A musical as well as a moral missionary, he believed that 'it was essential to have the amelioration of the people and their uplifting in view, in virtue and morals, as well as producing the best choral results'. He put his ideals into practice in 1853 by founding one of Wales's first Bands of Hope in Trebanos that met in the new reading room that he also founded, and the following year harnessed the enthusiasm unleashed by the temperance movement to form a choir of 200 to sing choruses and anthems like those of John Ambrose Lloyd. This was virtually a monoglot Welsh-speaking community that sang Ieuan Gwyllt's translation of the 'Hallelujah Chorus' for probably the first time in 1855. With unflagging zeal for the continued causes of temperance, social reform and ethical improvement, he initiated a series of temperance singing festivals in Pontardawe, holding the first one in 1860 on Gellionnen Mountain as a deliberate counter-attraction to Neath Fair being held the same day. He also founded or worked with choirs in Pontardawe's outlying villages further up the valley at Cwmgïedd and branching east to Onllwyn, which together formed in 1862 the basis of the Swansea Valley Choral Society (Cymdeithas Gorawl Dyffryn Tawe), incorporating chapel choirs from Glais at the bottom of the valley to Brynaman at its north-western extremity.

Unusually it was formed not to participate in a temperance festival but at an eisteddfod in Carmarthen, an arena into which some of the recognized choral gladiators of Rhymney and Aberdare were expected to step. Ivander's choristers shared with the Aberdarians most of the choral prizes on offer that day in front of an unheard-of 3,000 whose enthusiasm for the choral proceedings had forced the rector of Neath to draw his address to a premature conclusion.

It was this competition that established the choral movement in the Swansea Valley, but it was not a competitive movement merely, for Ivander obtained 250 copies of the cheap Novello edition of *Messiah* to give the first amateur performance in Wales, with orchestral accompaniment, at Panteg Ystalyfera on 10 January 1863.[33] With more choristers from lower down the valley added, Ivander's now 300–400-strong choir gave four performances in all, including three orchestral occasions with instrumentalists from Swansea and primarily Bristol. The physical effort and logistical problems involved in such an undertaking are not to be lightly dismissed, for the railway had not yet penetrated the Swansea

Valley, and to reach the Ystalyfera centre the choristers from Brynaman and Onllwyn had to walk six miles each way, those from Clydach seven. It was no less strenuous an undertaking for Ivander himself who walked eight miles each night to the rehearsals of the various subdivisions of the choir. In the absence of an instrument, the choristers relied on the ear and voice of the conductor, a dependence triumphantly vindicated when the Bristol orchestra arrived and showed the choir's pitch to be entirely secure.

Prominent gentry and local worthies were soon to be seen lending their support, and it was on the occasion of one of the choir's performances at the Swansea Music Festival in 1864 that H. A. Bruce, Lord Aberdare, spoke warmly of the promotion of music among the working classes which 'has induced them frequently to desert the public house, and no occupation surely can be purer or free from anything like dangerous influences or more successful in its results than the choral cultivation of music'.[34] Doubtless he approved the choir's acquisition of the bureaucratic trappings of a committee (of fifty four!) and two treasurers, making the choir in all respects the prototype of Caradog's South Wales Choral Union of 1872.

The Swansea Valley did not contribute to that later formation because by then its own choral union had dissolved. Ivander, increasingly preoccupied by his business affairs, had in 1867 moved to the Crawshay works in Treforest, and then in 1869 to the north-west of England, where he bought the Derwent Tinplate works in Workington, taking a Welsh colony with him.[35] There, as part of what he regarded as his 'music, temperance and other mission work' he established in 1872 the Ivander Annual Eisteddfod, which left an enduring legacy of musical competition on which Mary Wakefield built her Kendal festival in 1885, and on which the Morecambe Festival was founded in 1891.[36]

By the time Ivander returned to Pontardawe for a testimonial gathering to celebrate the fortieth anniversary of his choir in 1902, with forty-three former members in attendance, the musicality of the Swansea Valley had been further enhanced by soloists like the internationally renowned tenor Ben Davies of Pontardawe, *tenore robusto* Eos Morlais, who, though Dowlais-born, spent most of his adult life in Swansea and district, the tenor Dyfed Lewis of Gurnos, Barry Lindon of Ystalyfera, principal bass at Westminster Cathedral, and the remarkable cluster of compositional talent that emerged from the picturesque village of Cwmgïedd at the top of the valley: Eos Cynlais, Silas Evans, J. T. Rees, and most notably Daniel Protheroe (1866–1934), who emigrated to

Scranton in 1886 and cultivated a facility for composing choruses and part-songs particularly congenial to male choirs. Moreover, the choral culture which Ivander had established – not entirely single-handedly – was maintained by the ambitious programmes performed at sacred venues like the Morriston Tabernacle[37] and Capel y Cwm, Llansamlet, where Ben Hughes trained a 250-strong choir to perform *Israel in Egypt* with its large double chorus, the Brahms *Requiem*, and in March 1912 the Bach *St Matthew Passion*, an extraordinary feat for a choir from a Nonconformist chapel, with a by now Swansea-based orchestra.[38]

Post-war developments, signalled by David Vaughan Thomas's directorship of the music at the 1926 Swansea National Eisteddfod, and the rise of a choir comparable in size and even superior in achievement to Ivander's organization – W. D. Clee's Ystalyfera choir, which dominated the Welsh choral scene in the inter-war period[39] – built on the foundations laid by William Ivander Griffiths whose Swansea Valley Temperance Choral Union indicated by its very name a significant compulsion behind the rise of nineteenth-century Welsh choralism.

2

Storming the Fort of Sin

&

1. The Battle Afar Off

The decades between 1830 and 1860 were the temperance years in Welsh singing, though the movement retained something of its hold until the end of the century. At an eisteddfod in Pontypridd in 1893 when the test piece for male choirs was David Jenkins's 'The War Horse' that 'smelleth the battle afar off', one zealous chorister insisted on singing instead 'he smelleth the bottle afar off'.[1]

In the long view it is likely that after the first enthusiastic flush the temperance ideal was not taken too seriously by so-designated musical organizations, least of all by bandsmen, but its association with a musical activity reinforced responsibility, thrift and general social competence. Equally, it is likely that those most in need of those habits were least touched by music. From a historical perspective we know that temperance had lost its social force as its relevance declined by 1914, by which time the working classes were generally cleaner, better educated and less drunk, and their sobriety as much to do with reasons other than temperance, such as an improved water supply.

It was in 1835 that Wales's first temperance society was established, in a Liverpool chapel, and the first temperance festival on Welsh soil held in Mold in 1836. Its colourful and processional element attracted people to the cause, and temperance marches became popular in north Wales in 1836–7, while in the south parades became familiar features in Swansea, Carmarthen, Merthyr and Llanelli between 1838 and 1840.[2] One of the movement's achievements was to take the eisteddfod out of the public house; unfortunately there was nowhere to take it except to the chapel. The public house was one of the institutional and recreational symbols of continuity between pre-industrial and industrial popular culture, and it made the transition from being the traditional dispenser of entertainment in a predominantly rural society to becoming the focus of sociability for an industrial work-force. It continued well into the nineteenth century to be the home of amusement and entertainment, including literary contests, harp-playing and singing. Aberdare's earliest eisteddfodau were held in the Swan Inn in the late 1820s, while the Stag fulfilled a similar function in neighbouring Trecynon and adjacent villages in the 1840s.[3]

The middle-class provision of less morally damaging counter-attractions to the beerhouse, like lecture halls, libraries and reading rooms, and from the 1830s of outdoor amenities like public parks and allotments was slow to penetrate the industrial communities of south Wales, where Blackwood (Monmouthshire) had one beerhouse for every five people in 1842 and Dowlais had 200 public houses in 1847. Only in the 1870s did recreational alternatives begin to emerge in south Wales in the form of free libraries with their special newspaper rooms mostly voluntarily financed by the working people themselves, twenty-nine workingmen's libraries opening in east Glamorgan and Monmouthshire between 1870 and 1895. Working-class self-improvement was until then focused on the chapel, as much by default as by conviction, and the interdenominational temperance singing classes which began at Merthyr in 1843, composed of the most accomplished vocalists of the various chapels, provided the basis for the series of temperance eisteddfodau held annually for the next thirty years or more in local chapels.[4] Merthyr's Temperance Hall was built in 1852–6 to accommodate the town's pledge-takers, and two years later in the same town the Temperance Choral Union of Glamorgan and Monmouthshire came into existence to comprise, by 1862, ten choirs and 700 choristers.[5]

By this time Ivander's Swansea Valley Temperance Choral Union was into its stride and there was complementary activity in north Wales in Eryri, Snowdonia (1866) and Ardudwy, Harlech (1868), the latter unique in having at its disposal a castle for its mass meetings. The others had to make do with chapels, and there were plenty to hand: the number of Welsh places of Nonconformist worship rose from 1,300 to 3,800 between 1800 and 1850. They were opening at the rate of one a week.[6]

There are always antecedents, and the temperance-inspired choral unions were pre-dated by the musical societies established in the 1820s to reform and invigorate congregational singing, themselves the products of singing classes formed by itinerant musicians like John Evans of Llanrwst (1750–1834), John Williams ('Ioan Rhagfyr' of Dolgellau, 1740–1821), and Dafydd Siencyn Morgan (1752–1844) of Llechryd in Cardiganshire who travelled as far as Anglesey establishing small choirs and spreading musical education, holding three-month singing classes, charging men a shilling and women half as much, and teaching from William Owen of Newtown's *Grisiau Cerdd* (1828). Lacking a tune-book – music was costly to buy, transcription an uncommon accomplishment and in any case laborious for an itinerant musician – Morgan used his own compositions, and appears to have attached as much importance to musical posture as to principles, such as keeping the chin up and putting more weight on the left foot than the right.[7] There was a tradition of shoemakers and tailors as precentors, many of whom developed as much craftsmanship in working notes as in leather and metal. One old character from Glamorgan used to decorate the Old Hundredth with ninety-five to a hundred notes where there are in fact only thirty-two.[8]

The increase in popular musical literacy is generally considered to be one of the obvious gains of the nineteenth century, and the tonic sol-fa sight-singing movement in particular relegated the role of the aural-dependent, musically semi-literate but creative performer to a secondary status. Yet the shift from a predominantly aural musical tradition to a mostly literate practice must have had significant implications for the conceptualization and performance of music. It has been observed that just as literacy disables the oral poet from improvising and rhapsodizing, once a written language has entered his or her consciousness, so can written music have the effect of stabilizing the repertory, to the extent that the ability to read a musical notation is destructive of aural methods of musical creation and re-creation.[9] By the end of the nineteenth century the score-independence of musically illiterate Welsh choirs vexed critics inside and outside Wales, but the effect of musical literacy on significant sections of the working class was not always positive, and the loss of status, relegation and ultimate redundancy of elaboration, decoration and variation, which were features of the older aural tradition, count as a significant loss.

The drive towards the elimination of spontaneity came, not for the last time, from the Presbyterian stronghold of Aberystwyth which in the hands of Edward Edwards ('Pencerdd Ceredigion', 1816–97) acquired a reputation for choral and congregational singing. Edwards, a cobbler, first encountered oratorio when he went in his late teens to work in the north Gwent iron town of Tredegar. On his return he founded a choral society at the Tabernacle, Aberystwyth, which became well known in the early 1850s for its rendition, in English, of choruses like those sung at its First Concert of Sacred Music at the Assembly Rooms on New Year's Day 1852, from *Messiah, Samson, Judas Maccabaeus, St Paul, Israel in Egypt, The Creation* and Mozart's Twelfth Mass and, in Welsh, Richard

Mills's *Duw sydd Noddfa*. A hard taskmaster, Edwards had perfect pitch, a vocal range of at least three octaves and an uncompromising hostility towards alcohol and the weed, which he cared for even less than sol-fa.[10]

Over the Plynlimon range in Llanidloes the Mills family, a humble Welsh equivalent of the Bach dynasty, first came to the fore in the person of James Mills conducting the congregation of Bethel Chapel on principles drawn up by his kinsman John. As in Merthyr, Chartism and temperance in this then busy manufacturing town made for what was still a heady brew, and John Mills was sufficiently imbued with the spirit to embark on a lecture tour of Glamorgan and Carmarthenshire in the late 1830s, leaving newly founded musical societies in his wake. Similar kinds of societies emerged in north Wales, in Anglesey in 1835, Bangor (1837), Cerrigydrudion (1838), Llanddarog (1840) and Bala (1845).[11]

The revolutionary decades of the 1790s and 1840s saw major breakthroughs in the history of Welsh music bibliography. John Williams ('Siôn Singer')'s *Cyfaill mewn Llogell* (A Friend for the Pocket, 1797) was the first attempt made, in dialogue form, to explain music notation in Welsh, and the first printed book to contain music notes, though the notes were written in by hand on to a printed stave.[12] A major difficulty was the dearth of music in Welsh, a want that began to be met by collections like John Parry of Chester's *Peroriaeth Hyfryd* (Heavenly Music, 1837), Richard Mills's *Caniadau Seion* (Songs of Zion, 1838) and D. T. Williams ('Tydfylyn') of Merthyr's *Caneuon Dirwestol* (Temperance Songs, 1844) which contained older Welsh tunes, new compositions and English tunes. Musical grammar books also appeared from the late 1830s, notably John Mills of Llanidloes's *Gramadeg Cerddoriaeth* (Grammar of Music, 1838), whose initial print run of 2,000 soon ran out and seven subsequent editions sold 10,000 each.[13] Another textbook to enjoy a wide circulation was *Gramadeg Cerddorol* (1848) by David Roberts ('Alawydd'). Alawydd's Bethesda choir of quarrymen and their families was sustained by the Novello cheap editions of Handel and Mendelssohn obtained from a book club. His manual, published at Bala in three parts in 1848, reflected Bethesda's position as a focal point of choral accomplishment to match the musical bastions of Llanidloes, Merthyr and, soon, Aberdare.

Between 1816 (when John Ellis of Llanrwst published the first substantial edition of tunes to appear in Wales since the early seventeenth century, *Mawl yr Arglwydd*) and 1859 (the year of Ieuan Gwyllt's *Llyfr Tonau Cynulleidfaol*) sixty collections of tunes and anthems were published in Wales.[14] Between 1840 and 1900 over 120 Welsh tunebooks and musical grammars appeared, sixty-seven by 1870 and another sixty by the end of the century. They were reformist and revolutionary. Several of these publications, like R. H. Pritchard's *Cyfaill i'r Cantorion* (The Singers' Friend, 1844) were intended to wean the faithful from 'empty and defiling songs'; others, like Thomas Williams ('Hafrenydd') made a still more resounding contribution, for his two-volume *Ceinion Cerddoriaeth* (Musical Gems, 1852), as well as containing in the first volume 220 Welsh and English tunes, including some by John Ambrose Lloyd, a skilful exponent of melodic, diatonic and stately tunes, included in the second some seventy anthems and choruses. It was through Hafrenydd's *Ceinion* that choruses from Handel (*Messiah, Samson, Israel in Egypt* and *Dettingen Te Deum*) and Haydn (*The Creation*) became accessible to Welsh choristers and the means by which a later reformer like D. Emlyn Evans came to know and study the works of these masters.[15]

The ability to engage with the choral challenges these presented was facilitated by a musical literacy acquired through the textbooks and grammars produced by the autodidacts who laboured so heroically in the first half of the nineteenth century, by the spread of sol-fa, and by the campaign spearheaded by Ieuan Gwyllt that insisted on a sober, morally uplifting, reformed, devotional music consisting of a sonorous, classically harmonized psalmody that was regularly rehearsed and worked on. Such was the rationale of the *cymanfa ganu*, the hymn-singing festival which remains 'Wales' most distinctive contribution to the world of music'.[16]

2. *And He shall Purify*

The two most obvious public expressions of the collective musical proclivities of the Welsh by the end of the nineteenth century were the increased status accorded to choral singing, manifested in concert and eisteddfod, and the hymn-singing festival known as the *cymanfa ganu*. It was estimated in 1896 that nearly one in eight of the entire population of Wales had attended such a festival in the course of the previous year.[17]

The Welsh were not innately part-singers, despite the nineteenth-century discovery that Giraldus Cambrensis had apparently noticed that peculiarity seven hundred years earlier. Yet the idea of people in twelfth-century Wales singing harmoniously in 'the soft sweetness of B flat' according to the diatonic criteria of a later age is not inherently more ludicrous than Sir George Macfarren's claim that English part-singing originated with Hereward the Wake.[18] Congregational singing was a product of the Protestant Reformation when Martin Luther applied his concept of the priesthood of all believers to sharing the worship. Bach was the first composer to understand Luther, and if Bach did not reach the Welsh until the nineteenth century, that was only a hundred years after the Reformation had made itself effectively felt in Wales. The metrical psalms of Edmwnd Prys (1621) had been stiff and unfriendly to the singer, while the tendency of William Williams of Pantycelyn in the eighteenth century to write on the metres favoured by the English hymn-writers Wesley and Watts meant that English tunes, even ballads, were inappropriately adopted as melodies for Pantycelyn's profound words. However, the Methodist Revival of the eighteenth century had made the singing of hymns an important part of public worship, and the musical grammars and editions of tunes that appeared with increasing frequency from the turn of the century provided valuable resources for the singing classes instituted by itinerant musicians like Dafydd Siencyn Morgan of Llechryd and others.[19]

There is little evidence that this activity had much impact on congregational singing. There were ructions at a Merthyr chapel when attempts were made to change the system whereby not the men but the women sang the tenor line, an octave above.[20] The distinction between sacred and secular tunes, too, had yet to be established, witness the setting in Richard Mills's *Caniadau Seion* (1840) of John Ellis's 'Ai am fy meiau i?' (Was it for my sins?) to a version of 'On Ilkley Moor'. John Mills in 1848 sought to distinguish between music that was secular (traditional airs and national songs), morally uplifting (temperance), and sacred. It was John Mills too who first applied the term *cymanfa* in a musical context, a scheme whereby the representatives of musical unions, like the one that flourished in Carneddi, Snowdonia, from 1828, could convene, hear lectures and devise ways of improving the quality of musical worship, something far stricter and more focused than the later development of what was virtually community hymn-singing.[21]

This idea caught on. The Gwent and Glamorgan Music Temperance Union of 1854, founded in Merthyr, combined choral performance with lectures on musical topics, and the only difference between these choral festivals and the later singing festival was that in the former a union of various choirs combined, whereas in the *cymanfa* the whole congregation sang as one choir. What thrust the congregational element to the fore was the fusion of the tail-end of the temperance movement with the 1859 religious Revival and the surge of tonic sol-fa. Eleazer Roberts (1825–1912), novelist, astronomer, pacifist, temperance reformer and musician, father of fifteen children and of the sol-fa in Wales, is credited with its introduction into Wales in 1860, having been seduced by John Curwen's outlining of his scheme in Liverpool the previous year into translating his work into Welsh.[22]

It is probable that Eleazer Roberts was pre-dated, at least in Glamorgan, by local teachers using sol-fa. A similar argument surrounds the priority of claim to the first *cymanfa*, whether it occurred in Aberdare in 1859, or was one of several such meetings that can be traced back to culturally more acceptable Aberystwyth in 1830.[23] The transforming social changes of the mid-century – accelerating industrial and demographic growth, town and chapel building – gave the movement an irresistible momentum, sustained by the tunes of Sankey and Moody which injected *hwyl* into the singing. The *cymanfa* then became a popular institution, the focal point of entire communities, an occasion for dressing up (with its implicit social closure for those unable to do so), meeting and socializing, trans-gender surveys and encounters, in all constituting a festive highlight which helped structure the local year. By the 1880s it was intriguing influential visitors to Wales like Curwen himself, but what it had increasingly become was a source of formalized pleasure and entertainment which was certainly contrary to the intentions of the Revd John Roberts (Ieuan Gwyllt, 1822–77), a severe Presbyterian to whom enjoyment was suspect and to whom the purpose of the *cymanfa* was instructional, to improve the standard of congregational singing and not to promote singing merely for its own sake; certainly *not* entertainment.

Born near Aberystwyth and a member of Edward Edwards's choir, trained as a teacher at Borough Road, he was at various times of his life a teacher, editor, minister, journalist, lecturer, poet, composer and conductor.[24] The Methodist Church viewed with disquiet his sympathy for radical causes: his opposition to hanging and to the Crimean War, his support for a secret ballot and the legality of Welsh in courts of law. Rejected for the ministry on these grounds in Aberystwyth and Liverpool, he eventually gained entry in more enlightened Merthyr Tydfil.

He may not have been admitted to the ministry at Liverpool in the course of his six-year sojourn there, but he encountered Mendelssohn's rediscovery of Bach, whose influence is evident in his innovative congregational hymn-book *Llyfr Tonau Cynulleidfaol* (1859). It is difficult to over-emphasize the significance of this publication, which even in old notation sold 17,000 copies in three years on the back of the 1859 Revival. Containing 459 hymn-tunes, chants and anthems, it grouped tunes according to metre, included several tunes of European origin and promoted a severe and unadorned style at the expense of tunes (like 'Lingham', 'Calcutta' and 'Devizes') which although they had found favour with Richard Mills, who included them in his *Caniadau Seion* (Songs of Zion, 1840), Ieuan Gwyllt regarded as worthless. He was a mover and shaker who in accord with the reformist temper of the times sought to cleanse what he perceived as the augean stable of Welsh hymnody. Never one to reflect current practice merely, he wanted to improve it by seeking and setting new standards of performance and comprehension.[25]

Ieuan Gwyllt moved to Aberdare in 1858 to edit *Y Gwladgarwr* (The Patriot), thence the following year to Pant-tywyll, Merthyr, where in 1861 he persuaded ten Calvinistic Methodist congregations to form a union for the purpose of learning the same list of prescribed tunes in order thereby to improve the standard of congregational singing in the locality. The publication four years later of his 1859 *Llyfr Tonau* in the more accessible sol-fa confirmed its status as the most important book published in nineteenth-century Wales. It sold 25,000 copies almost overnight, and established the *ysgol gân* (singing school) as the most popular and influential instructional institution in the social as well as musical and religious life of Wales. Singing practice became as funda-mental an aspect of chapel and therefore community life as the prayer meeting, and even more accessible, irrespective of age or gender. The combination of books, musical language and notation taught the Welsh to sing. But as well as making the Welsh a singing people, it had other, unintended, divisive consequences.

Ieuan Gwyllt had founded a Congregational Singing Union (Undeb Canu Cynulleidfaol) in Aberdare Temperance Hall in April 1859 to sing from his new *Llyfr Tonau*. Similar unions sprang up across the country: Penllyn (Bala) in 1860, followed by Merthyr and Dowlais, Nant Conwy, Cardiff, Swansea, Llŷn and London, in 1861, and soon Rhymney, Corwen, Blaenannerch (Cardiganshire), Cardigan, Carmarthen, Pwllheli, Ffestiniog, Pontypridd and elsewhere.[26] The fire was in the thatch, and it sent the temperature of denominationalism soaring. The Independents produced a hymn-book in 1868 and 1879 before their standard *Caniedydd Cynulleidfaol* appeared in 1895; edited by D. Emlyn Evans, M. O. Jones and D. W. Lewis, it sold over 70,000 copies, 58,000 of them in sol-fa, by 1900. The Baptist hymnal (*Llawlyfr Moliant*, 1890) had sold 40,000 (36,000 in sol-fa) by the end of the century, while Ieuan Gwyllt's own Methodist hymn-book went through several editions and revisions between 1859 and 1897, when a new revised version edited by J. H. Roberts that year sold 50,000 sol-fa copies and 11,000 in staff notation by 1900.[27]

Since these figures relate only to denominational hymnals and exclude the individual collections of their own tunes and anthems by composers like David Jenkins (1894) and Joseph Parry (1898), they are testimony to the rising tide of Nonconformity: Glamorgan's 393 chapels in 1851 had become 1,217 by 1910, with 151 in the Rhondda alone. The Baptists had 230 chapels in Wales in 1830 and 896 by 1902 to accommodate a rise in membership from 40,000 in 1850 to over 100,000 in 1900. The Calvinistic Methodists had 2,794 chapels in Wales in 1895, with 145,000 members and 300,000 'hearers'. By 1905 there were, according to the Royal Commission of 1910, 4,716 Nonconformist chapels in Wales, a quarter of them (1,170) in Glamorgan.[28]

These, as much as their primitive sports grounds, were the people's theatres of late-nineteenth-century Wales – there were only four actual entertainment halls in south Wales in 1880 – and undeniably they purveyed a narrow set of values that impoverished as much as they enriched. Yet to fail to recognize their more positive contributions to the reform of popular culture, alongside their spiritual role, is historically myopic, for the prescriptive if unbending puritanism of Ieuan Gwyllt survived him. He would certainly have endorsed the principle enunciated by the organizers of a sacred concert at Gibea Chapel, Brynaman, in 1891, that only sacred pieces should be performed and all chanting and whistling forbidden, these agreements to be secured with soloists and audience beforehand; it was also suggested that the engaged soloists might wish to submit their items to a committee for approval if necessary, but 'we are pleased to say this proved unnecessary'.[29] Even Ieuan Gwyllt might have baulked at such intrusiveness, particularly since one of the soloists was the nationally famous David Hughes, but the chapel's expressed desire to distinguish the sacred from the secular was consonant with the views frequently to be found in the monthly *Y Cerddor Cymreig* (The Welsh Musician), one of the historic landmarks in Welsh publishing history and in the history of music in Wales.

Regular musical criticism of the journalistic kind was a product of the nineteenth century, with London's broadsheet press providing an informed and international coverage of the musical life of Europe that was rivalled only in Paris.[30] Wales could hardly hope to compete. Yet between 1852 and 1895 fourteen music periodicals were published in Wales – indeed, from 1861 to 1939 there was not a year in which a Welsh-language music periodical failed to appear – occasionally two or three running concurrently, and published equally in north and south Wales in areas of population density or acknowledged musical excellence: Holywell,

Wrexham, Llanidloes, Aberystwyth, Llanelli, Pontarddulais and Merthyr. Of those fourteen, only six survived longer than five years, and three beyond ten.[31] The most important was *Y Cerddor Cymreig*, costing 10*d*. a copy, published in Merthyr, then Wrexham, between 1861 and 1873, and consciously modelled by Ieuan Gwyllt, who had lived in London, on the *Musical Times* (1844). In addition to its other services, from reporting on the music scene in Wales and England to reviewing new compositions, its wide-ranging educational dimension included, from 1864, contributions by Eleazer Roberts, an enthusiastic advocate of the tonic sol-fa system, to which Ieuan Gwyllt, initially fairly agnostic about it, magnanimously allowed a free run.

Y Cerddor Cymreig also, importantly, included music supplements, comprising 137 different pieces, 93 of them by Welsh composers, as well as choruses, anthems, glees, madrigals and part-songs by Palestrina, Gibbons, Farrant, Tye, Haydn, Mendelssohn and Spohr. Ieuan Gwyllt's Welsh translations of the words of familiar choruses were carefully crafted fusions of the musical and scriptural metre, like 'Pob Dyffryndir' for 'Every Valley (shall be exalted)' and 'Eu Sain aeth ar led' ('Their Sound has gone out'). From 1865 *Y Cerddor Cymreig* began issuing supplements in sol-fa and thereafter alternated between the two notations.

The sol-fa system taught Wales to read religious music, and it is arguable that through its tendency to make the singer think in terms of chords rather than phrases it led to the emergence of a recognizably Welsh style of singing. Certainly *Cerddor y Tonic Sol-ffa* (Wrexham, 1869–74) modelled on Curwen's *TSF Reporter*, *Y Cerddor Sol-ffa* (1881–6) and *Y Sol-ffaydd* (Pontarddulais, 1891–2) indicated a widening gulf between the two notations, in anticipation of the comparable gulf between amateur and professional musicians represented by the respective careers of Dan Davies and Harry Evans in Merthyr.[32] While these periodicals published only the sol-fa, *Y Gerddorfa* (The Music Place, Pontypridd, 1872–81) was the only publication to issue all its supplements in both notations simultaneously. It was suggestive that where *Y Cerddor Cymreig* (*YCC*) published arrangements of Haydn, Mendelssohn and others, *Y Gerddorfa*'s supplements were almost entirely by Welsh composers, indicators of the fact that by the 1870s there were more Welshmen writing music than in any previous decade in history. *Cronicl y Cerddor* (The Musical Record, Treherbert, 1880–3) was edited by D. Emlyn Evans and M. O. Jones, and in its amalgam of biographical sketches, articles on sacred music and notes on old Welsh tunes acted as a bridge between *YCC* and the publication which brought the Welsh musical press to its fullest expression, *Y Cerddor* (The Musician), jointly edited by D. Emlyn Evans and David Jenkins until 1913 and by Jenkins alone until 1915, jointly by David Evans and W. M. Roberts from 1915 to 1918 and then by David Evans alone to 1921.

Of these, it was perhaps David Jenkins who was most deficient in the public warmth that Ieuan Gwyllt before him had notoriously lacked. Ieuan was a poor conductor, stiff in movement with no voice and a short fuse, dependent on the singers to have learned the music; when he discovered they had not, he became impatient and bad-tempered. A humourless perfectionist with an infinite admiration for Bach, as a composer he had little of Johann Sebastian's flexibility in harmonizing – his tunes are stately rather than fluent; both John Ambrose Lloyd and Joseph Parry were better harmonizers – and he certainly lacked Bach's humour. A stickler for propriety and with little room for the light-hearted, he was severe in his condemnation of one chapel eisteddfod that offered a prize for baking a loaf, 'the winning product the property of the committee'. On another occasion, in Merthyr, he asked the congregation to sing what he regarded as a tune of poor quality in order to demonstrate its inferiority. The choristers, however, allegedly put up to it by Rosser Beynon and some others, sang the condemned tune with evident enthusiasm, doubling and trebling the chorus until Gwyllt became enraged.[33]

He could be inhumanly stern, with no compunction about bringing an entire singing festival to an awkward halt until an embarrassed mother had left with her whooping baby. As a result of such instances, his notoriety preceded him to parts of the country where he received a less than enthusiastic reception: the congregation at Caeathro (Caernarfon), for example, already displeased at the omission from Gwyllt's 1859 hymn-book of tunes by the local favourite William Owen, Prysgol, deliberately slid on the notes in the fifth line of Owen's 'Bryn Calfaria' in a manner they knew to be wholly unacceptable to someone so in thrall to the German chorale style as Ieuan Gwyllt.[34] In his view the dignity (*urddas*) of hymnody was everything, and in its quest he ruined perfectly good folk-tunes by subordinating them to its demands, and ignoring others better suited to the melody than the tunes he forced to fit what were originally dance rhythms.[35] It is therefore a satisfying irony that one of his final acts was to publish in 1874 a Welsh version of Sankey and Moody's revivalist hymns and tunes, *Sŵn y Jiwbili*, as if the unbending patriarch of psalmody was making belated amends for so much excessive discipline. However, if he had already 'Teutonized the sacred music of

Wales', as one writer infelicitously put it in 1920, his attempt to Americanize Welsh music was less successful, at least initially, though by 1934 half a million copies had been sold. With their elementary harmony and rudimentary melodies they might be thought to represent precisely the meretricious elements in hymnody that the old puritan disliked; but of course he had switched from a successful journalistic career to the ministry in the Revival year of 1859.

Iconoclastic attempts to portray this particular idol as having feet of clay are destined to founder on the indubitable fact of Ieuan Gwyllt's centrality as pioneer and pivotal figure in the reinvigoration of choral and religious music in Wales, and perhaps even as the prime mover of the Welsh musical renaissance which was already under way at the time of his death in 1877. He had a deeper and longer influence than even Joseph Parry.

By the 1870s the Welsh were already, in no small measure thanks to Ieuan Gwyllt, a singing people; in the opinion of some, they were so to excess. In south Wales especially, it was felt, the people were 'singing themselves stupid'.[36] Ieuan Gwyllt's *Y Gwladgarwr* (The Patriot) warmed to this theme:

> Wherever you go in Wales, all you hear is singing: at work, without end in chapel, in the streets, and nothing *but* singing at the eisteddfod. Theology, philosophy, the sciences, antiquities and history are all neglected. Few receive, let alone read, our quarterly publications. A shilling book containing some worthwhile knowledge is scorned, but the author of a book of tunes, glees and anthems can ask a fortune and retire before his hair starts greying.[37]

That the Welsh were beginning to see themselves as a singing people owed a great deal to the events of 1872–3 and the inspiration of a man who, his dedication to choral singing apart, was the antithesis of Ieuan Gwyllt. Burly Griffith Rhys Jones ('Caradog') had a lusty appetite for life and living. He loved competition, the eisteddfod and the big stage, and at the Crystal Palace in 1872–3, and Pontypridd and Chicago in 1893, he found it. In the year following Ieuan Gwyllt's death (1877) this harmonious blacksmith-turned-brewery-director pronounced Wales to be 'the land of song'. Ivander had gone north, Joseph Parry had gone west (though since 1868 he was back). This land of singers was the creation first of Ieuan Gwyllt, then of Caradog, who was waiting in the wings.

Wales and the Tonic Sol-fa: A Note

In 1840 John Hullah introduced his fixed-doh system of sight-reading according to sol-fa methods based on a German model, only to see it eclipsed by the movable-doh system of his contemporary in the field of choral education, John Curwen. Curwen, realizing the limitations of the C major-related fixed doh in the matter of modulation and transposition, introduced the new sol-fa method to his Sunday school in 1841, the year in which he is believed to have learned it from Sarah Glover of Norwich. The singing lessons he published the following year attracted philanthropic interest, and by 1850 he had instigated a national movement. In 1853 he founded the TSF Association, in 1863 the Curwen publishing house, and in 1869 the TSF College, which became the poor man's university, awarding diplomas, licentiates, fellowships and advanced certificates like confetti to generations who had few means and less hope of ever entering the august portals of the Royal College or Royal Academy of Music.

By the 1890s the TSF College was receiving more support from Wales than any other part of the country: nearly 79 per cent (149) of the college's 187 advanced certificates awarded between 1891 and 1895 went to Welsh entrants. The college report for 1900–1 showed that forty-nine of its eighty-two matriculands and twenty-four of its twenty-five candidates to whom the advanced certificate had been awarded that year came from Wales. This led to strident demands for greater Welsh representation on the college Council, and even for a separate Welsh institution, a call intensified in 1911 when twenty-seven of the college's seventy fellows and 300 of its 500 licentiates were reckoned to be Welsh, as well as 260 of the 348 who passed its theory and practical examinations that year.[38]

The system had spread rapidly in Wales in the 1860s, thanks to the work of Eleazer Roberts, Curwen's Welsh translator (1862). Consequently, those musicians whose formative years were the 1850s, like J. A. Lloyd, 'Tanymarian' (Edward Stephen), Joseph Parry, D. Emlyn Evans, David Jenkins and D. W. Lewis, were not natural sol-faists though they quickly mastered it and appreciated its virtues, and the first Welshman to gain the advanced certificate, in 1869, was David Jenkins, who was sufficiently convinced of its salutary role in enhancing the musicality of his people vehemently to challenge the claim made in 1887 by Professor W. H. Cummings, principal of the Guildhall School of Music, that 'the sol-faists have . . . nearly killed music in Wales'. Jenkins pointed out that only 200 of the 2,400 choristers who had learned his *Psalm of Life* for the Crystal Palace Festival in 1895 were readers of staff notation.[39] These statistics can be confirmed from other directions: for instance, of the 1,130 singers that made up the seven choirs competing in the chief choral event at the 1894 National Eisteddfod, 87 per cent were sol-faists, and the proportion among the male choirs was 96 per cent.[40]

These figures were reported with evident satisfaction by the TSF organ *The Musical Herald*, but they had less happy implications for the ability of Welsh choirs to cope with harmonically more interesting works outside the standard oratorio repertoire.[41] The democratic, user-friendly sol-fa system did encourage an ignorance of staff notation that worked against the assimilation of increasingly chromatic, more adventurous modern compositions. Insofar as it generated and was best able to cope with rather soapy religious music, the sol-fa revolution must bear some responsibility for the welter of unimaginative works produced during the second half of the nineteenth century, in England as much as in Wales. It also had a tendency to cut off the wealth of Catholic music, whose decadent chromaticism made it as suspect musically as it was dubious religiously.[42]

The great advantage of the tonic sol-fa, as Dr Dave Russell has pointed out, was that it was more than a system of notation merely; it taught pitch, rhythm and a basic harmonic sense.[43] It was easily taught and in 1864 was adopted by Bangor Normal College as part of the teacher's instruction, and the inclusion of music in schools' provision after the 1870 Education Act, when sol-fa became the accepted method of teaching in most of the newly created elementary schools, is a key factor in the Welsh musical awakening in the late nineteenth century. By 1891 70 per cent of schoolchildren in England and Wales were being taught to sing from a musical notation that was generally the tonic sol-fa. Since the school-leaving age was only ten in 1880 (twelve by 1899), a possible association of singing with school, discipline and 'learning' generally could have led to a counter-reaction to singing, and this argues against seeing its centrality in the schools as accounting for the expansion of choral activity.[44] In Wales, however, the Sunday school enjoyed massive popularity, and it was there in its associated institutions like the Band of Hope that sol-fa was implemented.[45] It became such a common language that even rhetorical styles were described in sol-fa terms. In this way it was noticed that each cadence of the famous preacher John Jones of Talysarn ended ray soh; for example, m r s, r r s, or s r s in a modal style with the doh on C.[46]

If singing became the national preoccupation of the Welsh in the second half of the nineteenth century, sol-fa was the hinge on which the door to so much musical experience swung open. It attached itself to the very texture of much social life, especially the life of the chapels where it was learned in *ysgol gân* (singing practice). It contributed powerfully to the rise of the muscular four-part congregational singing which so impressed and occasionally overwhelmed visitors,[47] and provided a career structure for generations of self-taught musicians who, condemned by their poverty and lack of opportunity, might never have realized their potential. John Price of Rhymney, Tom Price of Merthyr, Alaw Ddu (W. T. Rees) of Llanelli and J. T. Rees of Bow Street had all been colliers; Emlyn Evans and David Jenkins were both tailors' apprentices, J. H. Roberts a quarryman. They spoke to their countrymen through the medium of sol-fa and in consequence their music is almost entirely vocal.

Does this imply that, instrumentally, Wales was a desert? Insofar as relatively few played orchestral instruments this is probably true, but the assertion that there was 'seldom an opportunity in Wales to hear an orchestra before the Second World War and few people played orchestral instruments'[48] is true only in the limited sense of a professional orchestra or one containing a full range of instruments performing solely orchestral works. The factors that militated against the development of an orchestral tradition are obvious enough: the absence of a courtly aristocracy, of a metropolitan milieu and of a music college, allied to the restrictions imposed by a materially underprivileged, culturally confined country in the grip of Nonconformity. Yet the closer we look, the more evidence we find: in the regular reports in the pages of the Welsh musical press; the orchestras engaged by the National Eisteddfod (thanks to the efforts of the great enabler Brinley Richards) from the 1860s; the orchestral bands that came down from Gloucester, Cheltenham and elsewhere to accompany choral performances in Swansea from the 1860s; the activities of Jules Rivière at Llandudno from the late 1880s; or the local orchestras in Cardiff, Merthyr, Swansea, Aberdare, Llanelli, Aberystwyth and Wrexham already in existence by then. John Marc Davies has looked and found even more.[49] If it was the case that 'the playing of musical instruments remained a mainly middle-class, amateur activity' in parts of England,[50] this was clearly not the situation in Wales.

3

From the Cynon Valley to the Crystal Palace

ℰↄ

1. The Harmonious Blacksmith

By the mid-nineteenth century the population of the 7½-mile stretch of the Cynon Valley from Mountain Ash to the extremities of Hirwaun had risen tenfold from 1,486 in 1801 to 14,998 by 1851. Within another two decades it would nearly treble again to 40,305. Its industrial development gave the Aberdare district the name, and reputation, of being 'the Australia of Glamorgan'. As in neighbouring Merthyr Tydfil this industrialization began with iron, and the Crawshay family were again the key players. The first ironworks had been established in Hirwaun in 1757, and acquired by Richard Crawshay in 1818. In like manner the Fothergills took over the works at Abernant in 1819 and Llwydcoed four years later, while Matthew Wayne, Richard Crawshay's manager at Cyfarthfa before moving to the Cynon Valley, in 1827 established an iron company at Gadlys.[1]

It was not iron but the discovery of the four-foot seam at Cwmbach and its exploitation by Wayne and Thomas Powell that launched the industrial trajectory of the valley. Powell, whose name is enshrined in the coal company Powell Duffryn, soon to be more of an empire than a business, sank five shafts in the 1840s, a decade which saw intense activity on the part of local entrepreneurs like William Thomas in Lletty Shenkin (1843) and David Williams ('Alaw Goch') at Ynys-cynon, Mountain Ash, Cwmdare and Aberaman, where Crawshay Bailey was in business from 1845, as were other immigrants to the district like Thomas Nixon at Werfa and David Davis from Carmarthenshire at Blaengwawr. As a result of this activity, the coal production of the Cynon Valley rose from 12,000 tons in 1841 to over two million tons by 1870. In other words, until the Rhondda's rapid industrialization from the 1870s, the heart of the south Wales coalfield was located in Aberdare.[2]

The social cost was ghastly: typhus, smallpox and cholera paid fatal visitations in successive years between 1847 and 1849, a decade when the expectation of life among working-class children was seventeen and a half. In the wake of the 1848 Public Health Act which demanded an inquiry in any district when the mortality rate exceeded twenty-three per thousand, two years later T. W. Rammell presented a report heavily freighted with damning statistics on the social conditions at Aberdare, attributing them to the absence of an established, self-conscious and responsible middle class. Unlike Merthyr, which was older, Aberdare hardly had, as yet, a professional element: before 1850 the town was little more than a haphazard cluster of iron and mining villages with neither a coherent middle class nor a substantial commercial core, and 'lacking that sense of community of interest that might enable it to build traditions of civic duty and function'.[3]

Rammell's report, however, following as it did on the heels of the Blue Books of 1847 which so castigated the moral shortcomings of the residents of Aberdare in particular, prodded the small but burgeoning middle class of shopkeepers, works managers, agents and lesser indus-trialists into action. A local Board of Health was set up in 1854 with David Davis, Blaengwawr, a prominent member, and the provision of public services was put in motion: sewage disposal, a water supply, laying out streets and erecting public buildings like Aberdare's Market Hall in 1853 and a Workmen's Hall at Mountain Ash (1864). High on the list of perceived priorities in Aberdare where there were 103 drinking houses in 1853 was a Temperance Hall, duly built in 1858 to accommodate 1,500. In neighbouring Trecynon in 1858 there was a public house for every 156 of the population, a place of worship for every 900. There were twenty-five officially licensed premises to assuage the thirst of the 7,000 residents of Abercynon in 1863, and 273 throughout the valley in 1872.[4]

They lubricated throats as well, for remarkably this crude social environment spawned cultural and intellectual societies devoted to the pursuit and enjoyment of eloquent expression that defied the surround-ing grimness. Welsh was the language of the locality as much as of the in-migrating fugitives from the agriculturally depressed counties of west and mid-Wales; it was the medium of literary and musical discourse at the Swan in Aberdare in the 1820s, and in the 1830s and 1840s at the Mount Pleasant and the Stag in Trecynon. Nonconformity and temper-ance, naturally, had little room for the public house, the fair or the ballad. Fifty chapels were built in Aberdare between 1840 and 1870; in the 1850s the eisteddfod migrated from the tavern to the chapel. Henceforth the singing of ballads to the accompaniment of the harp would be supplanted by choral singing and the harmonium, while the string band, amphibiously at home in either milieu, mediated between the more spontaneous older culture and the new.

For the two cultures were not wholly in opposition: seven small choirs were in competition at the Stag as early as 1846. It was the meetings of religious and library societies that began to mark out the calendar of the respectable working class and *petite bourgeoisie*, and their activities were fuelled by and reflected in an active Welsh-language press that made Aberdare in the middle decades of the nineteenth century the busiest publishing centre in Wales: from its presses came *Y Gwron Cymreig* (The Welshman, 1854–60), *Y Gweithiwr* (The Workingman, 1856), *Y Gwladgarwr* (The Patriot, 1858–82) and from 1875 until 1934 *Tarian y Gweithiwr* (The Workingman's Shield) that was selling around 13,000 copies a week at the turn of the century.[5]

Its industrial development, the four-foot seam, demographic growth and its cultural life were the building blocks of this Welsh Athens, 'Athen Cymru'. The quest for the uplifting and edifying in this grim environment was not easily undertaken, but it was a project to which the Revd Dr Thomas Price (1820–88) was prepared to devote his formidable energies. Baptist minister, theological scholar, literary producer, organizer and editor, he campaigned tirelessly to uphold the standard of Welsh Nonconformity against its detractors. These included the contemptible Revd John Griffith, the Anglican vicar of Aberdare from 1846 to 1859, who had fed the commissioners of the Blue Books a string of defamatory untruths concerning the morality of his parishioners. A four-hour lecture was nothing to Dr Price, whether on the Crimean War, the Indian Mutiny or, especially, industrial matters, a topic which he had made exhaustingly his own. In 1872 Aberdare's musical ambitions presented the tireless Revd Dr Price with a vehicle worthy of his energies.[6]

Aberdare was a musical hothouse. By mid-century the older, informal, often disorderly entertainment had for the most part yielded to a new musical culture which was still vocal and instrumental, but now choral and collective, driven by urban imperatives among which temperance was only one. As yet, the Cynon Valley had neither public halls nor libraries, no workingmen's institutes, no rooms for reading or billiards. There was hardly any commercial entertainment. Outside the public house, the chapel and to a lesser extent the church provided for the recreational requirements of the populace, and did so with assurance, for in the previous twenty years, Gwilym Ambrose has written, 'Aberdare had become a numerous and confident community' with the social organization and musical sophistication necessary for preparing and transporting to London the largest choir Wales had seen, the South Wales Choral Union, popularly known as 'Y Côr Mawr'.[7]

The Cynon Valley was itself confident, enterprising and radical. It was one of the last strongholds of Chartism, and in Cwmbach the first co-operative shop in Wales had opened in 1860. It was the Aberdare and Merthyr constituency that the Liberal Henry Richard momentously won in the name of the Nonconformist people of Wales in 1868. The Amalgamated Association of Miners which was based at Aberdare, especially Aberaman, had, within two years of its foundation in 1869, 4,300 members in the Cynon Valley. By common consent, it was in Aberdare that the first *cymanfa ganu* had been held in Wales, in 1859, with Ieuan Gwyllt conducting it.[8]

With the sacred and secular, the traditional and technological, the old rural and new industrial in juxtaposition, no area of activity was more lively than the musical, where business and capital invaded the culture of the ballad, and where professional outside instrumentalists and vocalists were welcomed as warmly as well-known local artists. The emergence of a choral culture cannot be laid at the door of the sol-fa movement, for this did not reach Aberdare before the 1860s. Nor was it only in the chapel that musicians made rendezvous; string bands were in demand for what passed for soirées even in mid-century Aberdare. Without doubt, however, the most robust musical recreation, combining the popular and the improving, was the eisteddfod, which developed apace in the 1850s, a form of collective popular entertainment that drew large crowds to the Temperance Hall and local chapels and reached a peak with the national gathering at Aberdare in 1861. That auspicious occasion began most inauspiciously when the purpose-built 6,000–seater pavilion blew down on the eve of the event, but it swiftly relocated to the Market Hall where solos to harp accompaniment, Welsh and English glees, choruses by Verdi, Mendelssohn and Tanymarian and three winning choirs from Aberdare and two victorious bands from Aberaman set a satisfying seal on the largest assembly ever seen in the valley. The reporter of one London paper was moved to observe, with prophetic insight that

> if the singers of this valley were ever to visit London, or the Crystal Palace, they would create as much astonishment in the performance there of their national songs as did the Orphéonists or Bradford choristers, and as they have done among the visitors here now.[9]

Neither the eisteddfod nor the chapel had an absolute monopoly on the formally organized music of the Cynon Valley. Thanks to the initiatives of the Revd Evan Lewis, vicar of Aberdare between 1859 and 1886, a tradition of choral services and festivals was established at St Elvan's Church where the combined choirs at the 1871 festival, for instance, comprised over 200 voices. Throughout this period, choristers from the district participated in the annual Llandaff Festival, while the Roman Catholic Church (opened in 1868) made its own contribution to extending the musical horizons of Aberdarians by in 1869 celebrating High Mass in its full liturgical context with the ecumenical assistance of the Aberdare United Choir and a string band; a setting of the Mass by Weber was sung in 1872, and Haydn the following year.[10]

Concert life throve as well with well-known vocal and instrumental performers from London and elsewhere winning the enthusiastic approval of large audiences at the Temperance Hall. In 1861 Madame Parepa, the wife of Carl Rosa, sang solo in *The Creation*, and paid a second visit the following year with Signor Pezzi, principal cellist at La Scala, their programme consisting of a Beethoven cello sonata, Mozart and Schubert songs, various operatic items and a 'bel canto' rendition of 'Llwyn Onn' (The Ash Grove) that reportedly induced near-delirium among the audience.[11]

These activities were all part of a mission to transform the older culture and impose a new pattern, a programme of cultural and moral improvement which incorporated the respectable working class as enthusiastic participants in its implementation. What above all else enthused the inhabitants of Aberdare was choral music, whose roots were constantly watered by the congregational singing of the Nonconformist chapels. It was in Bethania that Ieuan Gwyllt had pioneered the *cymanfa ganu* in 1859, and its success was made possible by David Rosser's preparatory work with the Bethania choir, the nucleus of the Aberdare United Choral Society under Silas Evans (1838–81) of Aber-nant. It was Silas who at the 1862 Mountain Ash Easter eisteddfod conducted the chapel choir of Nazareth, Aberdare, to victory over three other choirs, one of them Bryn Seion, Cwmbach, led by Caradog. It was again Silas and the Aberdare Temperance Choir who in 1859 had shared first prize with Aberdare United under Caradog. Caradog led this choir to victory at the Aberdare National Eisteddfod in 1861, but it then disbanded until Silas Evans resurrected it to compete at the Swansea National in 1863 where it won on 'Praise the Lord our God' (Spohr), a madrigal, and an arrangement of 'Men of Harlech'.[12] When Silas moved to Swansea soon

afterwards Caradog proposed himself as his successor and by 1869 had
built it up to a strength of 150.

Who was this Caradog? Other towns boast memorials to military
heroes and political tribunes, but for the cultured residents of Aberdare it
is a choral captain who is commemorated by the statue, paid for by
public subscription and executed by W. Goscombe John, that was
unveiled in the town's Victoria Square on 10 July 1920. By that date
Griffith Rhys Jones – Caradog – had lain in Aberdare cemetery for
almost a quarter of a century, but 120 of his former choristers, some
from as far away as the USA, Australia and even the Chinese mission
field, had assembled to sing in the rain to honour the memory of their
famed conductor, the one who can safely be credited with having laid the
foundations of the golden age of Welsh choralism.

He was born in the Rose and Crown, Trecynon, on 21 December
1834.[13] By the time of his death in December 1897 he had accumulated
sufficient wealth through his business acumen and deft manipulation of
profits from properties, particularly public houses, and the directorships
of sundry brewing and bottling companies, to be able to leave an estate
valued at more than £38,000. In other words, this beefy embodiment of
the close association between Welsh choralism, Nonconformity and
temperance was for most of his life associated with the drink trade.
Something of a musical nomad, he lived at various times in Trecynon,
Aberdare, Treorchy, Treherbert, Llanybydder (Carmarthenshire), Cardiff
and Pontypridd, and married three times. His first wife, Sarah, died aged
twenty-two years shortly after their marriage in 1879; but the third,
Margaret, whom he married in 1881, survived her husband until 1923.
To Caradog and Gwenllian a son was born in 1864; Major John Griffith
Jones became a chartered account and stood unavailingly in the Con-
servative interest at Pontypridd in 1922, dying six years later.[14]

'Griff y Crown' (Griff from the Crown), as he was popularly known in
early life, was a blacksmith, apprenticed to his father, who was a
mechanic at the Llwydcoed ironworks. Griff followed in his footsteps,
leaving school at twelve years of age to be a blacksmith's striker at the
Gadlys works, where the ring of the hammer striking the anvil miracu-
lously endowed him with a sensitive and musical ear. His hair cut short,
his face clean-shaven save for a tuft on his lower chin, he had broad open
features and the deadpan expression of someone barely able to suppress
mirth. He could apparently reduce his choristers to helpless laughter
while remaining wholly impassive himself. His language was, it seems,
colourful: one member of his choir thought him crude (*anghoeth*), and to

1. The former blacksmith, later breweries' director,
Griffith Rhys Jones, 'Caradog' (1834–1897), who
conducted the South Wales Choral Union to undying
fame at the Crystal Palace in 1872 and 1873.

the professionally trained Merthyr musician Harry Evans he was 'a born conductor, but uncultured'.[15]

The Trecynon into which he was born was pretty uncultured too: rows of workmen's cottages, a Unitarian meeting-house which his family attended, a few places of worship and a couple of public houses. Griff learned the violin from an older brother, who kept a school at the Bird in Hand before reversing the experience of his immigrant neighbours by quitting the Cynon Valley for the Australian gold rush. Whether or not Griff ever attained the virtuosity on the fiddle that earned him the sobriquet of 'the Welsh Paganini', clearly he was proficient, and it is an engaging illustration of his sense of humour as much as of his alleged lack of refinement that his party piece was 'The Farmyard' in which he imitated various creatures on the violin, to the huge delight of his audience though much to the consternation of the diaconate when performed in chapel concerts.[16]

Although he was a member of a string band that was often to be heard either accompanying or performing in its own right in the 1850s, it was as a choral conductor that Caradog gained celebrity in a career extending from 23 June 1853 when, at eighteen years of age, he took a choir from Trecynon to an eisteddfod in Aberavon, to 10 June 1873 when he conducted the South Wales Choral Union for the last time in the rather more spacious surroundings of the Crystal Palace; by coincidence, Beethoven's 'Hallelujah to the Father' was the test piece on both occasions. His first choir had been the Bryn Seion Chapel choir in Cwmbach, but it was in Aberavon that he secured his first eisteddfod victory with seventeen vocalists, some of whom had come over from Dowlais. It was customary for each choir to compete under a pseudo-nym, and since 'Caradog ap Brân' was the appellation chosen by the winning conductor from Trecynon, 'Caradog' was called forward to receive the princely prize of £5. The name stuck following this event in 1853, which might not have happened at all had it not been for the opening that year of the Vale of Neath Railway linking Merthyr and Aberdare with Neath and, then, Swansea. It was the 1,500 miles of railway laid in Wales between 1840 and 1870 that enabled the South Wales Choral Union to steam into history.[17]

This early success as a choral conductor did not induce Caradog to relinquish his instrumental ability. He joined Aberdare Philharmonic Society as a violinist and performed Mozart's Twelfth Mass with them at the Temperance Hall in 1858. He also formed a string ensemble to accompany services at the Unitarian meeting-house in Trecynon before moving to the Unitarian chapel at Cwmbach as *codwr canu* (precentor). Although Silas Evans was at the helm when Aberdare United won at the Swansea National in 1863, Caradog had been allowed the opportunity to conduct it on several previous occasions, for example at an eisteddfod at Pontypridd on Whit Monday 1861 when Ieuan Gwyllt's monthly journal *Y Cerddor Cymreig* (The Welsh Musician) declared it had never heard better singing in Wales than the victorious Aberdare United's perform-ance there of 'Thanks be to God' from *Elijah*.[18]

After hearing them at Llanelli in 1867 another correspondent deemed it advisable that every choir in the Principality hear this one so that they might have a clear conception of what choral singing was about. As the standard rose, so did the prize money. At Swansea on Good Friday 1868

2. String and wind bands had long been features of religious worship, and despite the introduction of harmoniums and pipe organs from the 1870s, they survived into the twentieth century, as shown by this photograph of Ebenezer, Trecynon's church orchestra, c. 1900.

Caradog's Aberdare United beat four others on 'O Great is the depth' (*St Paul*) to gain twenty guineas, a silver baton for the conductor and praise from the astounded adjudicator, Alfred Stone, the eminent Bristol organist and choirmaster, that he too, had never heard better.[19] When the choir presented a concert at the Drill Hall, Merthyr, in September 1869, the first half consisted of secular items and the second was devoted to the oratorio choruses at which it excelled like 'The Heavens are Telling', 'O Great is the Depth', and 'Worthy is the Lamb'. This last, and the 'Amen' chorus which follows it, secured the prize at Newport at the end of the year, forcing the *Cerddor Cymreig* to admit, 'Unless choirs from Glamorgan and Gwent make every effort to beat them, before long people will begin to think they are invincible. For that matter, perhaps they are . . .'[20]

In 1870 Caradog moved from the Fothergill Arms, Cwmbach to take possession of the Treorchy Hotel in the Rhondda, where he lost no time in forming a men's chorus, the forerunner of the famous Treorchy Male Choir that William Thomas took over in 1885. This was not a new experience for Caradog, for in order to vary a concert programme he would often reconstitute the men's section of his mixed choir into an autonomous glee party; at Llanelli in 1867, for example, they sang Adolphe Adam's 'Comrades in Arms' and Gounod's 'Soldiers' Chorus' which have retained their popularity in the male-choir repertoire to the present day. William Thomas agreed to accept the conductorship of the Treorchy choir in 1885 only on condition that they quit the public house for the schoolroom as a rehearsal venue.[21] Clearly 'Griff y Crown' had never imposed such a pre-condition; in any case there were few other facilities for practice. Similarly, the fact that in the absence of more suitable auditoria it was mostly in chapels, with boards placed across the front pews to create a temporary stage, that concerts and eisteddfodau were held explains the predominantly religious and respectable nature of the Welsh choral culture. It was in a Treherbert chapel rather than a spacious, purpose-built concert hall that Caradog on 13 April 1871 conducted what may have been the first amateur performance of a complete oratorio to be given in Wales, Spohr's *Last Judgement*.[22] This was an appropriate enough setting for such a work, but certainly there was a dearth of Crystal Palaces in the Cynon as in other Welsh valleys.

In 1872 the Crystal Palace Company in London announced its intention of holding a National Music Meeting in June and July that year. The Crystal Palace had been re-erected at Sydenham in south London after a brief period at Hyde Park where it was first put up for the Great Exhibition of 1851, and there it remained until it was destroyed by fire in November 1936. Its designer, Joseph Paxton, was not a professional architect but rather chief gardener at Chatsworth House, a position which enabled him to become something of an authority on glass houses. The Palace was not intended to be a place of musical enterprise, but for commercial display, and the royal and other ceremonial occasions held there required musical support from massed bands and enormous choral forces of six or seven hundred to provide fanfares, patriotic pageants and national anthems. Almost inadvertently the Palace became a centre for choral music, in effect the music of Handel whose 'melodic appeal, metrical simplicity, tonal stability and ceremonial nobility' ensured it could be presented by massed vocal and instrumental forces, 'as Bach's choral music could not'.[23] From 1857 audiences of 20,000 gathered to listen to united choirs of several thousands at the Palace's Handel Festivals, while the staging of the National Brass Band Championships from 1900 to 1936 was the climax of a development anticipated by the contests held there in the early 1860s, when the Cyfarthfa Band won first prize on the second day of competition in

1860. Willert Beale (1824–74) bears the responsibility for adapting this concept to the choral sphere. It was a short-lived experiment, but since Beale claimed Welsh ancestry it is doubtless fitting that it was a choir from south Wales that kept the National Music Meetings held in 1872 and 1873 from sinking without trace.

Beale's express intention was to promote a deeper national musical awareness, and he made no bones that he derived the idea from the Welsh National Eisteddfod and, after attending the Grand Concours International in Paris in 1870, the Orphéon choral movement in France. At the same time he insisted that his project was more educational than those, since it demanded a higher standard of musical knowledge. On New Year's Day 1872 the London press carried a list of sponsors, test pieces and conditions of competition in eleven classes. Chief among them was the thousand-guinea Challenge Cup, to be awarded to the winning choir of between 200 and 500 voices. There were competitions also for choirs of fewer than 200 and for male voices. The adjudicators' bench would be occupied by some of the foremost musicians in England, Julius Benedict, Joseph Barnby, Arthur Sullivan, John Liptrot Hatton and Henry Leslie. In the event, the judges in 1872 proved to be none of these but the no less eminent W. Sterndale Bennett of the Royal Academy of Music, the sol-fa pioneer John Hullah and the expatriate Brinley Richards.

The idea of forming a Welsh choir to compete prompted a letter to *Y Gwladgarwr*, with the consequence that on 17 February 1872 some of south Wales's leading musicians met at the Temperance Hall, Aberdare – a sure indication of the Cynon Valley's musical if not geographical centrality – to set the wheels in motion.[24] A steering committee was appointed under the chairmanship of Canon Jenkins, vicar of Aberdare, with the Revd Dr Thomas Price, inevitably, as treasurer and D. Brython-fab Griffiths, registrar of weddings for the Aberdare district and a local solicitor, as secretary. Despite the attendance at this first meeting of several able conductors who constituted the musical cream of south Wales like W. T. Rees (Alaw Ddu) of Llanelli, Lewis Morgan of Merthyr and Rees Evans, who had succeeded Caradog as conductor of the Aberdare United Choir, it was felt that none was more qualified to be appointed conductor of the proposed choir than Caradog himself, and Eos Morlais's proposal to this effect, seconded by Tom Williams of Pontypridd, was warmly endorsed. Despite some initial reservations about competing for a prize that he considered hardly worth the effort involved, Caradog accepted the nomination.[25] Those conductors who conceded to Caradog the position of *primus inter pares* now generously agreed to be responsible for the local sections that together would comprise the united South Wales Choral Union.

A hundred of the 450 originally – if none too fastidiously – selected fell by the wayside during the weeks of sectional rehearsal, but it was appropriate that a co-operative musical venture on a scale hitherto untried in Wales should have originated in the valley that also saw the first Welsh 'cop' (co-operative shop). It was equally fitting that Aberdare should be allocated the strongest representation, and the Cynon Valley in total a quarter of the entire choir, for here the idea had first germinated. The South Wales Choral Union would in 1872 include sections from Pencae (Ebbw Vale), Brynmawr and Blaenavon in Monmouthshire to Swansea, Morriston and Llanelli in the west, but above all it represented the peak of twenty years of strenuous and varied endeavour 'to which the musicians of Aberdare had notably contributed'. The Côr Mawr mapped and represented the musical topography of south Wales.[26]

It was an onerous and costly enterprise that would run to over £6,000 over the next two years, and it is improbable that the unrealistic expectation that choristers should pay a shilling (5p) towards expenses was ever strictly applied. The more practical expedient of charging the public for admission to the final rehearsals was adopted, and there were avid audiences on 4 June in Swansea, 12 June in Pontypridd and 20 June in Merthyr (arranged with those from the western valleys of Monmouth-shire in mind) with the final rehearsal at the Temperance Hall in Aberdare on 1 July. It was originally intended to hold this climactic send-off at 2 p.m. but to meet the consuming public interest and to allow for the different shifts operating in the district, the choir sang again at 5, 8 and 9 p.m., four concerts in the space of one afternoon and evening, which raised £200 towards expenses. Then a specially chartered eighteen-carriage train transported the choir to London – it was a venture impossible to conceive before the advent of the railway – though on arrival at Paddington it was a lusty performance of 'The Men of Harlech' rather than 'Sleepers Wake' that threw the staff of the station into confusion. Confusion would be the keynote of the 1872 descent on London of the South Wales Choral Union.[27]

2. The Many Rend the Skies

Of the eight pieces the choir was required by the rules of the competition to prepare, the adjudicators asked to hear three, Bach's 'In Tears of

Grief' (from the *St Matthew Passion*), 'Then Round about the Starry Throne', an oft-ridden warhorse on the south Wales eisteddfod circuit from Handel's *Samson*, and 'The Night is Departing' from Mendelssohn's *Hymn of Praise*. From their very first note the volume and richness of sound produced by the Welsh choir astounded the audience, who were also taken aback by the evident enthusiasm of the choristers, a zeal even exceeded by their supporters in the audience. The Crystal Palace, according to one witness, could never have heard a sound like it; another, from the *Tonic Sol-fa Reporter*, was compelled to the conclusion that one Welsh voice was worth three from London.[28] Reportedly, the choir's entry in 'Round about the Starry Throne', which most of the singers knew backwards, so surprised the accompanying players that their heads involuntarily jerked upwards, almost losing their place.

This misfortune, however, was the calamity that befell the choir who, conscious of the effect they had made, lost concentration, intonation or both. As the chorus proceeded, they went out of tune. 'Listen to the band!' shouted an increasingly desperate Caradog. Others thought this yelp emanated from Brinley Richards, one of the impartial adjudicators. The orchestra who had in any case managed only a few minutes' rehearsal with the choir before the competition, were too unnerved by the choral tidal wave to help restore the vocal intonation, and Caradog was obliged to ask permission to start again, which he was allowed to do.[29] The rerun went without mishap, and the audience went mad. The adjudicators seemed pleased too, though unofficial critics were less than enthusiastic about aspects of the performance: 'There was really very little expression of any sort; in the high notes the sopranos sometimes screamed and the tenors often forced the chest register in a very untuneful way. The Handelian runs were done in the gliding fashion of the rawest amateurs.' In the opinion of another, however, 'the subdued pianos, the inspiring fortes, the extended rallentandos, the slight variations of tempo here and there were all evidence of a teacher's eye.' *Quot homines tot sententiae* at the Crystal Palace in July 1872.[30]

The more observant could not but be struck by the skill with which Caradog, in white gloves, conducted the Bach which he had taught his choir to sing to three beats in the bar. It was written in 3/4 time, most of the notes were quavers, and this was how the Merthyr string band had played it in rehearsal. When it came to the actual competition, however, the leader of the London orchestra demanded that Caradog beat their accustomed six beats in the bar. Faced with a choir unfamiliar with six beats, and an orchestra unused to three, Caradog grandly proclaimed 'I

will do it in both ways', and proceeded to beat six with one hand for the
benefit of the players, while with the other giving his own choristers their
accustomed three.[31]

It was no contest, and the awarding of the handsome cup for a walk-
over hardly detracted from the wider significance with which the victory
was invested in Wales, where the calumnies of the Blue Books still
rankled but now were felt to be redressed. The Welsh were not so uncivil-
ized or deficient in virtue after all; they sought to elevate themselves
through a cultural appreciation of the arts, and through education; the
founding college of the University of Wales at Aberystwyth would be
opening its doors in October. Even *The Times* reined in its instinct to
patronize, preferring instead to praise:

> When it is remembered that this chorus is almost entirely drawn from
> the labouring classes of the Principality, miners, colliers etc., their
> wives, daughters and relatives, we cannot but wonder at the excellence
> they have attained, an excellence unattainable except through assiduous
> and continued study.[32]

Ieuan Gwyllt's monthly journal devoted to musical matters in Wales, *Y
Cerddor Cymreig* (The Welsh Musician) founded in 1861, took righteous
pride in this achievement of the Welsh working class, and that such
musical distinction – not the prize but the standard of performance – was
attained under the baton of a blacksmith:

> If they knew more about us in this Principality, they would just about
> understand that it is our labouring class that does everything. It is to the
> labouring class we look for our preachers, our writers, our poets, our music-
> ians . . . It is from the ranks of the labouring class that we raise the men who
> fill our pulpits, write for our newspapers and journals, compose our songs,
> anthems and choruses, conduct our choirs, adjudicate and compete.[33]

In full flow, Ieuan Gwyllt could sound like Marx and Mazzini as he
delineated the gendered Wales of this morally respectable, Nonconformist working class who by their music had raised the Welsh in the
esteem of their neighbours:

> The vast majority of the English have been accustomed to speak
> disparagingly, and generally have a low opinion, of the Welsh. When it
> comes to achievement, knowledge and imagination Wales is assumed to
> be as lifeless as the graveyard. [Caradog's choir] demonstrated there is

life here, and ability and achievement, and the Welsh in Wales are no longer to be despised . . . we are in a new era and the impact of this Welsh choral victory will contribute significantly to raising the standing of the Welsh both here and abroad.[34]

The choice of test pieces had been little less than providential: for Victorian Wales, truly the night was departing. and Aberdare's middle class could reflect with satisfaction on the completion of a civilizing mission that had begun in the 1850s. In the 1870s, in the Cynon Valley, coal theft, violent assault, prostitution and public disorder were common, but for the moment the notion of the Welsh Athens, an 'image of the whole of Aberdare created out of its partial reality', had been resonantly reaffirmed.[35]

There was no room for complacency, for all that. At a post-victory reception Henry Richard MP warned the choir members not to rest on their laurels: if they hoped to retain the cup they needed to 'go home and pay more attention'. It was a view endorsed by John Hullah, one of the adjudicators, who 'considered the Welsh great in the matter of voice, ear and musical feeling; but this was not quite enough; a great deal more was wanting before they did justice to the gifts God had given them', and that meant hard work heeding the advice of their conductor.[36]

The homecoming of the South Wales Choral Union was tumultuous.

At Mountain Ash hundreds of people assembled at the railway station, and cannon were fired. At Aberdare the greatest enthusiasm prevailed . . . some thousands of people filled the approach to the station: flags were suspended from the principal buildings and two or more bands of music struck up 'See the conquering hero comes'.

In fact the conquering hero had left the train at Quakers Yard to connect with another for Treorchy, where he was carried shoulder-high through the streets on a bardic chair thoughtfully provided for the occasion by the Revd Gurnos Jones. Time to take stock and consider the next move.[37]

One move was to establish the following year the Rhondda Valley Brewery Company, with himself as one of the five founding directors.[38] On the choral front there was less to consider. If the trophy was to be retained work had to begin immediately on the prescribed pieces – only five this time – for the 1873 competition, three of which were familiar: 'The Many Rend the Skies' from Handel's *Alexander's Feast*, 'See what Love hath the Father' from Mendelssohn's *St Paul* (which in the mid-nineteenth century eclipsed *Messiah* in popularity), the 'Hallelujah' from

Beethoven's *Mount of Olives*, plus 'Come with Torches' (Mendelssohn's *Walpurgisnacht*) and a Bach motet, 'I Wrestle and Pray'. Standards had not only to be maintained but raised, especially in view of the fact that there was competition this time in the formidable shape of Joseph Proudman's 350-strong London Tonic Sol-fa Society, the so-called 'Paris Peace Prize Choir'.[39] It was therefore unacceptable that certain sections, including Merthyr and Dowlais – surely a fall from grace – were 'lax and deficient in application', as was reported to the organizing committee in November 1872. It was decided to dispatch examiners to oversee the various sections, these visitations to be entrusted to Thomas Davies ('Eos Rhondda'), Dewi Alaw and Richard Jones (the Aberdare district), Alaw Ddu (Llanelli), David Francis (Merthyr), Silas Evans (Swansea) and for the Rhondda Caradog himself, who made an example of one contingent by excluding them altogether.[40]

Such an authoritarian approach – clearly necessary: singers had been picked up en route to London in 1872 who had not been to one rehearsal[41] – was no deterrent to those who still sought admission, so that there were around 450 voices by the time the second assault on the trophy was made in 1873.[42] As numbers rose, so did costs. Although an extra prize of £100 was added to the Challenge Cup in Class One, 'such sum being set off against expenses inseparable from preparing for competition',[43] it was still reckoned that each rehearsal the choir intended holding would cost £470, and a second London expedition £4,500. The choristers themselves raised £2,000 of this, with some gentry donations, but the bulk of the remainder came from the working class who knew that every chorister would have to forgo a week's wages and was likely to incur a week's expenditure while in London. This was a situation that came as no surprise to the musician and musical journalist D. Emlyn Evans, who believed that the upper and professional classes 'kept themselves entirely aloof and have no part in the aspirations and sympathies of the people'[44] – beyond, that is, the kind of pious belief expressed by Richard Fothergill, MP, at the meeting in February 1873 when the decision to compete at the Crystal Palace for the second time was formally announced, that choral singing was a means of easing the current industrial problems (there were 160,000 miners on strike in south Wales from January to March 1873) and that 'things would get back to normal once the workers recognized who their true friends were'.[45]

The strike made more time available for local practice, before the massed rehearsals cranked into action in Swansea in May, and another early in June in front of 20,000 who paid a total of £500 to listen to them in a rain-soaked Caerphilly Castle. Audiences were 'overflowing' at Newport and Merthyr, while 'such choral singing had never been heard at Llanelli', where two rehearsal-concerts at the Atheneum and a local chapel raised another £800. On 2 July they sang twice at Cardiff's Drill Hall, and gave the two final rehearsals at the Temperance Hall, Aberdare, on the seventh, when gifts of several hundreds of dollars from Welsh exiles in America were handed over. A further sum was raised through singing at the Colston Hall, Bristol, before an audience that included the renowned tenor Sims Reeves, and a less renowned singer, the Shah of Persia.[46]

The competition itself was held on 10 July, and this time it was Proudman's choir that broke down, in 'Come with Torches'. The Welsh performance, by contrast, was on this occasion a model of restraint; the singing never rose above *mezzo-forte* in the Bach, and the now disciplined approach insisted on by Caradog beforehand paid dividends when he conducted the second movement of the 'Hallelujah' more slowly than he had ever done before without disturbing the composure of the choir; in fact, while the London choir got through their programme in half an hour, it took the South Wales Choral Union forty-five minutes to sing the same items. John Curwen told Ieuan Gwyllt that 'it was not the same choir as the year before', and this was the positive impression its performance made also on the adjudicators John Goss, Julius Benedict and Joseph Barnby. So pronounced was the impact on Barnby that he told a delighted audience at Tonypandy in September 1874, when he heard five choirs singing the 'Hallelujah' – the Crystal Palace competition influenced choice of both test pieces and adjudicators – that Welsh choral singing was the best in Europe, and that his own choir, despite numbering 1,200 voices, could never produce the same effect as Caradog's had the year before.[47]

The Welsh choristers for their part were anything but overwhelmed by the solemnity of the occasion on their second visit to the Crystal Palace. They took forty minutes to assemble and take their seats on stage, until Caradog gave them the signal to stand. Then, to everyone's astonishment, he turned to face the audience. Caradog, however, did not intend conducting from this position – though it became the habit of Jules Rivière at Llandudno in the 1880s to conduct from a gilded armchair facing the audience – for it became apparent that a photograph was to be taken; another ten minutes elapsed before the choir actually sang. No attempt was made at imposing sartorial uniformity, and no distinctive ribbons or gloves worn; all wore what they chose, the women smartly attired in tight-waisted Sunday best, and the men in the dark cloth they too reserved for formal occasions. Few held scores either; as in the previous year, the pieces had been committed to memory.[48]

It was not the instantaneous attack that all eyes on the conductor ensured, nor, either, the powerful vocalization that struck listeners this time, so much as the choir's clear, consonantal articulation. English was virtually a foreign language to most of the choristers: 13 per cent of Aberdare, which contributed the largest contingent, was still monoglot Welsh-speaking at the start of the twentieth century. Yet English was the language of the oratorio in Wales, even though Ieuan Gwyllt's *Cerddor Cymreig* had provided skilful and musically sensitive translations of most of the best-known choruses. Unless there were original Welsh words, the Welsh sang in English, even when there were Welsh words available. Nearly forty years later, D. Emlyn Evans professed his inability to understand 'why . . . Welsh choirs, the majority of whose members have practically no knowledge of any other language than their own native Welsh, persist in singing their test pieces in English – a foreign tongue to them.'[49] Welsh choirs had been singing in English since the 1840s, but the success of the South Wales Choral Union at the Crystal Palace confirmed and reinforced the trend. It established another trend too, that of inviting London musicians to adjudicate in Wales: in 1873, even before Joseph Barnby ran the rule at Tonypandy, Joseph Proudman was pleased to accept an invitation to co-adjudicate alongside Caradog at a Christmas eisteddfod in Aberdare.[50]

Naturally, the wish was expressed during the heady night of victory to compete again in 1874. At home a repeat of the ecstatic scenes that had greeted the choir on their arrival back delayed a more measured assessment of the situation:

> On the arrival of the train at 8.30 p.m. the excitement became intense . . . Loud cheers were given by the assembled thousands, intermingled with the bursting of fog signals, the firing of cannon, and what with the ringing of bells and the playing of the band the scene may be more easily imagined than described.[51]

However, a decision whether to re-enter the following year could not be postponed. The competitive crucibles of Merthyr, Aberdare, Maesteg, Cwmafan and Llanelli were eager to defend the title yet again, to secure permanent possession of the cup (though in actual fact nothing in the rules stated this); and the revered Silas Evans was keen to compete against Continental choirs as well. But there were weighty voices against, too, like that of the equally respected M. O. Jones of Treherbert, supported by the representatives of Mountain Ash and Pontypridd. What carried most influence was the negative attitude of Caradog, and that ended it, at least as far as south Wales was concerned.[52] The urge to compete at the Crystal Palace had now spread to north Wales, and on 20 September 1873 the North Wales Choral Union was founded and structured on the southern pattern. The Bangor and Bethesda sections were quick off the mark with a concert at the Penrhyn Hall in March 1874, and the united choir of 440 voices assembled for the first time on Whit Saturday at Moriah, Caernarfon, under William Parry of Birkenhead. To no avail: no choral competition on the lines of 1872–3 was held again in the Crystal Palace.[53]

Despite strenuous efforts to revive it in 1885, this was the end, too, of the South Wales Choral Union, though not of the conducting career of Caradog, who went on founding choirs wherever he happened to be living.[54] His last years were spent at Pontypridd, where he conducted Haydn's *The Creation*, *Athalia* (Handel), the *Hymn of Praise* and Handel's dramatic and demanding *tour de force Israel in Egypt*, which he conducted with an orchestra of sixty at the Pontypridd National Eisteddfod in 1893. It was Caradog's decision also, from the chair of that eisteddfod's music committee, to use the orchestra to accompany the chief choral competition, the first time for this to happen at the National. That year, too, he received a tumultuous welcome from the American Welsh assembled at the Chicago World's Fair, where his presence was the occasion of near-pandemonium. He was the national choice as first chairman of the South Wales Society of Musicians in 1895, and that year pioneered the kind of concert which has retained its popularity in Wales until the present day, the festival of massed male voices: in November he fronted 500 choristers from Neath to Carmarthen in the evergreen 'Comrades in Arms', de Rille's 'Martyrs of the Arena', Joseph Parry's 'Pilgrims' and Gounod's 'Soldiers' Chorus'. They were still evergreen a century later.

3. 'Our Musical Hercules':[55] Rees Evans of Aberdare

When Caradog moved to Treorchy, his successor at the helm of the Aberdare United Choir was Rees Evans (1835–1916), a native of Cross Inn, Ammanford, who moved in 1852 to Aberavon, where he may well have heard Caradog's Bryn Seion choir competing at their first eisteddfod in 1853. In 1860 he married and settled in Aberdare to follow his vocation as a tailor and become precentor at Siloa Chapel. Like Caradog, he was a violinist and taught his singers their various parts by means of the fiddle. Unlike Caradog he disliked the idea of eisteddfodic competition, and in later life expressed the view that the success of the Côr Mawr had been 'unfortunate', for the exaggerated praise of London-based musicians had induced a dangerous complacency in Welsh choral circles when it should be realized that the era of '*hwyl* and climaxes' had passed.[56]

Cynonites, however, would not easily be persuaded that musical progress meant the abandonment of competition. Gwilym Cynon took the Aberdare choir to the Birkenhead National Eisteddfod in 1878 where at least it was placed ahead of Eos Cynlais's Rhondda representatives. But both had to yield on that occasion to the champions of Eryri (Snowdonia) whose gleeful supporters distributed mourning cards tearfully lamenting the passing of the musical glories of Aberdare and the Rhondda at 'Pen y Bercyn' (i.e. Birkenhead) on Wednesday 18 September 1878.[57]

This was not Rees Evans's choir, however, for he had taken the considered decision to forgo further competition, chiefly in response to insinuations in the English press that Welsh choirs sang single choruses but were incapable of mastering complete works. He now addressed himself to precisely this task, and his production at Christmas 1874 of Mozart's Twelfth Mass, accompanied by the Cyfarthfa bandsmen, the Aberdare String Band, two harmoniums and a piano, was the first in a notable series of annual concerts which he conducted until 1895, when he was succeeded by his son W. J. Evans. It was *Y Gerddorfa*'s measured opinion of the 1874 concert that in years to come Rees Evans's decision would be seen as 'inaugurating a new era in choral music in South Wales'. His annual concerts featured not only complete oratorios by Handel, Haydn and Mendelssohn but helped familiarize Welsh audiences with new or hitherto unfamiliar works like Rossini's *Stabat Mater*, George Macfarren's *Joseph* and Alexander Mackenzie's *Rose of Sharon*, and compositions by the two Parrys, Hubert and Joseph, whom the press were so prone to confuse. Soloists of wide renown were flattered to be invited to take part in the Aberdare Choral Union's annual oratorio concerts, including all the leading Welsh singers, many of whom had a nation-wide reputation like Mary Davies, Maggie Davies, James Sauvage, Maldwyn Humphreys, Ben Davies, Lucas Williams, Eos

TEMPERANCE HALL, ABERDARE.

PATRONS:

The Right Hon. LORD ABERDARE; C. R. M. TALBOT, Esq., M.P.; Sir H. HUSSEY VIVIAN, M.P.; HENRY RICHARD, Esq., M.P.; C. H. JAMES, Esq., M.P.; Rev. R. D. JENKINS, M.A., Vicar of Aberdare; JAMES LEWIS, Esq., J.P.; W. T. LEWIS, Esq., J.P.; D. P. DAVIES, Esq., J.P.; F. R. HOWELL, Esq.; J. C. BROWN, Esq.

Aberdare Choral Union.—Eleventh Annual Oratorio Concerts.

THREE GRAND PERFORMANCES

OF HANDEL'S

ORATORIO 'SAMSON'

WILL BE GIVEN AT THE ABOVE HALL, ON

Thursday & Friday, Dec. 25th & 26th, 1884

ARTISTES:—SOPRANO:

MADAME DUVAL-WORREL.

Contralto: MADAME SPENCER JONES.

TENORI:

FIRST DAY:
MR. TOM WILLIAMS
(EOS CYNON).

SECOND DAY:
EOS MORLAIS.

Basso: Mr. LUCAS WILLIAMS.

CHORUS: ABERDARE CHORAL UNION. ORCHESTRA: CYFARTHFA STRING BAND,

(By kind permission of W. T. CRAWSHAY, Esq.), assisted by MR. HOOPER, of Gloucester, and others. Leader: MR. G. C. BAWDEN.

Pianoforte and Solo Violinist: Miss META SCOTT. Harmonium: Mr. W. J. EVANS.

CONDUCTOR: MR. REES EVANS.

Admission:—Reserved Seats (2nd day only), 4/-; Front do., 3/-; Second do., 2/-; Third do., 1/-

Doors open at 2.30 each afternoon, and 7 in the evening. Concerts to commence at 3 in the afternoon, and 7.30 in the evening. Carriages may be ordered for 5.30 and 10 o'clock. The Hall will be comfortably heated. Entrance to Reserved Seats and Cloak-room through Canon Street.

☞ Tickets for Reserved Seats may be secured at Messrs. Farrant & Frost's, Canon Street, where a plan of the Hall may be seen. Tickets may also be had of Mr. J. Williams, Hairdresser, Commercial Street; Mr. D. E. Coleman, Mountain Ash; Mr. T. Howells (Hywel Cynon), Aberaman; Mr. George, Chemist, Hirwain; also of most of the principal tradespeople of the town, and members of the Choir.

W. LLOYD AND SON, PRINTERS, BOOKSELLERS, ETC., CANON STREET, ABERDARE.

3. The annual oratorio concerts begun in 1874 given by Rees Evans's Aberdare Choral Union attracted leading soloists, the plaudits of the critics and packed audiences to the Temperance Hall, built in 1858.

Morlais and David Hughes ('of whom an Aberdarian audience never tires').[58]

If further proof were required that, in the face of stiff competition from the Morriston Tabernacle Choir, Wales's premier musical society at this time was Rees Evans's Aberdare Choral Union, it is found in Joseph Parry's decision to take a hundred of its members to Cambridge in 1878 to perform his oratorio *Jerusalem*, a public performance of which in King's College Chapel was a prerequisite to his obtaining his prized Mus.Doc. (Cantab.). Another example of the high standards attained by this choir, and of Rees Evans's confidence in them, was his hiring of a trumpeter from the Royal Opera House to provide the accompaniment in 'The Trumpet shall Sound'.[59]

On the eve of the second Christian millennium, one more secular than the first, it requires a leap of the imagination fully to understand the popular appeal of a work like *Messiah*, which was loved and lauded as no mere product of harmony and counterpoint – Methodists, historically, disliked 'fugueing' music – but as a veritable immaculate conception. For unlike Bach in his Passions, Handel in his oratorios is not so much a religious composer as a musical moralist. *Messiah* owes its popularity among the amateur choral societies of the nineteenth and twentieth centuries to the fact that structurally it is built around the chorus, musically it is melodious and tonally stable, and textually, though it deals with the prophecy, birth and crucifixion of Christ, its universal spirit elevates it above the letter of doctrine. A conductor like Rees Evans recognized it for what it was, a spiritual epic, 'a compendium of basic Christianity set to music',[60] and he would have shared the conviction of his choristers and his audiences that, like the Bible, it was divinely inspired. An oratorio concert was ennobling, with Handel and Mendelssohn the leaders in the field. The captious critic dismisses the *Hymn of Praise* as a disastrous attempt to follow Beethoven's Ninth with its three instrumental movements followed by the vocal ones, but by the turn of the century audiences in Aberdare loved and knew by heart every note of its viscerally thrilling choruses. A performance might invite criticism but the music itself was above censure, and to participate in it as singer or listener was an act of faith.[61]

Rees Evans conducted the Aberdare Choral Union and other choirs in the district for thirty-five years. And not only in oratorio: in 1878 he produced the first performance 'in character' of Joseph Parry's *Blodwen*.[62] Before long a lively tradition of opera had been instituted in the Cynon Valley. In 1882 Daniel Jones, who was born in Cil-y-cwm,

Carmarthenshire, thirty years earlier, formed the Aberdare Glee Society to sing ballads and part-songs for male voices. Through persuading women to take the female roles, male parties like Daniel Jones's were responsible for putting on operas and cantatas entirely with local resources. At Easter 1889, inspired perhaps by an earlier visit of the professional D'Oyly Carte Opera Company, Daniel Jones presented David Jenkins's 'dramatic cantata' *David and Goliath* at the Aberdare Temperance Hall, the first occasion on which such a work was given 'in character, with full scenic and stage accessories' by any Welsh society. This led on to a series of annual amateur operatic productions: in 1890 Michael Balfe's *The Bohemian Girl*, followed by *Maritana* (Wallace), *Il Trovatore* (Verdi) in 1892 and in 1893 Flotow's *Martha*, by now with soloists from Carl Rosa and the Leslie Crotty Company in the lead roles. And as further confirmation of the extent to which in the 1890s the valley was seized by opera fever, an amateur company was founded in the village of Trecynon which launched its own series of Gilbert and Sullivan productions with *HMS Pinafore* in 1897.[63]

If it is with the Aberdare Choral Union that we associate the name of Rees Evans (of Rees Evans and Son, Ladies and Gentlemen's Tailors, 45 Commercial Street, Aberdare), the 'Son', W. J. (1866-1947) was making a name for himself with the Cwmaman Choral Society formed in 1900. Cwmaman was a close, isolated, single-industry community that grew up around and depended entirely for its livelihood on the local colliery, whose officials played an active role in the social life of the locality. The manager, D. E. Davies ('Dewi Mabon'), was a keen *eisteddfodwr*, the conductor of the Aman Glee Society and a popular as well as respected figure. By 1912 Cwmaman Choral Society was well established, even if, ostensibly, caught in a time warp: the offerings that Christmas were Handel's *Jephtha* and J. H. Roberts's *Bryn Calfaria*. The audience still had a clear sense of standards: on this occasion the tenor Mr Francis Glyn, his 'B.A. (Oxon.)' notwithstanding, was deemed to be

not of the class to which Cwmamanites are accustomed, and was decidedly a non-success with the audience . . . Welsh audiences very soon show their approval or disapproval of an artist and the fact that he was not encouraged by the crowd had a tendency to dishearten Mr. Glyn.[64]

By this time W. J. Evans had conducted both the Cwmaman Choral Society and the Cynon United Male Choir, leading the latter to a notable victory over the illustrious Manchester Orpheus Choir at the Royal Albert Hall in February 1905. He had conducted the Rhondda Orchestral Society to victory at the Pontypridd National Eisteddfod in 1893, and was by 1913 also conducting the choir of Siloa Chapel, Aberdare. On 25 December 1913 the Siloa choir performed Bach's *Christmas Oratorio*, a remarkable achievement for a chapel organization, especially so in view of Henry Walford Davies's frequent insistence in the 1920s that the Welsh had yet to discover Bach.[65] Caradog, too, would have had something to say on that score – had not the South Wales Choral Union sung Bach on both triumphant occasions at the Crystal Palace?

Caradog did not survive the century into which he was born. The new one would intensify the challenge already being presented to the institutional basis of Welsh Nonconformity by secularization and social and political change. He died on 8 December 1897, the first modern musical hero of what he himself had in 1878 dubbed 'the land of song'.[66] Its first choral flowering had bloomed in the Cynon Valley, but its roots lay over the mountain, in Merthyr.

4

Music and a Musician of Merthyr Tydfil

ଏ

1. The Frontier Years

If Wales is the land of song Merthyr is the capital of that happy land for
it is the centre of a great district, thickly populated with a large Welsh-
speaking section where music is the very breath of life to the majority of
the people and where the eisteddfod is the most popular form of social
entertainment, its methods being imbibed from earliest childhood.[1]

As the twentieth century opened Merthyr could indeed claim to be the
musical capital of Wales. It had produced composers, conductors,
choristers and bandsmen whose fame extended from Dowlais to
Danville, and from Pentre-bach to Pennsylvania Avenue: in 1904 the
choral conductor Dan Davies was entertained by President Theodore
Roosevelt at the White House itself.[2] It was its musicians that defined
Merthyr and its people to the world from 1850 down to and beyond the
First World War.

By then Merthyr had been a busy musical centre for over a century
as ballad singers and harpists mediated between an older rural culture
and the new industrial surroundings of a predominantly Welsh-speaking
population. The adjoining village of Cefncoedycymer on its northern rim
had held a chair eisteddfod in June 1816; from the early 1820s Merthyr
itself was the location of a series of competitive meetings and entertainments held variously at the Patriot, the Bell Inn, the Swan, the George,
the Dyffryn Arms, the Bush Hotel, the Glove and Shears, and the Boot,
which hosted Merthyr's own first chair eisteddfod on New Year's Day
1824.[3] Not to be outdone by the chaired poets, vocalists were allotted
their first solo competition the following year.[4] The societies which sought
to structure and impose a measure of control over these events were as
much literary as musical, and Cymdeithas Cadair Merthyr, Cymdeithas Cymmrodorion Merthyr and Cymdeithas Lenyddol Merthyr

(respectively Merthyr's Chair, Cymmrodorion and Literary Societies) overlapping with other literary groups like the Prydyddion, Llenyddion and Cymreigyddion, were not averse, until temperance exerted its sober influence, to patronizing the customary venues of a popular culture more bibulous than bardic which still bore traces of its roots in the festive disorderliness of *taplas* and taproom.

The first of a series of annual eisteddfodau sponsored by the Merthyr Cymmrodorion was held at the Vulcan in July 1826, shifting in the 1830s to the White Horse. The first Dowlais eisteddfod was held in February 1835 at the Dowlais Inn under the auspices of the Brythonic Society (Cymdeithas y Brythoniaid) where solo vocal competitions were interspersed among the literary jousts, and taverns and public houses were the venues until 1848, when a Merthyr eisteddfod was held for the first time in a chapel. The ballad culture of rural Wales found its last haven in the pubs and beerhouses around Jackson's Bridge and China, where harpists, fiddlers and balladeers like Dic Dywyll ('dark' because blind) were the agencies by which an older dispensation was transposed to an industrial environment.[5]

There seems little doubt that it was the incursion of the temperance movement into Merthyr around 1836 that was responsible for this shift and boosted choral activities, so that singing and temperance went hand in hand for over forty years. Clearly Merthyr was already vocally active by the 1830s when small groups of singers travelled in the relative comfort of the Coach Mawr (if lucky; if less lucky in Susan Morley's cart on its weekly trip to market) to the Abergavenny eisteddfod held by Cymmrodorion y Fenni under the patronage of Lady Charlotte Guest. It was the fine voice of William Morgan (father of David Morgan, 'Dai o'r Nant', later miners' agent of Aberdare) that attracted the attention of the musically aware Lady Charlotte, who in turn secured him a sought-after position at the Dowlais blast furnaces at £6 a week. William received his tuition from Ieuan Ddu (John Thomas, 1795-1871), Carmarthen-born, a central if elusive figure in the musical history of Merthyr from the early 1830s, when he settled there as a schoolmaster, a commanding swarthy man whose distinguished mien 'gave you the impression of a genius'.[6] Reckoned by the first historian of Welsh choralism to be 'probably the pioneer of choral singing in South Wales',[7] certainly in Merthyr, and by extended influence on adjoining Rhymney and Aberdare and further west on the Swansea Valley, Ieuan Ddu was credited with being the real influence behind the Crystal Palace triumphs of Caradog's South Wales Choral Union in 1872–3. A keen *eisteddfodwr* as competitor and, in later years, adjudicator, he won more prizes than anyone else at the Abergavenny eisteddfod between 1838 and 1845, and was the author of a prize essay on music history which was very likely incorporated into Thomas Stephens's *Literature of the Kymry*, the first critical history of Welsh literature. But he viewed the competitive urge with a healthy cynicism, as is evidenced by his satirical *Cambria on Two Sticks* (Pontypridd, 1867), the two crutches being the eisteddfod and penny readings. As one-time clerk to the notorious deist and Chartist leader Zephaniah Williams, as schoolmaster successor to Taliesin Williams (ab Iolo), the Unitarian son of Iolo Morganwg, and as editorial assistant on the first Welsh working-class newspaper, *Y Gweithiwr* (The Welshman), Ieuan had seriously radical credentials. He was serious about Handel too, buying for himself the 12s. *Messiah* and then copying out by hand – a colossally laborious task – the different voice parts for each of his choir of forty. The shortage of music copies was not peculiar to Merthyr, since in the 1830s and 1840s even the Huddersfield Choral Society sang and played from hand-copied parts. The elusive first performance in Wales of *Messiah*, which Ieuan and his choir are alleged to have given at Merthyr in the 1840s, and for which, as Professor Gwyn Alfred Williams observed, he must bear 'a heavy historical responsibility' for introducing it to Welsh audiences, is most likely to have been a selection of choruses. The inability or at least reluctance of Welsh choirs to sing complete works, as opposed to individual choruses,[8] was therefore half a century old when it became the object of unfavourable critical comment in the 1890s. At least Ieuan's choir was good enough to be invited by Lady Charlotte to give concerts at her own expense in London, Cheltenham and Liverpool.

As a Unitarian, Ieuan had little opportunity for direct involvement with the growing congregational singing movement, though as the trainer of a generation of local musicians he exercised a decisive influence on Merthyr music for three generations, one which was felt particularly by Abraham Bowen (1817–92), who was born in the Castle Hotel and then moved to Dowlais, where he led the singing at Bethania from 1846 until 1887. The possessor of a substantial library of music as well as a piano, the first ever seen by many Dowlaisians ('Oh! with what rapture I gazed on it and listened for the first time to the magic tones which came from it' recalled Megan Watts Hughes),[9] Abraham Bowen's centrally located house was for many years 'a sort of Jerusalem to the lovers of music in the locality', and the works he taught his Bethania choir to sing included John Ambrose Lloyd's *Gweddi Habacuc*, the Twelfth Mass attributed to Mozart, and choruses from Tanymarian's *Ystorm Tiberias*, Beethoven's

Mount of Olives and Handel's *Samson*. He was not without honour in his own locality for in January 1891, the year before he died, he was presented by the High Constable of Merthyr with an illuminated address and portrait of himself and a silver tea and coffee service for his wife, bought with the proceeds of a testimonial concert the previous October.

One of the innovations that established Abraham Bowen as the pioneer of choral singing in Merthyr was getting the women (rather than the tenors) to sing the melody; another was to encourage the use of musical instruments in churches.[10] This assigning of the melody to the ladies in his choir was seen, later, as striking an early blow for women's rights.[11] In point of fact the issue of the sopranos singing the tenor line and the tenors the melody in the English fashion had already occasioned a bitter rift in Merthyr. Moses Davies had been born in Defynnog, Breconshire, in 1799 and moved to Merthyr at five years of age.[12] A plasterer by trade he sought work in England in the 1820s, returning to Merthyr in 1827 to galvanize the choir at Pontmorlais chapel by framing and applying a set of rules that required each of the two hundred choristers to pay 3*d*. (1p) a month for the coal and light used in rehearsal, and to build up a music library.[13] Entirely self-taught in music, he seems exceptional in not having come under the influence of Ieuan Ddu, but taught sight-reading by a method of painted cards before Hullah's sol-fa system became known and certainly before Curwen threw singing classes the lifeline of the movable doh. The vexed question of whether women or men should sing the tenor line caused Moses Davies to leave Pontmorlais in 1850, though he had also been reprimanded by the chapel's notoriously strict diaconate for going to a picnic in Vaynor.[14] Pontmorlais's stern puritanism extended to the tonsorial: forty-eight members were ejected because of the younger men's habit of brushing their hair back from the forehead (characteristically high in Merthyr) rather than bringing it forward. 'If our Saviour became a member at Pontmorlais he would surely be excommunicated', complained Edward Matthews, himself a Calvinistic Methodist from Ewenni in the Vale of Glamorgan.[15] It was not in Pontmorlais, therefore, that Moses Davies found an ally in allocating the tenor line to the sopranos, but at Soar, a chapel that first assembled in the Long Room at the Crown in 1794 and whose singing was led from 1835 by the gifted Rosser Beynon (1811–76) whose family had moved from Glynneath to Merthyr in 1815.[16]

Of the meanest origins – 'un o blant y llwy bren', born with a wooden rather than a silver spoon – what Ieuan was to choralism Rosser was to congregational singing. Again self-taught, Rosser had already been conducting at Soar for six years when Ieuan came to Merthyr to offer him further instruction. Rosser proceeded to establish his name as a conductor, teacher and editor. On the basis of the evening classes he started teaching in 1840, he built up a male party of twenty, one of Wales's first; as a teacher he instructed a shoal of Merthyr musicians, including Abraham Bowen, Dan Price and D. T. Williams (Tydfylyn), who formed his own temperance choir in 1843–4 and composed several works for it; in his writing capacity he was music editor of *Y Diwygiwr* (The Reformer) from *c.*1830 to the 1850s, and edited *Telyn Seion* (Zion's Harp) in 1845, a narrow long book of 200 pages containing 22 anthems, and 130 hymn-tunes. This was an eclectic and innovative collection including tunes by Bach, Mozart and Haydn, though the kind of German chorales admired by Ieuan Gwyllt found far less favour than tunes then in vogue: some by his Merthyr contemporaries, several snatched from Merthyr's pullulating ballad and tavern subculture, and also for the first time hymn tunes by J. A. Lloyd ('Eifionydd' and 'Groeswen') as well as metronome markings. Rosser opened a bookshop in Merthyr in the 1840s but was reckoned to have 'spent too much time in the loft with the breve, semi-breve and minim', which resulted in the failure of his business, and he spent the last twenty-six years of his life from 1850 as an under-supervisor at the Dowlais Ironworks. [17]

That year he changed not only his vocation but his chapel, leaving Soar for Ynysgau over a temperance dispute. By then musical Merthyr was taking institutional shape and temperance was largely responsible. Shrewdly highlighting the colourful and ceremonial, its early features were street parades and singing, as on Christmas Day 1837 when a long procession descended on Pontmorlais from Dowlais, an event repeated annually for several years on Easter Monday. In 1841 twelve banners could be seen to represent different contingents from Aberdare and Rhymney as well as Merthyr and Dowlais, and an early indication of the shift to the choral-eisteddfodic is suggested by the fact that choirs from Merthyr and Aberdare shared the prize at the first Carw Coch eisteddfod in Trecynon (Aberdare) in 1846. [18]

Two years later, and 1848 is the European year of revolutions in the musical and eisteddfodic history of Wales too, on several counts. One of them is the graduation of the choral competition to the major eisteddfod programme: at the Abergavenny eisteddfod held over two days in October, four choirs competed for a prize that went to a Rhymney choir conducted by William (Billy Shôn) Morgan from Penderyn above Merthyr and Hirwaun, and it is entirely plausible, certainly appropriate in view of the heroic choral feats associated in the 1890s with John Price's great Rhymney United Choir and then with Dan Owen's rival Gwent Choral Union from the same north-west corner of Monmouth-shire, that it is to Rhymney that the credit belongs for producing the first choir victorious at a representative eisteddfod – just as it is to the perhaps unlikelier venue of Abergavenny that the credit, or otherwise, belongs for the musical innovation which steadily but surely began to elbow out the long-standing literary competitions.[19]

It was also on Christmas Day 1848 that the first temperance eisteddfod was held, not of course in a public house but in the Primitive Methodist chapel, Morganstown, Merthyr, where the programme included a competition for composing a hymn-tune, an event which continues to attract large numbers of entries to eisteddfodau a hundred and fifty years later. The event was followed the next year at Bethesda Congregational chapel when the previous year's seven items had increased to twenty-one, including a choral competition at which J. A. Lloyd adjudicated. The chapel remained the concert hall of Merthyr even after the Temperance Hall was built in 1852 in time for the following year's temperance eisteddfod, where seven choirs competed on Lloyd's 'Teyrnasoedd y Ddaear' and at which the twelve-year-old Joseph Parry sang with the Bethesda choir. Over-cautiously, but perhaps judiciously, Dr Evan Davies of Swansea adjudicated that the seven-guinea prize should be shared by all seven choirs.[20] It is evident that by the 1850s Merthyr's eisteddfodau were routinely being held in chapels; it is apparent, too, that they were successful early on in attracting leading Welsh musicians as judges: John Ambrose Lloyd adjudicated regularly from 1848, John Mills of the famous dynasty of Llanidloes musicians in 1854, Ellis Roberts, the royal harpist, in 1855 and Owain Alaw in 1858, with Sir Henry Leslie becoming the first English adjudicator in 1872. By 1858 this eisteddfod featured solos, duets, quartets and glees, and a lull in the course of the proceedings was sharply enlivened, we are told, when the pride of Anglesey, Llew Llwyfo, sang 'The Maniac' with great effect.[21] The next year Merthyr's now well-established temperance eisteddfod held a brass-band competition and in 1865 it pioneered the trail that would be followed for the next hundred years by initiating the first competition for children's voices as well as a sight-reading contest won by Eos Morlais's Dowlais choir.

Among those whose musical career was shaped by temperance was Megan Watts, who became Megan Watts Hughes after her marriage to Lloyd Hughes in June 1872.[22] She was born at 2 Ivor Street, Dowlais in

1845 (not in 1847, as she herself claimed). Neither of her parents, who originated from the Fishguard area of Pembrokeshire, had any education beyond what they had learned from the Welsh Bible, of which her mother could recite large portions. The Dowlais of the mid-nineteenth century consisted, apart from a sprinkling of tradesmen, almost entirely of colliers and ironworkers, among whom the death rate by industrial accident was fifty per annum, and the average age at death was 40.[23] With the exception of a few English immigrants and a small Irish colony, the majority of the inhabitants were virtually monoglot Welsh. Despite the ubiquity of the chapels, which were the sole places of worship apart from an Anglican and a Roman Catholic church, their ameliorative influence hardly affected a rough element addicted to drinking, brawling and prize- and cock-fighting on Sundays on what were known as 'The Tips', but in the household at 2 Ivor Street religion and music prevailed. As Megan Hughes remembered it,

> Our cottage home was certainly what might be called musical, for every one of its members could sing . . . in tune and in time – no musical instruments of any description except a tin whistle had ever been seen inside it but some very fine voices were heard.[24]

Even courtship rituals acquired a musical complexion, for on Sunday the interval between Sunday school and evening service was devoted to the singing of Welsh hymns, in which mother and father sang soprano and bass and the tenor part was usually taken by one or more young men, like Robert Rees (Eos Morlais), especially since Megan's two sisters were 'prima donnas' with, it appears, beautiful voices and an exceptional talent for singing. Joining the Bethania singing class as a young girl, before the age of ten she had learned the cantata *Y Mab Afradlon*, the early Welsh oratorio *Gweddi Habacuc*, the anthem 'Duw sy'n Noddfa', and selections from Mozart's Twelfth Mass. Then her interest shifted to the Dowlais Temperance Number One choir who met in Hermon chapel and with whom she sang until the age of sixteen, by which time she had become acquainted with all the great oratorios and Welsh anthems and cantatas like Tanymarian's *Ystorm Tiberias* (The Storm of Tiberias) and Owain Alaw's *Y Ddaeargryn* (The Earthquake), a typical example of how chapel and temperance choirs provided the 'institutional infrastructure' for nurturing local talent.[25] The people with whom she sang knew little of the technicalities or vocabulary of music. The words contralto, mezzo-soprano and baritone were foreign to them, while 'as to a knowledge of the art of singing they were as ignorant, most of them, as the birds that sang in the trees. They knew nothing of vocal ranges, registers, breaks and the fixed rule laid down in books.' It was almost entirely a working-class choir and frequently the men employed at the ironworks came to practice on their way to the night shift, their moleskin trousers, soiled aprons and jackets modishly adorned with a small breast-pocket hand-kerchief. The modern reader cannot but share some of Megan Watts's sense of humility: 'As I listened to them singing from Beethoven's *Engedi* 'Worlds unborn shall sing His glory', they seemed to me to be trans-formed into Musical Gods and I felt scores of times as if I should curtsey to them'[26] – to Thomas Hughes a miner, to Evan Samuel a shoemaker, to Dafydd Lloyd a rough puddler, and not least to Eos Morlais himself, who at the age of twenty wielded the baton and conducted that sizeable choir with all the artistic instincts of the educated singer he was yet to become (asked later in life at what musical university he had received his musical training, he replied, 'Number Two Dowlais colliery').[27] Initially his familiarity with English cannot have been too intimate: Megan Watts recalls the great difficulty the choir had in singing in a language few spoke, so that the words had to be effortfully read in addition to the music. Nor was it only a matter of reaching a uniform pronunciation, for 'in singing English and Latin words one could not help missing a spirit which was ever present when singing Welsh – with the native tongue the music became life and true feeling, as from a deep well of intelligent emotion.'

Suspicions that the temperance movement was humourlessly dedica-ted to the suppression of pleasure and enjoyment are dispelled by the sense of lively social occasion that annual excursions could engender and the opportunity which the larger, more formal choral societies fully exploited later in the century for sociability and the company of the opposite sex. 'The excitement was great' as the day of the trip to Rhymney dawned:

> At a very early hour the people were astir, groups standing at the corners of the streets to witness the departure of the fiery-souled singers . . . Gigs, phaetons, carts, wagons and every sort of vehicle had been requisitioned to convey them to their destination. As they wended their way over the mountain roads the young singers, dressed in their best Sunday apparel and in the highest of spirits, would burst forth into song . . . to be followed by merry laughter caused by Shencyn Morris the wit of the party. It was song and laughter all the way until they reached their destination.[28]

It was on that particular trip that members of both Dowlais choirs decided what could be done to give Megan Watts a musical training: concerts would be held in her aid and she would be sent to Cardiff for a general education and training before a series of further concerts raised £500 to send her to London's Royal Academy of Music in 1864.[29]

She soon embarked on a concert tour over the length and breadth of Wales from 1863 to 1865. In the course of December 1863 she sang in Liverpool, Bath, Dowlais, Newport and Carmarthen; in Rhymney the following January her rendering of 'He was Despised' reportedly reduced hundreds to tears. In south Wales she was accompanied by other soloists like the 'Welsh nightingale' Edith Wynne, and by instrumentalists like the renowned flautist Signor Paggi.[30] The opportunity was seized to elevate rather than pander to popular taste, to the evident gratification of the columnist of *Baner ac Amserau Cymru* (possibly Moses Davies's son, and therefore a Dowlais man) who complimented the vocalists' good taste as well as their vocal abilities, and especially the endeavour to bring instrumental music to a wider public. It was only in the recent past that a piano solo used to be the signal for total indifference if not indiscipline, but the audience now listened with rapt attention to trios, fantasias and solos on combinations of piano, flute, cornet and voice. No doubt it helped that the fantasia should consist of national airs, and that Miss Watts's rendition of Rossini's 'Cavatina' was the musical equivalent of Blondin's high-wire act.

Dowlais itself may not have been the natural venue for high-class concerts but celebrated artists were not unknown there: Welsh singers like Edith Wynne, Owain Alaw and Llew Llwyfo, as well as the renowned Madame Parepa who sang excerpts from *The Creation* with the Dowlais choirs before Megan Watts went to Cardiff in 1863.[31] She was also among the crowd of two to three thousand at the 'grand concert' that concluded a two-day eisteddfod in Merthyr in September 1859, the most prestigious musical occasion in the town until the National Eisteddfod of 1881, when two to three thousand listened to solos, duets, trios and quartets from Sainton-Dolby, Pollitzer, Schreurs and Paque, who reportedly 'astonished the audience with their artistic skill', even though Sainton-Dolby felt slighted at being eclipsed by Edith Wynne in Welsh dress singing the plaintive 'Mae Robin yn swil'.[32]

When the Temperance Hall was opened in Market Square, Merthyr, in 1852 it contained rooms for concerts, eisteddfodau and practice rehearsals, and inaugurated a series of Saturday-night concerts to keep workmen away from the tavern, of which there was one for every twenty-

four houses in mid-nineteenth-century Merthyr, whose population of
46,000 was served by 305 drinking establishments, with another 137 in
Dowlais. The new hall was an immediate boon to a musician like Rosser
Beynon, who lost no time in rehearsing his choir there on Sunday
afternoons effectively enough to win on two choruses from *Messiah* at the
hall's first eisteddfod in June that year (1852). Longer periods of practice
enabled Rosser's choir in August to treat an audience at the new Baptist
chapel in Aberdare to a rich repast of movements from *St Paul*, Handel's
Te Deum, *Israel in Egypt*, *Messiah*, Mozart's *Requiem* and *The Creation*. 'It
is a credit to the locality', ran one report, 'that so much has been done of
late years for the management of choral singing', an impression confirmed when choirs from Merthyr and Swansea joined forces at the
Temperance Hall in June 1854 to sing Mozart's Twelfth Mass, perhaps
the first choral *and* orchestral performance done in Wales of this work,
and one attended, so he claimed, by the young Joseph Parry.[33]

The Dowlais Temperance Choir was one of the most formidable competitive forces in the land following the formation of the East Glamorgan
and Gwent Temperance Union in 1854. It held its annual festival in
Hermon, Dowlais, in 1857 and 1861, and in Bethania, Dowlais, in 1867.
It fostered the talents of Megan Watts, David Rosser and Eos Morlais, so
that Watts, Rosser and David Francis won on the vocal trio at the Aberdare National Eisteddfod in 1861 when Dowlais also shared the ten-
guinea choral prize with Aberdare, arguably the premier choral body in
the country at that time. The following January (1862) the committee of
the Union decided to raise money to further Megan Watts's musical
career – she herself playing a part by becoming the first winner of a £50
scholarship at the Swansea National in 1863 – and trustees were
appointed to supervise her affairs until 1868.[34]

Another offshoot of the Dowlais temperance movement was its
eisteddfodau, held at Dowlais schools. In 1864 the choral test piece was
the demanding double chorus 'Dyma'r Gwyntoedd' (Behold the Winds)
from *Ystorm Tiberias*, whose execution was assessed by three adjudicators
well known in the Merthyr and Cynon valleys, D. T. Williams (Tydfylyn),
Thomas Davies (Eos Rhondda) and David Rosser.[35] The following year,
to indicate the event's growing status, a choir travelled from Mountain
Ash to beat four others for £12 on 'Yr Haf' (Summer), a glee by 'Gwilym
Gwent'.

Musical notes dropped so spontaneously from the pen of Gwilym
Gwent (born William Aubrey Williams in 1834) that 'it probably cost him
more effort to write a postcard than to compose a glee'.[36] One of the

4. Temperance exerted a powerful influence throughout this period. Here the Dowlais Temperance Choir is seen on the steps of the Crystal Palace where it won the premier competition for Temperance Choirs in July 1895. The conductor (with baton) is A. J. Rees.

most prolific and popular composers for much of the second half of the century, this 'Welsh Rossini' was hitting his stride in the 1860s. 'Yr Haf' and 'Y Gwanwyn' (Spring) were the most widely sung of a stream of glees and part-songs that flowed from his pen in this decade, and he achieved instant success with his prize-winning cantata *Y Mab Afradlon* (The Prodigal Son) at the Aberystwyth eisteddfod in 1865. A native of Tredegar, he migrated in 1872 to Pennsylvania where he died in 1891. His career thus ran parallel with, though geographically in the opposite direction to that of Joseph Parry who returned to Wales from the USA to take up the newly created chair of music at Aberystwyth in 1874; and there was no love lost between them. Writing home across the Atlantic in 1880 after hearing that 'Joe and his "Emmanuel" had been successful in London', Gwilym expressed the opinion that 'unless Joe's work was better than his personality it could not be up to much. He's one for the money. Let the world go to the devil.'[37]

In November 1867 the musical journal *Y Cerddor Cymreig* looked in vain for a Welsh composer. Brinley Richards was too French and John Thomas (Pencerdd Gwalia) too Italian. Neither was able to convey in his music the desired delicious melancholy, and given their education, mental disposition and social milieu it was futile to expect anything Welsh from them; neither was likely to fulfil the hoped-for role. If and when this musical Messiah should ever appear,

> and there is precious little evidence of his appearing in the immediate future, he will be rooted in the heart of his nation, the living embodiment of his country's emotions, religious, social and political, so that his works will be an accurate and vital mirror of the soul of the nation.

Y Cerddor Cymreig saw no likelihood of such a composer emerging in the foreseeable future; but it was wrong. Joseph Parry from Merthyr Tydfil was on his way.

2. 'Something Wrong with the Balance': Joseph Parry (1841–1903)

Joseph Parry was born to a poor, Nonconformist working-class family in Merthyr, a town floating on a sea of song, excrement and human effluvia, and facing appalling problems of social order and public health, in the decade that ended with a cholera epidemic that caused eighty-one deaths in his own neighbourhood of Georgetown and killed four out of ten

5. Dr Joseph Parry (1841–1903) of Merthyr, 'Pencerdd America', Aberystwyth's first professor of Music, flawed genius and national icon.

children before the age of five.[38] Though born in Chapel Row, he grew up not to the strains of hymns but of the Cyfarthfa Band that practised in the Lamb and Flag in Georgetown; he followed it through the town on ceremonial occasions and listened out for it as it entertained at the social round of fêtes, balls and garden parties on the terraces at Cyfarthfa Castle.

This was Robert Thompson Crawshay's private band, founded in 1838 for his personal edification and social elevation, which pioneered arrangements of Italian opera, notably Rossini and Donizetti, as well as Meyerbeer and transcriptions of entire symphonies of Beethoven and Haydn, which were as much a novelty as the Sunday concerts the band introduced in local parks.[39] It would achieve national exposure on the second day of the first National Brass Band contest at the Crystal Palace in July 1860, playing the overture to *Nabucco* in front of 22,000 and beating over forty bands, including the previous day's winner, John Foster's Black Dyke Mills, for a first prize of £30, a silver cup and a complete set of Boosey's *Brass Band Journal*. Ten years later Charles Dickens's *Household Words* reported the wonderment of a visitor to Merthyr on hearing boys in the Cyfarthfa Works whistling airs rarely heard outside the drawing-rooms of fashionable metropolitan society. By the time Joseph Parry reached the age of eleven the *Musical Times* was reporting on concerts given at the castle by the Cyfarthfa Band, whose repertoire included Rossini's overture to *The Thieving Magpie* and a march from Meyerbeer's *The Sorceress*. The band survived longer than Parry, and though it was taken over by Merthyr Borough Council in 1908 – a striking example of musicians becoming civic property – very soon afterwards it slid into obscurity, its glory days of the years between 1850 and 1870 long gone.[40] Joseph Parry, though, was exposed early to its sound and its repertoire, and the influence can be detected in most of his published work, not merely in the 'go' which his first biographer identified in his music but in its distinctive rhythmic, often martial characteristics, too.[41] Why he should be criticized for this is unclear: the last movement of Beethoven's Ninth suggests he was in the best company.

A collier boy at ten years of age, a Cyfarthfa ironworker at twelve, earning 6*d*. (3p) for a twelve-hour shift, in 1854 Parry emigrated with his family from a Merthyr that, according to an official report of 1850, 'was a place to quit for a healthier spot once you had made a competence',[42] to Pennsylvania where he worked in the rolling mills at Danville until 1865 and received what little educational grounding he acquired beyond Sunday school from his Welsh-born music teachers, John Abel Jones of Merthyr and John M. Price from Rhymney. Parry would later portentously claim that 'if I have succeeded in anything in music it is due to these men, my own industry and God'.[43]

His work as a puddler for ten years gave him the opportunity to write down the musical ideas taking shape in his head, and he cultivated a prodigious ability to remember. This was achieved at some cost, for that remarkable retentive faculty made it difficult, later, to distinguish between the tunes he heard in his head and those he had heard outside it; charitably we may say that it is merely echoes of Donizetti, Bellini and Rossini that we find in his work, of Verdi in tandem with Rossini, in his opera *Blodwen*, and with Wagner in his oratorios, while the rich four-part vocal scoring of Handel and Mendelssohn penetrated the whole fabric of his musical being.

From the early 1860s he began sweeping the board at American eisteddfodau, then at the National Eisteddfod in Wales itself, though when he arrived at the Aberystwyth National in 1865 it was to see the prizes scooped by his rival Gwilym Gwent because his own entries had been lost in transit.[44] His winning five-part motet 'Gostwng o Argwlydd dy glust' ('Incline Thine Ear, O Lord') at Swansea – where in the guise of various *noms de plume* like 'Bachgen bach o Ferthyr erioed, erioed' (A little lad from Merthyr, always, always), and the more self-regarding 'J. P. Bach' he won every other competition prize as well in 1863 – was immediately adopted as a test piece at Llandudno the following year, and this was to be the pattern for the remainder of his career.[45]

Parry had a facility for melody and tunefulness, and his period at the Royal Academy from 1868 to 1871, which he financed by organizing a concert tour for himself – an accomplished pianist and singer – and supporting artists throughout Wales in 1868–9, taught him structure and organization but not control and discipline. His London teacher, William Sterndale Bennett, had studied with Mendelssohn in Leipzig, which enabled Parry to tell his own pupil David Jenkins at Aberystwyth that Jenkins himself was through him indirectly a pupil of Mendelssohn ('You know that Mendelssohn is your musical great-grandfather. It is this way: he was Sterndale Bennett's teacher, Bennett was mine and I am yours').[46] He called his sons Joseph Haydn, David Mendelssohn ('Mendy') and William Sterndale, but whether or not he saw it in those terms himself, it was a matter for regret that Parry did not have the opportunity to study on the Continent as Brinley Richards had under Chopin, and Pencerdd Gwalia did at Leipzig, where David de Lloyd went later, or later again, like Grace Williams in Vienna. Had Parry been able to associate with European composers in France and Germany instead of Sterndale Bennett at the Academy, he might have found an original voice as opposed to imitating Mendelssohn, Rossini and Verdi from a distance. He might also have thereby avoided the fusty academic and sentimentally religious atmosphere of Victorian musical life that pervades much of his work, though in this respect he was fortunate that his Welsh Nonconformity safeguarded him from some of the more detrimental effects of the Anglican organ loft and the well-stuffed drawing-room.

It seems clear enough that up to the 1870s Parry's music, eclectic when it was not overtly sub-Handelian,[47] was stylistically as good as, if not superior to, contemporaries like Balfe, Benedict, Goss, Smart, Ouseley and Steggal, representatives of what we might call the English proto-renaissance who had received a musical education to university

level. But from the 1880s Hubert Parry, Charles Stanford and the archi-
tects of the full-blown English musical renaissance (so-called), none of
them great composers, began preparing the field in terms of compositional technique, musical education and public receptiveness for the
authentic genius of Elgar, Delius, Holst and Ralph Vaughan Williams.
Parry, by contrast (*Joseph* Parry: even the Welsh press could confuse him
with his English namesake Hubert) wrote for the musically uneducated
ordinary working people of Wales, the *gwerin*, whose reciprocal venera-
tion for 'Y Doctor Mawr' combined adulation with genuine love and
admiration for Wales's first university-educated professional musician.

He composed tirelessly from about 1860 until his death in 1903, forty
years entirely lacking in self-criticism, but productive of 300 songs and
innumerable anthems, chorales, glees, choruses, instrumental and large-
scale choral works in which, or in many of which, he touched, exposed
and expressed the frequently cheap and occasionally deep emotionalism
of the Welsh. Personally naïve and childlike as he was reckoned to be, it is
possible that his best work is his children's *Ymgom yr Adar* (Cantata of the
Birds, 1871). His own emotionalism frequently surfaced when hearing his
own works: when his oratorio *Jerusalem*, submitted for his Cambridge
Mus.Doc., was performed in King's College Chapel and A. A. Mann
played the overture which incorporates his hymn-tune 'Llangristiolus' on
the solo-flute stop, Parry wept like a child.[48] That he should have
reintroduced it, however skilfully, into the double choral fugue further on
in the oratorio was exactly what D. Emlyn Evans had in mind when
criticizing Parry's 'musical gymnastics',[49] for subsuming hymn-tunes (not
always his own) into large works was one of his favourite ploys: 'Crugybar'
appears in *The Maid of Cefn Ydfa*, and 'Moriah', 'Dusseldorf',
'Meirionnydd', 'Bangor' and 'Abertawe' in *Emmanuel*. At least, the
derivation was obvious and no attempt was made to disguise it. But his
fatal lack of a self-critical faculty meant that he never changed anything
once it was on paper. Thus, when the tenor Ben Davies told him that
Saul's solo in prison in *Saul of Tarsus* was exactly like Wolfram's 'Evening
Star' aria in *Tannhäuser* Parry did absolutely nothing about it.[50] This
effortless facility to produce tunes allied to an inability to be more self-
critical rendered virtually worthless Parry's own 1898 hymn-book, since
most of the 500 tunes in it were pale echoes of his dozen best.

Joseph Parry's faults as a composer have been rehearsed by Dr Dulais
Rhys: he lacked adventure (not least in changing key), his songs never
rise above the Victorian parlour-song variety, and he could be
embarrassingly derivative, as in the quotation from 'Hen Wlad fy

Nhadau' in the first four bars of the piano introduction to 'Suo Gân' (1883) and from 'In Dublin's Fair City' in bars eight to twelve.[51] His teacher Sterndale Bennett had a pronounced fondness for the Mendelssohnian 6/8 foxtrot, but could avoid giving it a sentimental inflection; Parry could never compose in 6/8 without sentimentality. Increasingly susceptible in his later years, like his pupil David Jenkins, to Wagner, in his cantata *Cambria* (1896) his attempt to use a leitmotiv is vitiated by his inability to vary it according to the musical or dramatic context, varying instead the harmony of the accompaniment according to the words. His eclecticism could baffle the critics. When his *Saul of Tarsus* ('an oratorio for the Welsh' in the *Musical Times*'s description) was given its première at the Rhyl National Eisteddfod in 1892, the *Musical Herald* recognized that this 'dramatic oratorio' was not quite Handelian or Mendelssohnian; in its use of motifs, elaborate instructions for the placing of the chorus and in its complete scenes rather than arias and cut-and-dried separate numbers, a pronounced Wagnerian influence could be detected. On the other hand, the last movement of scene 1 'would not (have been) out of place in an opera of the Verdi school'. The *Herald* concluded: 'In spite of this stylistic mélange it is all wonderfully striking and effective, the orchestration being often fresh and piquant, though one is not always sure whether he is listening to a sacred oratorio or to a military band playing on parade.'[52]

He saw his role as that of national educator, with his own works as exemplars. He spoke of his own compositions as if they were the work of someone else, a third-person device often affected by the conceited, and when he published a useful *Theory of Music* in Welsh in 1888 to wean young people away from a sole dependence on the tonic sol-fa so that they might become acquainted with the works of the masters, he clearly included himself among them. He had an undoubted sense of mission, but was not the best missionary, as his *Emmanuel* testifies. In his preface he introduced it to the lovers of music throughout the Principality in the hope that 'they may derive pleasure and profit in perusing and rehearsing it and that it may serve in some measure to foster and elevate and reform the taste of the rising generation in connection with sacred music'. *The Times*'s notice of a performance at St James's Hall in May 1880 thought the music 'well adapted . . . for such an educational purpose', pointing to the choral fugue in the third part and the concluding double chorus as examples of contrapuntal skill and genuine part-writing 'more than sufficient for the educational purpose referred to'. But it also could not ignore the appalling libretto (never Parry's strong point; this one was by

Gwilym Hiraethog) nor the fact that apart from what it diplomatically referred to as 'a few Wagnerian reminiscences', Parry had ignored the musical developments of the previous thirty years.[53]

Parry wrote *Emmanuel* at Aberystwyth where he held the chair of music from 1874 to 1880 and offended even those well disposed towards him by flaunting his Cambridge gown on every occasion (he erroneously believed he was the first Welsh Mus.Bac., Cantab.), and when it came to contemporary Welsh compositions, performed only his own works, ignoring J. A. Lloyd, Tanymarian and Owain Alaw.[54] He ultimately fell foul of the college authorities through a combination of envy (his students constituted a quarter of the total enrolment), accusations of indiscipline (he was no disciplinarian and an apparently hopeless teacher except to a favoured few), and complaints at his frequent absences adjudicating (though his mercurial judgements made him an erratic adjudicator)[55] and conducting (to which Parry argued that this was an obligation to his fellow countrymen, like Principal T. C. Edwards preaching).

The fact remains that virtually all Welsh musicians of distinction of the pre-1914 period were students of his: composers and conductors like T. Maldwyn Price, W. T. Samuel, R. C. Jenkins, J. T. Rees, Daniel Protheroe, David Jenkins and D. C. Williams; singers like William Davies, James Sauvage, Hettie Davies, Jennie Alltwen Davies and David Hughes. Forced to renounce his chair at Aberystwyth, he ran a private music academy (the Aberystwyth School of Music) until he accepted an invitation to be organist of Ebenezer Chapel, Swansea, where he composed a tune every Sunday and taught privately. Once again he continued to ignore the work of other Welsh composers except when he required their services as examiners, and created antagonism by characteristically monopolizing the music contribution to the royal opening of Swansea Dock in October 1881. Then he moved to Cardiff in 1888 and established another music school (address: Beethoven Chambers), his fourth in twenty-five years after previous establishments in Danville, Aberystwyth and Swansea.

It was in Aberystwyth, however, that his popularity was at its zenith and his muse at its most prolific: male choruses for conspirators, colliers and sailors, the celebrated love-song 'Myfanwy', the opera *Blodwen*, the cantata *Joseph*, the oratorio *Emmanuel* and innumerable hymn-tunes and songs for solo voice. At Aberystwyth Parry composed not only the hymn-tune that bears its name – in the minor key of which Parry was too fond ('Aberystwyth' fixed the minor-key hymn-tune as a Welsh speciality) – but also the opera with which his name is indelibly associated. Two years after the first full performance of *The Ring* in a specially built opera house in Bayreuth, *Blodwen* was first presented on 21 May 1878 in the Temperance Hall, Aberystwyth, where religious sensibilities would not permit acting with singing on stage, so that it was performed without costumes or action. Several of his students (Hettie Davies, Annie Williams, William Davies and R. C. Jenkins) took the leading roles, Joseph Haydn (Parry), aged thirteen, provided piano accompaniment and twelve-year-old David Mendelssohn Parry was at the harmonium. It was given its first performance 'in character' in more liberal Aberdare the following month and then took the country by storm. It is precisely its colourful setting in a faux-medieval Wales that would have made it instantly recognizable to any European representative of the nineteenth-century nationalist Romantic school. By August 1879 it had been performed forty times, and on Christmas Day that year was staged, in Welsh, in Cincinatti.[56] On 12 May 1880 it was produced at St James's Hall and at the Crystal Palace a month later (9 June), though the Alexandra Palace had staged a concert performance two years before (5 June 1878). By 1896 Parry estimated that there had been some five hundred performances in Wales and the USA of *Blodwen*, the only one of his nine operas to survive him.

Parry, fully aware of music's potential as a social force, and anxious to bring it within reach of an unprivileged working class, presented it to the nation in these terms:

> The composer has, in the present instance, entered on a department of the art which has hitherto been entirely neglected by Welsh composers. He has for some time felt the want of a composition like this in the music of Wales which is so rich in other aspects. This class of music has been developed to such an extent by other nations that he thought the Welsh, who are pre-eminently a musical people and have a strong predilection for dramatic representations, ought certainly to be stimulated to cultivate it. Such are the Composer's reasons for placing the opera before his countrymen.[57]

Despite its four-square structure, its obvious derivations and plagiarisms (almost lifting direct from Rossini and, in the case of the duet 'Mae Cymru'n Barod' nakedly so from the now unfamiliar Vincenzo Gabussi's *The Fishermen*, as Daniel Protheroe and David Jenkins were quick to recognize at the time); for all its obviously Italianate pattern of recitatives, arias, duets, ensembles and choruses; for all its humbling comparison with its direct contemporaries, including *Die Walküre* (1870), *Aïda* (1871), *L'Arlésienne* (1872), *Boris Godunov* and *Die Fledermaus* (1874), *Carmen*

(1875), *Parsifal* and *Samson et Delilah* (1877) – for all these, Joseph Parry was blazing a trail uncharted by earlier Welsh composers, and one down which only a few intrepid souls would venture over the next hundred years. After all, opera had been current in Italy, France and Germany since the seventeenth century, and despite developing apace in England in the eighteenth, English opera in the first half of the nineteenth century had been little more than a sequence of popular melodies, pointless plots and poor libretti which eventually yielded to the light operas of Bishop, Balfe and, in time, Gilbert and Sullivan. While the Savoy Operas were in a class of their own, even they were only derivations of Offenbach and the mid-century Parisian *opéra bouffe*. It was not until the 1870s, thanks to Carl Rosa, that grand opera caught on in England.

The first opera Joseph Parry had ever seen was *Fidelio* in Philadelphia in 1863. Welsh soil, by contrast, was distinctly unpromising: adjudicating the libretto for a cantata in 1862, the poet Ceiriog had remarked that theatre-goers were a rare breed in Wales and habitués of the opera even rarer. From this perspective, Parry's idea of a Welsh opera on a Welsh theme with Welsh words was strikingly innovative. The sensible comparison, then, is not with Johann Strauss or Saint-Saëns but with Arthur Sullivan, whose popularity Parry rivalled and whose musical output ran along similar tramlines of cantatas, oratorios, hymns (though Sullivan was far less prolific in this respect than Parry, who boasted that he had written more tunes than even J. B. Dykes) and part-songs for male choirs. *Blodwen* has been favourably compared with Sullivan's *Ivanhoe*, though the latter failed because the composer had broken his collaboration with W. S. Gilbert. Had Parry sought a better librettist, as Sullivan or Edward German had, *Blodwen* might better have survived the test of time, but late-nineteenth-century Welsh composers – hymn-writers apart – were ill-served by their 'books of words'. But there is no doubt that what contributed most of all to *Blodwen*'s appeal in Wales was its tuneful accessibility, and because it was written in Welsh. Certainly its success was as unprecedented in the history of Wales as its composition was a musical landmark whose melodious, richly harmonic appeal to the patriotic instincts of the Welsh gave them a sense of musical identity at a time when the unhistoric nations were asserting themselves across Europe. A contemporary gained the impression that 'the thousands' had gone half crazy over it, performances interrupted by people waving scarves and handkerchiefs, shouting and stamping, 'until the learned doctor had to implore them to let the work proceed'.[58] If Rossini was apt to wax eloquent on the immense responsibility borne by popular musicians, it was a responsibility that Parry, who was stylistically so indebted to him, took no less seriously.

It is not without significance that the single choral number to have survived from *Blodwen* is 'The Huntsmen's Chorus', still sung by Welsh male choirs a century later despite, or because of, its strong overtones of Weber's chorus from *Der Freischütz*. Few Welsh composers had written specifically for male choirs by 1870, though by 1900 no self-respecting Welsh composer neglected to do so if only for commercial reasons, and it was the *Männerchöre* that Parry heard among German immigrants in America that were his inspiration. Adopting the German style rather than the English, which gave the melody to the male alto, Parry wrote with technical assurance and melodic accessibility for the Welsh choir, the distinctive pattern of the musical narrative structured by the opening scene, the prayer and meditation beseeching divine aid in the confrontation ahead (no Welsh composer prayed as much in his compositions as Parry, according to David Jenkins)[59] before the dramatic finale. This structure – itself derived from the French *orphéoniste* composers like Laurent de Rille and Ambroise Thomas – became the template for other Welsh composers for the male choir, Daniel Protheroe, D. Christmas Williams, T. Maldwyn Price, even Parry's posthumous nemesis Cyril Jenkins; but a rousing performance of Parry's 'Pilgrims' Chorus', more so than his syrupy 'Jesus of Nazareth' written for the Cardiff National Eisteddfod of 1899, still retains its capacity to thrill a Welsh audience that can find the cloying close harmonies of 'Myfanwy' too sentimental by half.

The young composer and *enfant terrible* that was Cyril Jenkins (1889–1978) professed himself 'suffocated by the artistically mephitic atmosphere' that arose from Parry's music. To Jenkins, at its best it was only second-rate; at its worst it was beneath contempt. *Blodwen*, whose libretto was 'feeble' and its plot 'offensively silly' only confirmed that Parry was fated 'never to understand the meaning of poetry; almost any words were good enough for him'. Nor, in Jenkins's view, did *Blodwen* stand alone in its 'almost tragic inferiority', for all Parry's music has 'the stamp of an inferior mind', and most of it smeared in a 'disagreeable emotionalism'.[60] Thus Cyril Jenkins, whose vendetta against Parry made him, after Caradoc Evans, the most hated man in Wales.[61]

Whether Joseph Parry's greatest lack was an adequate librettist or emotional depth, the plain fact is that his music was melodic, and he spoke to his people and entered their souls as few other composers could. When his 'Pilgrims' was selected as the test piece for male choirs at the Swansea National Eisteddfod in 1891, the ten-choired competition lasted four hours. Eventually Pontycymmer were declared the winners, receiving especial commendation for the bass solo of Gwilym Thomas, whose voice Parry had in mind when composing the piece. Thomas had been one of the rescue team at the Tynewydd colliery disaster in the Rhondda in April 1877, when five miners were recovered from a ten-day entombment cut off by flood waters underground.[62] When a service of thanksgiving was held at Cymmer Chapel, Porth, on 12 May 1877, Parry was commissioned to write a special anthem. Such invitations fuelled his perception of himself as a national figure: when in 1896 he applied for the principalship of the Guildhall School of Music (unsuccessfully; W. H. Cummings was appointed), he solicited references from the mayor of Cardiff and several MPs.

Ever since being forced out of Aberystwyth, Parry had become resigned to professional disappointment, his deepest regret being at his failure to secure a lectureship at Cardiff in 1883, when an unknown Englishman, Clement Templeton (BA Cantab.), secretary to Harrow Music School, was preferred to David Jenkins (Mus.Bac., Cantab.) and Joseph Parry (Mus.Doc., Cantab.). If Jenkins's list of testimonials reads like a *Who's Who* of English and Welsh musicians of the time (Macfarren, McNaught, Henry Leslie, John Curwen, Brinley Richards, Tanymarian, Eos Morlais), Parry trundled even bigger guns into position: Macfarren (again), John Stainer, Randegger and Garcia (professors of singing at the Royal Academy of Music; Randegger was also conductor of Carl Rosa), John Thomas (Pencerdd Gwalia, professor of the harp at the RAM and harpist to the Queen), Principal T. C. Edwards of Aberystwyth, several other Welsh academics, composers and ministers of religion, MPs, and notables like the Marquis of Bath and Lady Llanover. The resounding roar from this battery of heavy artillery only intensified the unanimous protests of Welsh public opinion when the indignity (*sarhad*) of Parry's rejection became known.[63]

Emotional, egotistical, hard-working, prolific, Parry, in the words of a fellow native of Merthyr, was 'a genius . . . but something was wrong with the balance'.[64] Yet despite, or more likely because of, his human failings, the esteem in which he was held by the people of Wales in the last quarter of the nineteenth century was equalled only by that enjoyed by Lloyd George in the first quarter of the twentieth. Arguably there is no good music or bad music, but music whose melodies appeal and survive. For all their apparent banalities, Joseph Parry's accessible tunes are sung a hundred years after his death, and unless a more pressing claim is made on behalf of Ivor Novello, until the second half of the twentieth century the greatest Welsh composer remains Joseph Parry – alas.

5

Imperial Merthyr, 1880–1914

80

1. Music, Class and Community

The *Merthyr Express* assumed a natural interest in musical affairs on the part of its readers. When in March 1880 Joseph Parry's *Ymgom yr Adar* (The Cantata of the Birds, for children) was performed at Moriah, Dowlais, readers were regaled with a lengthy account of the structure of the work and informed of a few slight mistakes on the part of the soloist who was constantly singing an F natural instead of an F sharp.[1] R. S. Hughes's newly published cantata *Bugeiliaid Bethlehem* (The Shepherds of Bethlehem) was similarly closely analysed in form and performance at Penydarren with all twenty-one choruses and solos subjected to extensive attention, the blending of voices coming in for especial scrutiny.[2] Criticism could be especially virulent when laced with the kind of denominational arsenic dispensed after a performance at the Oddfellows Hall the following year. One correspondent hoped that 'the next time our Baptist friends treat the population of Dowlais to a sacred cantata they will not ruthlessly mar it', while another critic 'who did not know who sang the part of Asariel . . . would certainly advise him not to attempt the role again'.[3]

It was competition, however, that stoked the most intense passions. The preparation of Dowlais choirs for a forthcoming national or semi-national eisteddfod was 'the chief topic of conversation' in the works for weeks beforehand, and rehearsals became public events to which admission was charged; Dowlais Harmonic Society admitted listeners to their final rehearsals for the 1885 National Eisteddfod for 3*d*. and 6*d*.[4] The rail authorities were obliged to suspend all goods traffic and put on special alert to cater for five times the usual number of passengers expected to travel from Dowlais to Brecon on the day of the main choral competition at the 1889 National Eisteddfod, especially since the Dowlais Harmonic and the Dowlais Choral Society were competing in their respective sections.[5] For if one thing more than another is calculated to arouse the spirits and awaken the interest of the average Dowlaisian it is the anticipation of a choral competition of the first water, and for some weeks preceding the event the Porth Eisteddfod held on Whit Monday when the [Merthyr] Philharmonic Society entered the lists absorbed the attention of all.[6]

Dowlais and Merthyr generated immense local interest in choral singing. At the National Eisteddfod of 1901, held at Merthyr, with the choirs of 170–200 voices each having prepared all of the *Hymn of Praise* from which the adjudicators would select any three choruses to be sung with full orchestral accompaniment, the crowd was 'so thickly jammed' that the 11,000 could not move and sixty reporters were on hand to cover the clash of choral gladiators.[7] That these events were peculiar to the Welsh – 'the phlegmatic Saxon across the border had no adequate conception of the intense interest and excitement associated with these contests for supremacy in the eisteddfodic arena' – intrigued the Welsh themselves. C. H. James MP dilated on this at the Mountain Ash semi-national on Whit Monday 1880:

These assemblies [Welsh eisteddfodau] are unique, they are not to be found anywhere but in Wales, and I defy our English friends to bring together such assemblages of working men as are generally met with at these meetings . . . It is a thing they do not attempt because they know they cannot do it. Meetings of this kind keep up a love for the country. We do not want anything like home rule but we like to keep up a love for 'Hen Wlad fy Nhadau'.[8]

The notion that national identity did not require institutional expression of a political kind would retain its attraction for many of the Welsh for at least the next hundred years.

There were sound moral grounds for promoting 'meetings of this kind'. The Abergavenny eisteddfod had been one of the best known in Wales from the 1830s to the 1850s; it had then languished until its revival in 1873. Presiding the following year, one of the local gentry, Mr J. C. Hill of The Brooks, Abergavenny, declared:

Acquaintance with classical music of this kind must of necessity have a beneficial influence upon the hardy sons of toil who are gathered together today. The Welsh are, as a people, acknowledged to be a peaceful race, lovers of order and respecters of our laws. I attribute this in a great measure to their innate love of music, for to contend with any chance of success they must practise regularly and earnestly . . . How much better is this, both morally and physically, than wasting their time and their substance in the public house.[9]

Similar sentiments underlay the formation of the Merthyr Philharmonic Society in 1891 when, at a meeting chaired by a local solicitor, the motives for doing so were clearly articulated: to do good to the town and to rival the Rhondda (even in a small place like Treorchy a choir could be found to take a prize at the 1889 Brecon National Eisteddfod; Merthyr with a population of 58,000 in 1891 had no competitive choir from 1881); while among the many advantages the formation of a choir would confer on the community was that 'the young people had no place to go and he thought that was the reason why many of the rising generation attended public houses. If a choir was formed in the town they could be able to help them from going into temptation' (applause).[10]

This could cut both ways, as a correspondent to the *South Wales Daily News* noted in 1880, to the effect that the impulse given to the cultivation of music in recent years had had a serious if not dangerous effect on the young of both sexes, so that choral practices and preparation for eisteddfodic competitions had taken the place of the praises of the sanctuary.[11] Musical moralists could be left contemplating an ethical conundrum of the kind presented to them by Merthyr Orpheus Society's pleasure in 1887 at receiving help for their forthcoming London trip not only from the Chamber of Trade, a welcome indication of civic patronage, but also from the well-known pugilist John Knifton, 'a man of great musical talent' who had sent a sovereign and attended a rehearsal.[12]

All too often, however, such assemblages of working-people as the Abergavenny gentleman viewed through his presidential, rose-tinted lenses could behave in ways which he would hardly have commended. At the Aberdare National Eisteddfod of 1885 they frequently interrupted the proceedings on chief choral day to demand 'y prif ddarn' (the main (test) piece), out of an impatience which the organizers might have anticipated by devoting the whole day to the six choirs, each of around 180 voices, instead of opting to crowd the programme with competitions in which the 12,000 present 'had no more interest than in the change of government in Guatemala'.[13] The choral competition – the test pieces were 'Hark the Deep Tremendous Voice' (from Haydn's *The Seasons*), 'Beloved Lord Thine Eyes We Close' (Spohr, *Calvary*) and 'Vengeance

Arise' (David Jenkins, *David and Saul*) – saw Dowlais Harmonic conducted by Dan Davies beat not only two formidable Rhondda choirs, D. T. Prosser's Rhondda Philharmonic and M. O. Jones's Rhondda Choral Union, but Ebbw Vale, Llanelli and, sweetest of all, Merthyr United. The Llanelli choir numbering over 200 choristers on stage was the largest, but when their sopranos came in early on the last page of the third piece 'a wild shout broke out from the audience', which was renewed when the conductor, R. C. Jenkins, turned to face the audience at the end. The betting outside the pavilion had been 'six to one on Llanelli', and it could well have been disappointed punters who threw the reported clumps of earth from the floor of the pavilion at the heads of others. This first National win for a Dowlais choir was hailed locally as the victory for a young, self-taught amateur conductor over professional musicians like R. C. Jenkins and earned the choir a rapturous reception on its return, the inhabitants of almost every house in Dowlais at the door waving, fireworks exploding and improvised triumphal arches hastily erected as if for an imperial re-entry to Rome after an all-conquering transalpine campaign.[14]

When things went less well, Dowlais's good spirits were less in evidence. At a Swansea eisteddfod in 1884 Neath United Choir's deliberate delaying tactics in taking twenty minutes to arrange themselves on stage were seen as an attempt to intimidate the volatile Dowlais choristers. Then, when Joseph Parry (of Merthyr, of course, not Dowlais) applied a liberal dose of salt to the wound by awarding Neath the prize, a member of the Dowlais choir leapt on the stage 'and accused Dr Parry to his face of having delivered a most glaringly unjust and partial adjudication'. This was followed with the threat that a Dowlais choir would never in future attend an eisteddfod where he was to adjudicate – at which Parry, apparently, only smiled, probably in relief.[15]

Dowlais choirs brought their supporters in such numbers, however, that their participation was much sought after in eisteddfodau; after the Swansea débâcle the competition secretary wrote to the aggrieved Dowlais choir offering a rematch.[16] The necessity of good behaviour was emphasized to the choir as they set out for competition success at Easter 1887, and if need be to suffer defeat creditably. The Corinthian ideals of restraint in victory and losing with good grace were clearly proving as difficult to instil in working people whose popular culture embraced a robust competitive ethic in the choral as in the sporting arena.[17]

This applies as much to their followers as to the choristers themselves. Even the presence of W. Pritchard Morgan MP at the Dowlais Harmonic

Society's 1888 Christmas concert failed to curb rowdy behaviour in the gallery where the actions of some were compared to 'the conduct of the frequenters of the back part of a strolling theatre'; 'hobble-de-hoys' in the gallery also marred the Dowlais Temperance Choir's pre-Crystal Palace concert at the Oddfellows Hall in 1895.[18] Choristers and their supporters occasionally acted in concerted hobbledehoydom. Police were called to clear the stage when the names of the winning and second-placed choirs were inadvertently transposed at Porth's annual eisteddfod in 1896, and since the choirs involved were Dowlais and Merthyr, utter bedlam ensued. The leaders of both choirs marched on to the platform surrounded by a strong bodyguard of followers and advanced on the adjudicator, the respected but on this occasion hapless Dr Roland Rogers of Bangor.[19]

Dowlais's excesses grated on some nerves, especially when they seemed to be accompanied not merely by hobbledehoys but hobblede-hoydens as well. At an eisteddfod in 1891 in Treharris, some six miles lower down the valley from Merthyr, the barracking of other choirs was conducted with evident enthusiasm by Dowlais, with the female members especially prominent 'in a manner which even abashed their male companions. They presented quite an army of Amazons', whose bad language led to their expulsion from the eisteddfod. Even at the train station they continued to behave in an unseemly manner. 'The art of music', reported an eyewitness ruefully, 'had not the usual effect of soothing the savage beast in this instance.'[20]

If, then, music was meant to be synonymous with morality and civility,[21] 'musical Merthyr' was a problematic construct to those anxious to promote it as a positive social descriptor, and the town's middle class determined to have no truck with such behaviour. The driving forces behind the formation of the Merthyr Philharmonic Society later that year (1891) were the church organist T. Westlake Morgan and the solicitor John Vaughan, a prominent Liberal and manager of Pritchard Morgan's by-election campaign of 1888, who proceeded to secure for their new organization the aristocratic patronage of Lords Aberdare, Tredegar, Windsor and Wimborne and Sir John Llewellyn, while enlisting also the ironmasters Robert and Richard Crawshay as honorary members.[22] Thanks to his musical contacts Westlake Morgan was able to add the impressive name of C. V. Stanford to the list of patrons and, in a daring leap from Pontmorlais to the Pont-neuf, announce that M. Guilmant, 'the greatest of all French organists', had also agreed to lend his patronage, a major coup by the inevitably modest standards of late-nineteenth-century Merthyr.[23] At its inception in 1893, the affairs of the Merthyr Choral Society were in the respectable hands of a provision merchant, a bank manager, a newspaper proprietor and a brace of solicitors.[24] Similarly when Harry Evans was preparing the Dowlais Choir for the Llanelli National Eisteddfod in 1895, its officers were David Rees, a shop-owner, as president, R. P. Rees, a chemist, as treasurer, succeeded later in the year by J. W. Edwards, a draper, and David Williams, a grocer, as registrar.[25]

This lower-middle-class involvement reminds us that while choirs were mostly working-class institutions, the support of the more affluent members of the community was seen as important, whatever the motives that inspired it, whether self-aggrandizement, a desire to secure political support or acquiescence, or merely something as uncomplicated as a love of music. And choral music above all other forms of national recreation was pre-eminent in constructing a civic identity and projecting an inclusive image of the community. For a significant aspect of music's social appeal was its ability to attract different constituencies. Prestige in the local community went usefully hand in hand with prominent association with one of the choirs, as John Vaughan found when it came to council elections, just as it was the *petite bourgeoisie* of shopkeepers and solicitors' agreed image of respectability and social cohesion that had earlier played a moderating, mediating role between company and men during periods of industrial friction like the Dowlais strike of 1853.[26]

A similar congruence between the respectable working class and a progressive element in the middle class was to be seen in the encouragement of self-responsibility and progress in the classic rational recreational forms of eisteddfodau, reading rooms, savings banks, benefit and friendly societies and adult education. After the years of social crisis and class formation that Europe had witnessed between the 1820s and 1840s, the *petite bourgeoisie* took the lead in establishing voluntary societies directed at stabilizing the working class. Whatever the national variations – French sports associations, English brass bands, German gymnastic clubs, Welsh choirs – what we see are institutions of sociability solidly rooted in working-class industrial communities and organized by committees of small businessmen acting as secretaries, administrators, trustees and treasurers. Here was an alternative sociability for the aspiring minor middle class, giving them the kind of social importance locally that larger-scale philanthropists provided in the bigger towns and cities. It was in small towns and urban districts like Merthyr that shopkeepers and artisans had the most coherence and identity, reinforced by personal

Lawrence was at 2 Courtland Terrace where his niece Miss Hilden Hagen also was 'receiving Young Pupils to carefully prepare them for later tuition under Mr Lawrence's personal care'. Alfred J. Silver, FRCO, organist of St David's and late assistant organist at St George's, Windsor, was giving lessons at 8 Park Terrace, while the up-and-coming Harry Evans was at 'Beethoven House', Dowlais, and D. Christmas Williams in Prospect Street. Doubtless all directed their pupils to the busy music emporia of Thompson and Shackell in High Street, William Burr at Pontmorlais Circus and John Lewis's Music Warehouse in Penydarren.[42]

By 1903 Harry Evans had acquired the national reputation which led to his being offered the conductorship of the Liverpool Welsh Choral Union that year, the Fellowship of the Royal College of Organists, and a three-manual organ at his new home in 'Cartrefle', from where he taught singing, piano, organ, harmony and counterpoint. Christmas Williams was offering these subjects too, now at 30 Upper Thomas Street, while five doors along William Lewis, conductor of the Merthyr Orchestral Society, gave lessons in violin, organ, pianoforte and theory. Gwilym Lewis, another well-known local musician, also taught piano, while Dowlais, where Harry Evans originated, could boast E. T. Davies, ARCO (the FRCO would soon follow) at Handel House, Morlais Street, W. J. Watkins, LRAM, ARCO (as yet), organist of Dowlais Parish Church, in 6 Glendower Street, and Miss E. Newton-Smith, violinist, of Upper Union Street, while around the corner in 42 Union Terrace Mr J. W. Baker gave lessons in violin.[43]

There was no dearth of music or of musicians in late-nineteenth-century Merthyr. Nor of controversy, as the turbulent career of one of them would testify.

2. The Wellington of Choral Singing

The most celebrated Merthyr musician of the last two decades of the nineteenth century (Joseph Parry left in 1854 and never returned to live there), was Dan Davies, 'who may justly be called the Wellington of choral singing'.[44] Entirely self-taught musically, baleful-eyed 'terrible Dan' was endowed with a fiery temperament from birth, which was in Merthyr in 1859. At nine years of age he was conducting a party of boys at Moriah, Dowlais. From his first public appearance as 'the young and promising conductor' of the Dowlais Glee Party at Gwernllwyn School-room in 1881,[45] for the next twenty years he made Merthyr choralism

6. 'Terrible Dan' – Dan Davies (1859–1930), the
volatile conductor of the Dowlais Harmonic Society and
Merthyr Philharmonic Choir, whose fiery temperament
made him the focus of national controversy in the 1890s.

synonymous with his own volatile personality and dramatic conducting style. In June 1881 the party performed Eos Bradwen's cantata *Owain Glyndwr* and on gaining the advanced certificate of the Tonic Sol-fa College later that year he augmented his choir and brought the Dowlais Harmonic Society into existence to do *Judas Maccabaeus* with Edith Wynne and Eos Morlais among the soloists.[46] He then decided he was ready for competition and achieved the first of many successes with the Dowlais Harmonic in 1882 at Abergavenny, when he beat six other choirs on 'The Many Rend the Skies' (Handel), the vanquished including seasoned performers like the Rhondda Philharmonic, the

Merthyr Harmonic, and the rival Dowlais Choral Society conducted by John Evans ('Eos Myrddin'), father of Harry Evans.

He followed this with a highly charged *Elijah* at the Oddfellows Hall at Christmas 1882. Another victory was achieved at Abergavenny in 1885 when Ebbw Vale, Pontypool and Abersychan were beaten. Though they would twelve years later exact revenge on the national stage in controversial circumstances, Abersychan on this occasion, to the delight of the Dowlais contingent, went out of tune on the set piece. We gain an inkling of the intense rivalries generated by these competitions from the fact that when Dowlais were rehearsing at a local chapel in Abergavenny, Thomas Davies, a well-known Ebbw Vale musician (composer of the anthem 'Dyddiau Dyn sydd fel Glaswelltyn' – 'All Flesh is Grass' – that sold 320,000 copies between 1890 and 1920)[47] was spotted in the audience, the choir refused to sing a note until reassured he was not attached to any rival organization. The competition over, the defeated Ebbw Vale conductor accosted the victorious Dan Davies in the street and 'threatened all manner of things when he next had the opportunity of meeting him at a future eisteddfod'.[48]

This was the first series of incidents that dogged Dan Davies's musical career. National success at first eluded him, and after coming fifth at Cardiff in 1883 a chagrined contemporary was moved to note that 'Goddess Fortune disdains to allow a Dowlais choir to be successful at the National Eisteddfod of Wales'. Eventually Dowlais Harmonic's 'Deep Tremendous Voice' came out victorious at the Aberdare National Eisteddfod in 1885, the other pieces being, in addition to that chorus from Haydn's *Seasons*, 'Beloved Lord Thine Eyes We Close' (Spohr, *Calvary*) and 'Vengeance Arise' (David Jenkins, *David and Saul*). The £150 prize was divided into £20 to the conductor, £5 to both accompanists and the remainder divided equally among the 192 choristers who each received 12*s*. 6*d*. (62p).[49]

Purely in financial terms Dan Davies's Dowlais Harmonic Society – popularly known as 'the Invincibles' – was the most successful in Welsh musical history and took pride in its accumulating monetary prizes. By 1887 after three successive victories at Abergavenny (1885–7) and on Easter Monday 1887 snatching the £200 prize, the biggest ever offered in south Wales up to that time, at Pontypool, the choir had won £680, the conductor himself the recipient of four gold medals and an ivory baton.[50] A meeting of the choir was then held at which it was decided to divide the spoils among the members, a process fraught with difficulty. Batons could themselves be contested property. The *Musical Times* in March

1891 reported the case of the Caernarfon choir whose conductor maintained a gold baton belonged to him, whereupon fifty-two choristers went to the County Court and successfully demanded that the baton be sold and the proceeds divided among the members, who benefited to the tune of between 12s. and 15s. (60p to 75p) each. In the same way, in 1892 members of the Dowlais Harmonic unable to travel were indignant that 200 newly won guineas (£210) should all be banked in a reserve fund for the trip to the Chicago World's Fair the following year, an ambitious undertaking that in the event was unrealized.[51]

By Christmas 1888 the choir's tally was already £1,000 and eight gold medals.[52] Dan Davies kept winning at Abergavenny and picked up £100 and a gold medal a time at Neath and Ferndale in 1891 where, prophetically, the choir was warned about over-accentuation and exaggerated effects. Then in May 1892 amid acrimonious accusations in Dowlais of treachery, betrayal and desertion,[53] Dan Davies, ostensibly for business reasons (he dealt in meat, or, to quote one hostile witness, 'pigs')[54] left Dowlais and joined his 'new-found friends in Merthyr' where his arrival had an immediately galvanizing effect on its musical life. He formed a new choir which proceeded to sweep all before it. The chief choral prizes at the major south Wales semi-nationals, at Bridgend, Porth and Ferndale, swiftly fell to Merthyr Philharmonic. After only seven weeks' practice, Dan took his inexperienced choir to Porth, where defeat was inflicted on established choirs from Rhymney (John Price), Morriston (W. Penfro Rowlands) and the Rhondda (Eos Cynlais's Rhondda Philharmonic and Tal Hopkins's Porth and Cymmer). 'I and my fellow-adjudicators have been awe-struck by the performance', remarked the chairman of the judges, the English musician Dr E. H. Turpin.[55] On their return the choir faced a tumultuous reception at Merthyr. The conductor sought to escape by a side exit from the station, but crowds tracked him down to his house, brought him out and carried him round the town, until he agreed to address the throng 'speaking from an open window after the fashion of a successful parliamentary candidate'.[56]

Merthyr Philharmonic's continued success began to arouse the envy of others. At Treorchy in 1895 the choir was roundly booed and hissed as soon as it appeared on stage, and Dan Davies had a stone thrown at him (by an aggrieved Dowlaisian?) in Merthyr High Street after winning at Porth in 1896.[57] By then national success too had come his way, when he shared first prize with Rhymney at the Llanelli Eisteddfod of 1895, for which he had prepared with that professionalism of attitude that was his hallmark. (We might add that condemnation of 'pot-hunting' and unseemly competition for big prizes came from middle-class observers who viewed the idea of contesting for money with the same disdain as they regarded professional sport.) For Llanelli, Dan Davies took the precaution of getting the eisteddfod orchestra up to Merthyr to accompany the choir as they would be required to do in the competition itself, an innovation introduced, on Caradog's insistence, at Pontypridd in 1893, a sign of Wales's growing orchestral awareness.

The 1895 Llanelli chief choral competition was viewed by contemporaries as the most important choral competition since Caradog's own historic victory at the Crystal Palace, with six choirs out to stop John Price's vaunted Rhymney United from making it a hat trick after Pontypridd (1893) and Caernarfon (1894). Merthyr sang last at 6 p.m. after four hours of competition, and lost intonation as the impetuous 'veteran conductor' – though not yet forty years old – accelerated the tempo. Music with Dan Davies was never safe or dull; he lived dangerously and took risks. Joseph Barnby adjudicating with Joseph Parry and R. C. Jenkins congratulated Wales on having such magnificent choirs as he had heard that day for he had not supposed for a single instant 'that any other part of this great kingdom could show seven choirs as magnificent a seven as they had just heard'. But were they going to be content with merely getting pieces together to win prizes? Welsh choirs might be known in Wales but not in England and certainly not on the Continent, though if the Germans or French heard their singing 'they would be amazed'. Arguing for a national festival where Wales's 'magnificent choirs' could continue to perform major works in their entirety, Barnby feared that in Wales the Nasmyth steam hammer was being employed in the paltry work of cracking nuts.[58]

After the announcement that the prize was to be shared between Merthyr and Rhymney, W. Pritchard Morgan gave a gold baton to each of the two conductors, but the imperious Dan Davies was never well disposed towards his rival from the next valley after that; the amateur ideal of grace in victory was markedly at a premium at the Porth eisteddfod in 1896 when Davies cabled John Price, berating him for 'cowardly sending your singers to assist Dowlais choir'.[59] Nor had he lost any of his appetite for the big prizes, though he feigned otherwise. He told his choir that he hoped they did not attend rehearsals with any monetary objective – while making it plain that he would not compete at any eisteddfod that offered a prize less than £100![60] Dan Davies was as mercenary as any professional sportsman, telling a deputation from Porth 'which waited upon him at his residence' in the hope of persuading him to compete at the forthcoming eisteddfod that he was getting tired of £100 prizes but if they would increase it to £150 he would promise faithfully to compete.[61]

Now the 1896 National Eisteddfod beckoned at Llandudno. Despite the location, of the six choirs competing in the chief choral competition, Holyhead Choir was the only north Wales representative; there could be no greater demonstration of the dominance of south Wales choralism at the end of the nineteenth century. It was, though, unprecedented for *five* big southern choirs to go north: Llanelli (now under John Thomas after R. C. Jenkins's choir broke up in 1892),[62] Merthyr (Dan Davies), Dowlais (Harry Evans), Rhymney (John Price), and geographically just qualifying as a south Wales entrant, though chorally not taken too seriously as a rival to the others – yet – Builth (Llew Buallt).

Of these, the main threat to Merthyr was constituted by Rhymney United who had achieved their first notable success at the Pontypridd National Eisteddfod after only fifteen months' existence. Formed to compete at the 1892 Caerphilly Whitsun eisteddfod, which they won out of five choirs on 'Yr Haf' (Gwilym Gwent), they followed this with victory at Porth out of six, shared with Dowlais at Treharris, and beat them at Abergavenny later in the year. They then won at Pontypridd in 1893 on their first National appearance. They were renowned for their good order, partly attributable to the fact that a segment of the choir consisted of a Rechabite glee party, and were far less inclined than other choirs to dispatch sections of their choir to help out others, a common enough practice at the time for which they had suffered at the hands of less scrupulous rivals.[63] Defeated at Porth by Merthyr in 1893, Rhymney faced many of the same choristers in the National at Pontypridd in the guise of Cardiff Choral Society under Jacob Davies (grandfather of Ivor Novello) whom they had the satisfaction of beating into second place. At Brynmawr, just before Llandudno, the Abertillery choir had been received 'with a perceptible outburst of antagonism' from a section of the audience (mostly their great rivals, Abersychan) because Abertillery had been trained by Dan Davies and augmented by a cohort of his Merthyr choristers. When they were announced from the stage as 'the Abertillery choir', shouts of 'Abertillery and Merthyr' were hurled from the audience, 'Côr Dan Davies yw e' (It's Dan Davies's choir), and 'Throw them out'.[64] Despite Dan Davies's attempt to pin a similar accusation on Rhymney, they for their part seem to have remained aloof from this kind of wheeling and dealing normally associated with football teams. John Price's choir, composed almost entirely of colliers, their wives and

7. The Rhymney United Choir, formed in 1892, was composed almost entirely of colliers and their families. Photographed here in 1894 with their conductor John Price, they were Chief Choral winners at the National Eisteddfod three years running between 1893 and 1895.

daughters, was held in the highest esteem in the community. An appeal
for funds to enable the choir to proceed to Llandudno was met by all
classes, who lent conspicuous support to a 'monster' tea party held to
defray the costs of travel. Tickets were printed, tables at the Victoria Hall
laid out with glistening silver and costly china tea sets, various ladies were
detailed as 'tray holders' and it was deemed newsworthy that even 'Mrs
Jones the Vicarage was responsible for brewing the tea': an assault on the
country's premier choral competition required the interring of denominational differences. Thus was Rhymney indeed United.[65]

The Llandudno expedition was a matter of no small concern in
Merthyr too, where Dan Davies's final rehearsal was attended by leading
representatives of the middle-class élite, professional, managerial and
military, like Colonel Lewis who on being asked to say a few words,
expressed the view that 'the heart of the community beat in sympathy
with Merthyr in the week which lay before it', and Alfred Brown,
manager of the local ironworks, who like many others admitted to
catching the competition fever, and having already accompanied the
choir to the Porth Whitsun eisteddfod intended travelling with them
to Llandudno.[66] Choral singing, the rational recreation *par excellence*,
attracted such patronage because of its close and salutary association
with a religious, respectable, self-reliant working population, so that press
reports frequently alluded to the 'crowded and fashionable' audiences at
musical events.[67]

A special train was chartered to take the Merthyr choir to the north
Wales resort – Dowlais and Rhymney did the same – with two 'admirably
appointed' saloons laid on for the lady members, and the party arrived in
time to give a concert on Monday night arranged by the Llandudno
impresario Jules Rivière.

The competition took place the following day, with the adjudicators
Sir Frederic Cowen, Joseph Barnby, J. H. Roberts and David Jenkins
perched half-way up into the roof of the pavilion, as far removed as
possible from the subterranean burial chamber to which the judges had
been consigned the previous year in Llanelli. From this elevated vantage
point they listened to the rival choirs competing on 'When his Loud
Voice' (Handel), 'How Sweet the Moonlight Sleeps' (Henry Leslie) and
David Jenkins's 'Trip we Gaily', which only Holyhead chose to sing in
Welsh though the great majority of the south Wales choirs too were
Welsh-speaking, certainly Welsh-singing, and their English pronunciation
far from ideal, to the frequent amusement of English adjudicators
unused to hearing 'Arice O Lord'.

In the event Rhymney's unbeaten run was ended, though not by Merthyr, or by Dowlais or Llanelli, but – despite sounding to an incredulous Merthyr listener like 'a juvenile choir'[68] after the vehement south Wales renditions – by Builth. First, or Merthyr, impressions to the contrary, they had not risen from nowhere, though the population of the small Radnorshire market town was barely 1,500. There was busy choral activity there associated with Rhymney-born Alfred P. Morgan, a student of Joseph Parry's at Aberystwyth, whose choir would win the second competition at Newport in 1897 and share the main prize with John Williams's Caernarfon at Ffestiniog in 1898. Furthermore, Llew Buallt's choir had already won the second choral competition at Llanelli in 1895.

In Llandudno, once Buallt's choristers, though fewer in number and, to an English observer, with little of the typical Welsh choir in their appearance, had sung the first piece, the judges exchanged significant looks. 'The second piece', wrote one of them, 'confirmed our opinion that only a particularly good choir would have a chance against them. No such choir remained to be heard.'[69] Frederic Cowen's delivered adjudication pronounced it a magnificent contest, the finest since London in 1887. He indicated what he and his fellow judges were looking for: not merely a body of tone or violent effort or 'tricky reading', but high artistic quality, refinement and an accurate conception of the composer's intentions.

Merthyr immediately complained that Cowen had not dealt with the choirs seriatim or given a detailed adjudication but had fallen back on 'useless generalizations'. Their conductor took it very badly. Many years afterwards, Cowen recalled being accosted by 'the conductor of a choir that had been at the top of the poll at nearly all previous meetings' – clearly the intemperate Dan Davies rather than the mild John Price – who 'black with rage and disappointment . . . advised me, if I valued my reputation, never to set foot in Wales again'.[70]

Some disconsolate Merthyr choristers sought to raise their spirits by visiting a local theatre to see 'a side-splitting comedy', which doubtless produced a thin smile among the deflated and exhausted singers, before heading for the station by 11.30 and the long journey home. The truths that Cowen had enunciated about erratic tempi, faulty intonation and vocal straining were less hilarious, as Dan Davies was to discover once again the following year. For if only his pride had been dented at Llandudno in 1896, he was to suffer mortal wounds at Newport. In 1897 the choral Wellington would have his final come-uppance.

3. *Wellington Meets his Waterloo*

With the routine scalps of the Porth and Bridgend eisteddfodau under
their belt, in August 1897 Dan Davies's Merthyr Philharmonic now put
their minds to turning the choral world the right way up at the Newport
National Eisteddfod, after the carnivalesque reversal of the previous year.
They were one of the six choirs competing on 'Now All Gives Way
Together' (*St Ludmilla*, Dvorak), and 'They that Go Down' (*The Mariners*,
David Jenkins). 'As the great struggle approached', wrote the *Musical
Times*, 'thousands crowded into the pavilion and excitement ran high, for,
next after a football match, Welshmen enjoy a choral fight', and the
estimated 12,000–14,000 spectators included a phalanx of Welsh MPs:
T. E. Ellis, Lloyd George, Brynmor Jones, D. A. Thomas, Pritchard
Morgan and the local member, Albert Spicer.[71]

These choral fighters wore no distinctive uniform, but Merthyr caught
the eye (of the Merthyr correspondent) with their colourful appearance,
the ladies all in Jubilee bonnets and white blouses, the sopranos wearing
red and the contraltos lilac sashes, while the men looked 'quite distingué'
in their white waistcoats. This was Merthyr at its most imperial. The
Builth choir also looked well, with the ladies in white sailor hats and
white dresses, with pink sashes for the sopranos and blue for the contraltos: the public performance of mixed choirs, trans-gender as well as
pan-class institutions but not necessarily socially inclusive ones if codes
of dress were strictly adhered to, provided an opportunity for the display
of female sartorial elegance rarely available on other occasions. Rhymney
were distinctive too, for a more poignant reason: in memory of one of
their leading tenors killed underground only the night before, the ladies
wore black bows on their blouses and skirts 'of a sombre hue'.[72]

For Rhymney and Merthyr they could not have been more sombre
than Dr A. C. Mackenzie's adjudication, which indicated that the judges
'had not allowed themselves to be carried away by mere force or by
strength and mere power of sound'; in fact – and this was seen as directly
aimed at Merthyr – 'we wished that some of the choirs would moderate
their ardour just a little more'.[73] The winning choir was the one that gave
the most musical rendering; it was not coarse and yet it was strong, as
neat and clean and excellent a piece of vocalism as he ever wished to
hear. Once again Dan Davies had to face defeat: these qualities had been
shown by Abersychan and Pontypool, conducted by Walter Protheroe
who, according to Joseph Bennett in the *Daily Telegraph*, 'had trained his
singers to refinement and delicacy rather than noise . . . The showy

qualities of Merthyr most struck the common fancy, but to the connoisseur the best choir won.'[74]

It soon became apparent that there were deep questions at issue here beyond what the *Daily Chronicle* represented as 'emotional colouring versus technical accuracy'. Although the *Musical Herald*'s special correspondent tried to confine the issue to one of technique, 'not . . . of loud singing as against fine singing, but of impure as against pure singing . . . not a question of enthusiasm and Celtic fire but of exaggeration and lack of self-control',[75] the cry soon went up that the ostensibly technical objective of purging Welsh singing of its defects was only part of a larger campaign to Anglicize the eisteddfod. Even the *Western Mail* complained that adjudicators should judge according to choral standards in Wales not what was in vogue elsewhere, and that the adjudication was aimed at extinguishing Welsh *hwyl*, the traditional fire which distinguished Welsh singing from that of other nations. 'If the Cymry', it warned, '[should] ever permit their choral singing to descend to the cultural yet lifeless level it occupied in England and elsewhere they would lose that which made their country the land of song.' To compel Welsh choirs to sing in the style preferred by the adjudicator would not suit the Welsh, and to compel them to do so would, it editorialized, 'surely be doing violence to the enthusiastic Celtic temperament'. Force, it concluded, was characteristic of Welsh singing and the adjudicators were brought to Newport to pass judgement on the singing according to Welsh standards. (It appeared to forget that the winning choir itself came from the industrial valleys of Monmouthshire.)

It was alleged, too, that the unemotional nature of the two Scottish adjudicators could not be expected to favour anything savouring of poetic intensity. Or as a correspondent from Abertillery informed the *Daily Chronicle*:

Wales is a land of song because the Welsh are an emotional people . . . It is [therefore] as wrong to place English and Scottish adjudicators to judge Welsh music as it would be to hand over those essentially English offices, the Board of Trade and the management of our Colonial Empire to the Archdruids.

Little could that correspondent have anticipated that two virtual archdruids, in the form of D. Lloyd George and J. H. Thomas, would respectively become President of the Board of Trade in 1905 and Colonial Secretary in 1924![76]

The debate raged across the columns of the daily and musical press in both languages, and the location of musical alignment became a touchstone of national loyalty. The eminent Swansea flautist Frederic Griffith whose *Notable Welsh Musicians*, which included Dan Davies, had only recently been published, defended the adjudication declaring that 'Welsh music must be worthy of comparison by any standard and that all the opinions expressed by our best-known Welsh adjudicators . . . fully anticipated the result'. These must have included Alexander Mackenzie's fellow adjudicator D. Emlyn Evans (the third was Walter Macfarren), but the press was not long in compiling a list of those who thought Merthyr should have won, a register intended to impress including Harry Evans (Dowlais), W. J. Evans (Aberdare), Tom Stephens (Rhondda), William Thomas (Treorchy), J. T. Rees, L. J. Roberts, John Thomas (Llanelli), the baritone Ffrangcon Davies, instrumentalists E. J. Roberts and Arthur Angle, and, the *Merthyr Express* added for good measure, T. Marchant Williams, Clara Novello Davies and Clara Butt. 'All Wales is talking about it and all Wales indignant', it added, and none was more indignant than Dan Davies.

The notion that English standards of cultured yet lifeless de-emphasizing of dramatic colouring worked against 'the Welsh style' of choral singing would surface at irregular intervals for the next forty years, but the agenda had been set in the 1890s. Alexander Mackenzie was already a noted critic of Welsh choral singing, having boldly exercised his position as a newly created Bard ('Pencerdd Alban') to point out the weakness in Welsh choral singing which eisteddfodau unwittingly fostered through the over-concentration on test pieces.[77] The elaborate manner in which they were prepared (he was basing his conclusions on his single but significant experience of the 1893 Pontypridd National Eisteddfod) had

> brought them to a pitch of perfection which almost amounted to exhaustion; a zeal which was apt to provoke, after the music itself had been mastered, a desire to polish away, to elaborate, to gild refined gold and paint the lily until art may be lost sight of and artificiality may take its place.[78]

After so controversially depriving Merthyr of the prize that afternoon in 1897, Mackenzie was leaving the building by the main exit when he was advised that it might be unsafe to appear in the street and that 'certain groups of men' were waiting for him; as a result he was shown a rear door and escorted along side roads to his hotel.[79]

Joseph Bennett was no stranger to the eisteddfod scene either, though a recent experience had left a sour taste in his mouth too. At the Dolgellau New Year eisteddfod he had complained that defeat was accepted with bad grace: 'there were in Wales fighting choirs and fighting choirs were an abomination.'[80] He was supported in this by the Welsh musician David Jenkins, a stout opponent of 'musical prize-fights', and by the fear expressed by others that the rough behaviour of some defeated contestants was turning choral competitions into 'bullfights'.[81] Bennett's love of Welsh music, however, did not extend to embracing Dan Davies who ' . . . believes in exaggeration. He is all for noise, for forced emphasis, and the double-scoring of every direction given', and it was with ill-concealed *schadenfreude* that Bennett, having contrasted 'the emphatic, strenuous, noisy method of Merthyr' with the 'refined, eminently artistic rendering' of the choirs from Builth, Pontypool and Anglesey, was able to report that 'the great fighting choir of South Wales again went empty away'.[82] Dan Davies believed himself to be the victim of 'intolerable prejudice' and had not forgotten that Bennett was one of the adjudicators at Llandudno the previous year, 'where the first of those faddistical awards which deprived my choir of its rights was made', and which had cost him £400 in the last two years. If required he could find the names of 200 musicians of acknowledged ability in Wales who expressed surprise at the decision, a verdict based on 'a bastard standard of musical excellence' that commanded only a small measure of support even in England. Furthermore, as Dan swelled to his crescendo,

> it may interest your special correspondent to know that during the last fifteen years I have with the Dowlais and Merthyr choirs won more than three thousand pounds in prizes, a sum more than twice as great as that won by any other conductor in the whole world.

Since he had more choral expertise than either Mackenzie or Bennett he would cheerfully take his choir to compete against any body of singers conducted by either of them, the winner to be decided by a jury of English choral conductors who he was sure would prefer Welsh 'fire and dash and emotionalism . . . to the clothes-prop style of singing favoured by modern faddists'.[83]

It was a gauntlet Bennett chose not to pick up; instead, with disdain he kicked it away, remarking that the naïvety

> which supposes that the relative merits of Sir A. C. Mackenzie, Mr Davies and myself as choir-masters can have any conceivable bearing

upon the question whether or no the winning choir sang better than their Merthyr rivals is so delicious that I leave it to the reader's enjoyment without further comment.[84]

By his extraordinary behaviour during his bitter disappointments of 1896 and 1897 'terrible Dan' had forfeited both national and even local support. David Jenkins had articulated the feelings of many when Dan's persistent sour grapes led him to conclude that 'the boast and bombast of these people' was pitiful and their attempt to meddle with adjudications 'contemptible', while the editorial advice of even the *Merthyr Express* was that 'the Merthyr Choir should accept its defeat with good grace'.[85]

It was almost, though not quite, the end of Dan Davies. He picked up another £250 at semi-nationals in 1898, and in November 1899 he took a Merthyr and Dowlais combined choir to London, where the audience at the Queen's Hall were amazed to hear a choir of 180 singing part-songs. The sopranos were shrill, it seems, and breath not always taken in the best places. But presented with the information that this choir had won twenty-seven prizes amounting to over £3,000 in the last sixteen years, the correspondent of the *Musical Herald* was forced to the reluctant conclusion that 'nevertheless, this must be described as a great choir'.[86] Dan Davies continued to conduct the Merthyr Choral Society and prepared the Merthyr section of the eisteddfod choir for the 1901 Merthyr National. But his *Elijah* concert, the nineteenth occasion in the previous twenty-five years for this to feature in an Eisteddfod concert, was roundly criticized as the worst in living memory. 'Terrible Dan's' shortcomings as an orchestral conductor were embarrassingly exposed, while the choir was manifestly under-rehearsed. Chastened by this experience, especially in the context of Harry Evans's masterly *Israel in Egypt* with the same choir and orchestra in one of the other concerts, Dan Davies recognized the reality that was staring him in the face and announced he would not be taking the Merthyr Choral Society to the Llanelli National in 1903.[87]

He continued to conduct oratorio and singing festivals; in 1893 he had already conducted the biggest ever held, a *cymanfa ganu* of 20,000 at the Pontypridd National, with an orchestra of 200. Since this was an undertaking of American proportions, it was fitting that his reputation preceded him to the United States, where in 1904 he found himself besieged by 4,000 enthusiasts in Scranton and received in the White House itself by a President Roosevelt sufficiently well briefed to profess himself delighted to meet a Welshman who was 'a most successful conductor and who had won . . . more prizes than any other conductor in his country'.[88]

But with all passion spent, the battle-scarred general of the former Dowlais 'Invincibles', though only in his early forties, faded from the major competitive scene. There was now a younger champion in the lists, one with the kind of formal musical qualifications that he himself heroically lacked. And he knew it.

4. Elgar's 'Great Conductor': Harry Evans of Dowlais

While Dan Davies lived on in decent obscurity until 1930, he saw Dowlais-born Harry Evans hailed as a choral conductor of genius well before his premature death at forty-one years of age in 1914. The accompanist at the combined Merthyr and Dowlais Queen's Hall concert in 1899, Evans had already formed and expressed his views on the alleged partiality of adjudicators for the English over the Welsh style. It was not so much a matter of national styles as of musical technique, of accuracy, purity of tone, intelligent phrasing and 'a potent restraint', at all of which English choirs excelled. Opposed to this was the excessive noise and enthusiasm of Welsh choirs, who still had the better voices and a more musical temperament. They also had conductors of insufficient technique. Notice had been served on Dan Davies; the era of the brilliant but short-lived Harry Evans had dawned.

Early in his career Harry Evans was known as Ap Myrddin after his father Eos Myrddin (John Evans) who had been born in Pendine, Carmarthenshire, in April 1841 and come to Dowlais very young.[89] Orphaned at five, at nine working in a colliery, he later became as refining an influence on the locality as the iron furnace he spent his adult life tending. Eos Myrddin's musical career was typical of that time and place, in his teens singing in the Dowlais Number One Temperance Choir attached to Hermon Chapel and taking elementary lessons with Ieuan Gwyllt, along with fellow pupils Eos Morlais and David Rosser. He learned to play the flute, violin and cello well enough to play in a small orchestral group, and became precentor of Bethania when Eos Morlais left Dowlais in 1869, a position he filled until his death in 1905.[90]

Having conducted the Dowlais section of Caradog's choir, Eos Myrddin was the first to conduct a complete work there, David Jenkins's *Arch y Cyfamod* (The Ark of the Covenant), the prize cantata at the 1877 National Eisteddfod, and this was followed by the first Dowlais performance of *Messiah* followed by a string of works like *Judas Macca-baeus*, *Gweddi Habacuc* and *The Creation*. An ordinary ironworker rolling steel plates for the Admiralty with only a pair of tongs separating him from a heat as intense as the Dowlais passion for singing, when working nights he would rush to conduct choir practice in his moleskin apron and leather clothes until he had to return to the furnace. He commanded immense respect from his peers in the choir which consisted entirely of working people like himself, colliers and ironworkers, and even most of the sopranos worked at the pit-head or in the ironworks; the altos were boys. And since hardly any of them could read music, he had them to the house in batches of six or seven at a time, and taught them by ear.

He knew no sol-fa, unlike his children, and Harry, the fifth, learned it from an elder sister while his father taught him staff well enough for him to make his first public appearance playing a harmonium solo aged seven, three years later becoming appointed the organist of Gwernllwyn Chapel, a post vacated by the gifted Dan Price's move to London. The instrument he was required to play was no more than a harmonium, but it was too large for the young organist and a special blowing apparatus was rigged up behind it. Instead of payment the congregation at Gwernllwyn paid for him to have two years' tuition with Edward Lawrence, a local musician who had studied with Moscheles at Leipzig, but since the Evans household possessed no piano, the young Harry practised twice or three times a week at the house of a member of the chapel.[91] The congregation then organized a concert from whose proceeds they bought him a piano of his own: thus did these communities cherish and selflessly promote their talented children.

Increasingly in demand as a pianist and accompanist – in reporting Rhymney United's victory at Pontypridd in 1893, the *Merthyr Express* felt obliged to congratulate it not on winning but 'in having so accomplished a musician as Mr Harry Evans of Dowlais for its accompanist'[92] – he was urged by many, though not his father who wished him to have a 'proper' education, to further his music career in London. For health reasons – he was never robust – he heeded the parental voice, a decision made easier by the fact that in 1887, the year he became a pupil-teacher at the Abermorlais School, Merthyr, he became organist of one of Dowlais's most imposing chapels, the 1,300-seater Bethania Welsh Congregational where his father was precentor. The organ became his passion, and Harry Evans was one of Wales's first public organ recitalists, his prestige greatly increased by his gaining the ARCO in 1893 and the FRCO four years later. By the end of 1894 Harry Evans, ARCO of Beethoven House,

8. The brilliant but short-lived Harry Evans (seated, centre) with his victorious Dowlais Male Voice Choir at Liverpool in 1900 where, according to the Merthyr Express, 'Dowlais saved Wales from utter obliteration'.

Russell Street, Dowlais, was accepting at moderate terms engagements for organ recitals, concerts, eisteddfodau and lessons in organ, pianoforte, harmony and theory, with the Rhymney district visited on Wednesdays. He was a professional musician.

In 1892, when Dan Davies deserted Dowlais for Merthyr and the Harmonic Society was acrimoniously disbanded, there was agitation for Harry Evans to form a choir to recapture for Dowlais its former glories.[93] Henry Smith's smaller choir, the Dowlais Music Lovers, was worthy, but they were not winners. This was a community and a society that set great store by winning, and Dowlais since the days of Rosser Beynon saw choral triumphs as the defining characteristic of its existence. In September 1893 the phoenix that was the Dowlais Philharmonic rose from the ashes of the Dowlais Harmonic, and by December Evans had built it up to a strength of 200 to do Handel's *Samson* with full orchestra. The following Christmas he introduced the concept of a Handel Festival and did *Messiah*, *Acis and Galatea* and *Samson* over two days, Dan Davies's Merthyr choir confining itself to *The Creation* on Boxing Day.[94]

Gradually Harry Evans made inroads into Dan Davies's entrenched position by advocating a much less histrionic, exaggerated performance, an objective he found easier to attain with the fifty young women, privately educated and able to read music – single middle-class young women from the town's social élite had been a feature of the Merthyr Philharmonic Society since its inception – who now proceeded to form his Dowlais Ladies' Choir in 1898.[95] The following year he founded a male choir twice that size to compete in the Liverpool National Eisteddfod in 1900; then in 1901 the Dowlais Ladies, 'all of social position', combined with the socially inferior men, half of whom were colliers and the rest in various skilled occupations and trades, to do *Hiawatha's Wedding Feast*. Perhaps it took one only recently civilized, frontier society fully to enter into this colourful portrayal of another, though we ought to pause before rushing to elevate this social mix as the classic Victorian ideal of a pan-class recreational institution. If the middle class and their social inferiors who had saved 2*d*. a week to spend at Liverpool sang in the ranks of the same organization, it did not follow that they spoke (though in Dowlais it is unlikely that they did not), and if singers from differing social backgrounds did mingle, this suggests the existence of a climate already conducive to a measure of trans-class activity. Harry Evans spoke approvingly of 'the levelling influence of music', as many of the women sang with working men employed by their fathers.[96] The men, in any case, were no ordinary choristers: through their victory over ten other choirs, including the formidable Manchester Orpheus, at Liverpool they had saved the honour of the nation when all the other choral prizes, chief, second choral and ladies, had gone to England, plunging Welsh choralism into agonies of self-doubt and anguished breast-beating over *cyflafan Llynlleifiad* ('the Liverpool massacre').[97]

At the Merthyr National Eisteddfod in 1901 Harry Evans conducted the eisteddfod choir of 500 in a performance of *Israel in Egypt* that was reckoned to be far superior to Randegger's at Liverpool in 1884, the contrast all the more marked with Dan Davies's lamentable *Elijah* during the same week. A further, and as it proved, final competitive triumph awaited Harry Evans when he taught a Dowlais and Merthyr combined choir the whole of *St Paul* for the 1903 Llanelli eisteddfod, and swept to victory over seven other choirs. He was by all accounts the coolest man in the audience of 20,000 as he collected the winners' cheque. Some of his exultant choristers put 'winner' cards in their hatbands and tried to raise their conductor aloft but he 'deprecated any insanity'. On reaching Dowlais that night, however, what he dismissed as 'the shoulder-high business' could not be avoided as the Cyfarthfa Band, with the High Constable heading all the town's worthies and its workers, participated in scenes 'of almost indescribable and unparalleled enthusiasm'. It was 'indeed a sight for the gods'.[98]

This was Harry Evans's last competitive appearance but his choir continued to uphold the highest choral standards. When they gave a concert at the Queen's Hall, London, in April 1904 the *Musical Herald* commended 'its first rate training. Their tone is pure and round . . . the execution was always artistic and never defaced by the exaggeration that often characterises the performance of Welsh choristers.' It added that their conductor was a restraining influence who believed that the uncritical acclaim of a few English judges for the thrilling effect of Welsh choirs singing with all the power of their lungs, because they had never heard such a mass of sound from a choir before, had been positively harmful.[99] 'I dare not allow my choir to sing their loudest', Evans had asserted, provoking a measure of frustration among those who felt that he kept his choir on too tight a rein – 'one could have done with more Welsh fire', complained one critic. Whether this was over-restraint or not, it was achieved by stern discipline.[100] In Harry Evans's choir no one dared joke, laugh or even talk in practice; a look from those penetrating dark eyes so froze the object of their gaze that twenty years after his death one of his women choristers confessed to a physical tremor whenever she thought about him.[101]

He kept the choir together for some time after that date, but a significant development had already occurred in 1902 when he was offered the
conductorship of the Liverpool Welsh Choral Union, whose members
had to be of Welsh descent. Since there were at least 100,000 so qualified
on Merseyside there was no problem with recruitment, and Evans
doubled the size of the choir to 300, tested each member, and soon dispelled the notion that Welsh choristers could sing only Handel and
Mendelssohn by doing Sullivan's *Golden Legend,* Bach's *St Matthew
Passion,* Elgar's *Dream of Gerontius* and *The Apostles,* and the third-ever
performance of D. Vaughan Thomas's *The Bard.* For four years he
travelled from Merthyr each week to train the choir until in 1906 he
decided to uproot himself and settle in Liverpool, a move facilitated by
his appointment as organist and choirmaster at Great George Street
Congregational Church.

It is true that he attracted considerable contemporary attention as a
composer: his *Victory of St Garmon* for baritone and chorus was well
received by the public and the critics at the 1904 Cardiff Festival, for
instance, and his *Dafydd ap Gwilym,* commissioned for the Llangollen
National Eisteddfod of 1908, was also critically acclaimed. But it was as
an inspiring, technically accomplished choral conductor that he
introduced new, hitherto unattained professional standards of accomplishment into Welsh choralism. With his male choir he had rigorously
concentrated on voice production and intonation: for purity of tone he
took *pp* scales three times up and down in the same breath to get the
scale sung in tune. The thirds are notoriously flat in the singing of scales
by amateurs but 'all our practices were unaccompanied so we did not
flatten'.[102] He got his first tenors to use the head voice only, without
forcing the chest and becoming throaty, thus ensuring that all his top
tenors could sing an effortless B flat.

In particular he brought a wider perspective to Welsh choralism. He
claimed to have learned most by 'picking up', meaning the experience
gained through contact with singers, composers and conductors, and
'getting about' in London, especially to Covent Garden, the Queen's
Hall symphony concerts, and leading English festivals like the Birmingham, Leeds and Three Choirs. As a boy he had thought none could sing
choruses as the Welsh sang them but on hearing complete works at
various English festivals 'my eyes were opened to clear pronunciation,
phrasing and tonal purity'. He was insistent that more intelligent singing
was necessary if Welsh choral supremacy was to be maintained and drew
up distinct proposals for reforming the musical side of the eisteddfod,

recommendations that a later generation would consider unacceptably *dirigiste*, such as establishing a board of twelve musicians to publish an agreed list of test pieces for choirs, solo voices and instruments, and that these should in turn be graded for local, larger and national eisteddfodau. Free of the astigmatism which skewed the vision of his iconoclastic one-time pupil Cyril Jenkins, the more clear-sighted Harry Evans recognized the faults of the Welsh in music as arising from a lack of formal musical educational opportunities, a product of their wider social and economic impoverishment. But it was not a spiritual poverty, as Welsh congregational singing testified. He could never rid himself of the memory of once conducting 16,000 at the Caernarfon Pavilion – 'some of this combined singing is truly wonderful' – but characteristically he eschewed sentimentality or complacency, preferring instead a robust reformism: 'more might be done in these gatherings to instil the right artistic ideals into the people.'[103]

In terms of production, his performances with the Liverpool Welsh Choral Union showed what the implementation of his principles could achieve. Edward Elgar pronounced him 'a great conductor' after hearing a performance of his in September 1909,[104] though it was in his last two years that he attained the Parnassian heights when he took up the formidable challenge presented by the newly composed unaccompanied choral symphonies of Granville Bantock. There were no more difficult works, at least to amateur choristers, than Bantock's secular oratorio *Omar Khayyam*, his semi-religious *Atalanta in Calydon*, given its second-ever performance in 1912 by the Liverpool Welsh with the Manchester Orpheus Choir, whose combined forces were then redivided into four choirs singing up to twenty parts, and the fiendishly taxing *Vanity of Vanities* for twelve unaccompanied choral parts, especially dedicated by Bantock to Harry Evans and his Choral Union and given its première by them at Liverpool in February 1914.[105] It was predicted at the time that this 'would kill poor Harry',[106] and it did. He was in fact about to take up the conductorship of the North Staffs Choral Society in September 1914 when he died of a brain tumour in July, at forty-one years of age. Among the scores of tributes paid him, it was W. G. McNaught who most accurately identified his genius as intensity of emotion controlled by a powerful musical intellect.[107]

Merthyr choralism had moved on from the turbulent theatricality of Dan Davies who would yet survive Harry Evans into the inter-war period, when a new generation of composers, conductors and performers came of age to burnish further the musical reputation of the by then beleaguered town of Tydfil the martyr.

6

'This Valley of Coal and Song': Musical Rhondda, 1860–1914

୧୦

1. Impassioned Shatterings

There was no dearth of entertainment in the Rhondda Valley in the unexceptional year of 1907. As the year opened the Toy Terriers topped the bill at the Palace of Varieties at Porth, supported by Marie Collins, sister of Lottie Collins of 'Ta-ra-ra-boom-de-ay' fame, as well as by Dene and Dawson's mirth-provoking sketch, Harry Birt the society humorist, Bandoni the one-man band, the Four Sisters Sligo, Belford and Mars, Carlotta Lunn, Elliott and Warne and other acts. Barely two miles away Tonypandy's Hippodrome offered fare of a more exotic nature with Kyoto the Chinese marvel contortionist, the Australian Troubadours, and Tom Odlin the odd comedian who would 'sing two very good songs'; there were also two comedy duos, a boy impersonator, a charming comedienne, and at both venues the by now ubiquitous Electric Bioscope, Payne's in Tonypandy, the Palace's own in Porth.[1]

Meanwhile sons of the Rhondda were taking their own particular and, to some, preferred form of entertainment to the world. Since October in the previous year the Royal Treorchy Male Choir, only seventeen in number, nearly all unmarried colliers, had been touring North America. They had spent the outward voyage in singing, giving concerts, tug-of-war and pillow-fighting, and one chorister had acquired a certain notoriety by declaring himself to a conspicuous female fellow passenger to be 'the *capten* of the *llong*'. By the time they returned in March 1907 they had given sixty-six concerts in sixty-four days including performances at Harrisburg (Pa.) State Penitentiary and Neuberg (Cleveland) asylum. It was as punishing vocally as it was strenuous physically, especially for the first tenors who had to sing falsetto in those pieces written for male altos. The *Milwaukee Press*, the organ of a city that was a hotbed of male and lyric clubs and the home of Dr Daniel Protheroe, thought the Rhondda choristers 'brought *a capella* singing to the most exquisite perfection possible'. Such fine pianissimos, such shading and working up to grand climaxes had apparently never been heard there before.[2]

On their return they found a valley still resounding with the sounds of music that entertained, elevated, inflamed and inspired in equal measure. Some enthusiasts would have wished to make this claim on behalf of the Llwynypia Prize Flute Band which since its inception in 1893 had become one of the most successful musical organizations in the United Kingdom, a fact which persuaded their president, W. W. Hood, the Llwynypia colliery manager, in 1905 to make them an interest-free loan in order to buy £530 worth of instruments for £300 cash down. They had already repaid £105 by June 1907 when they beat seven other bands at the Ulster Hall, Belfast, a venue where this music was meat and drink.

But with due respect to the wind players of Llwynypia there was an even more momentous development in the next township, where Clydach Vale was, at this relatively late date, having its first taste of oratorio when Calfaria Baptist Choir performed *St Paul*. There were two pianos instead of an orchestra, an absence regretted 'on the introduction of oratorio to the district', and even the well-known David Chubb of Pontypridd had 'been heard to better advantage' as Paul. For it was hardly the case that orchestral music was unknown in the district: Percie Smith's Rhondda Orchestra had been in existence for five years by the time of its annual dinner in January 1907, a period in which they had given twenty-six concerts throughout the valley, and it was about to accompany Siloh Choral Society, Pentre, in Sir Arthur Sullivan's *The Light of the World*. In February and March Rhondda choralism burst forth with resplendent force: Moriah, Ton, echoed to the warlike strains of *Judas Maccabaeus*, although the conductor O. T. Jones ('Alaw Ffestin') had moved to the area only the previous summer. 'The work brims with the heroic,' exclaimed the local correspondent as he contemplated pieces of vocal artillery like 'O Father whose Almighty Power' and the rousing tenor aria 'Arm, Arm ye Brave'; Percie Smith's orchestra was on hand to provide the accompaniment. At Noddfa Baptist, Clydach Vale, Finlay Lyon's *The Great Light* was being performed, again with orchestral accompaniment; at Carmel Treherbert (accommodation 900), M. O. Jones was conducting *The Creation*, while all 850 seats in Ebenezer, Tonypandy, were taken for Stainer's *The Daughter of Jairus* and Mendelssohn's *Psalm 42* with Arthur Angle's orchestra.

The Rhondda Fach, not to be outdone, saw in April Tom Evans's 100-strong Horeb Chapel (Tylorstown) Choir do Mozart's Twelfth Mass, and at the local Workmen's Hall the Ynys-hir Choral Society performed Haydn's *The Creation*, assisted by Percie Smith's thirty-three-piece orchestra, which two weeks later would again be in demand in Pentre to accompany the choral society of the 1,140-seater Siloh chapel in *The Light of the World*.

Soon another shipload of the valley's second best-known export – singers – was heading west, this time with the twenty-strong Rhondda Gleemen aboard, some of whom had been members of Tom Stephens's victorious choir that won undying fame at Chicago in 1893. They landed on 4 October and immediately embarked on an impossibly arduous schedule of seventy-four concerts. To the irritation of the recently returned Royal Treorchy choristers the *Wilmington Record* pronounced the current phalanx superior, blending better and free of 'the rather cloying sweetness of the Treorchyites'. Better vocalists, they also had a superior accompanist in the young prodigy A. M. Setter.[3]

By this time the Rhondda was singing opera as well as oratorio. In November 1907 Ferndale Harmonic gave their second annual operatic performance, this time of *Il Trovatore* and *Maritana*, the principals coming from the Moody Manners company, apart, that is, from Mary King Sarah, a native of Talysarn in north Wales, a double winner (soprano and alto) at the Caernarfon National Eisteddfod of 1906, here making her operatic debut as Leonora: nothing gave greater pleasure to a Welsh audience than seeing one of their own in a starring role. Later the same month, lower down the Rhondda Fach, the Ynys-hir Operatic Society also gave two performances of *Maritana*, with the aid of the indefatigable and apparently indispensable Percie Smith Orchestra.[4] (That Rhondda orchestral life was not confined to providing accompaniment in choral concerts was demonstrated in October when the Tonypandy Orchestral Society conducted by David Morgan gave its first concert at the local Jerusalem chapel).[5]

This outpouring of musicality was enabled by a concentration of population which provided a market and an audience, by middle-class patrons and philanthropic employers, and most of all, by the all-pervasive influence of Nonconformity. So, in December, 1907 came full circle in another orgy of oratorio.[6] Salem, Porth, Musical Society did *Hymn of Praise* and *The Creation*, when a 'totally inadequate' string band (not Percie Smith's) was compensated for by T. D. Edwards at the organ and the popular London bass David Hughes; Tonypandy Harmonic Society performed Handel's *Acis and Galatea*, while the formidable and ambitious Noddfa Choral Society in the Rhondda's citadel of song,

Treorchy, outdid them all with Gounod's *Redemption*, the *Hymn of Praise*, Elgar's *Light of Life* and Cherubini's *Dies Irae*, a work with especial appeal, so it was believed, 'to the spirit of Welsh choral singing':

> The unutterable awfulness of the last day, the wails of despairing sinners, the prayerful appeals for mercy from the more hopeful, and the calm majestic confidence of the climax are fit subjects for those powers of song that have made Wales famous throughout the world.[7]

The year 1907 was not an untypical one in the Rhondda, where the enjoyment of music was hardly a minority pastime but a pursuit that generated enormous levels of enthusiasm and commitment. We ought not, however, to lose sight of the fact that the self-made musical culture of these self-making mining communities was expressed via a plurality of codes – vocal, instrumental, orchestral, operatic, comedic, choral, eisteddfodic, artistic and trans-Atlantic – that were points of contact with a consciously apprehended past, symptoms of a social energy that had been propelling the Rhondda's rising trajectory for as many, or as few, as four decades by 1907.

A conveniently arbitrary date from which to trace the history of music in the Rhondda as the popular cultural activity of a recently created industrial society would be 1899 and the publication of its first weekly newspaper. The inaugural number of the *Rhondda Leader* (2 December 1899) included a 'Musical Notes' column 'in view of the great interest taken in musical matters in the Rhondda'. The column's author, 'The Man about the Hills', was not long getting into his stride and by the second issue he was regretting 'the absence of work which is sadly neglected in the Rhondda Valley, the study and practice of the complete works of the great masters'.[8] Oratorio performances in Mid-Rhondda, he complained the following year, were 'as rare and as few and far between as the proverbial visits of angels'.[9] When Tom Stephens, whose success as conductor of the Rhondda Gleemen earned him the sobriquet of being 'the Musical "Bobs" of Wales', proposed, by way of reform of the eisteddfod, a semi-national event to be held at Ystrad in May 1907, with competing choirs to sing two choruses from *Messiah* learnt in its entirety, the author of the 'Musical Notes' column opined that 'conductors would be chary of facing so exacting a work' in view of the fact that 'good readers are not over-plentiful in the hill districts' and perhaps 'a less pretentious and less difficult work would have been more practicable' for test purposes.[10] Remarkably, therefore, at the start of the twentieth century Handel's masterwork had yet to impose its stranglehold on the Rhondda's choral preference.

Not that there was a dearth of raw material with which to do it justice: it was 'a matter of regret that with such splendid vocal resources in this district so important a branch of musical study should be so woefully neglected'. This was a view expressed in July 1900. Within a month a performance of Handel's *Jephtha* in Tonypandy (2 August) by the choir of Salem, Llwynypia, conducted by the newspaper's editor Tom John, and with an orchestra organized by Paul Draper, made that correspondent choke on his words. But 'while it was a pleasing sight to see such an immense crowd of all classes drawn to listen', the suspicion remained that this kind of work was not audience-friendly and that sooner or later Handel's masterpieces would have to be rearranged since 'they were deemed to presume too much upon the patience of audiences in these go-ahead days'.[11] He would have to eat those words as well: *Jephtha* was in the Rhondda to stay. For the next fifty years the valley's audiences would thrill to the grandeur of the majestic opening movement and the rollicking fugue of the second, listen intently to the tenor solo 'Waft her Angels', and bask in the mighty diapason of Rhondda's finest letting rip in what was to be the work's best-known chorus, 'When His Loud Voice in Thunder Speaks'.

The chapel choirs of his youth with their choruses that 'could swing one off the earth' made an indelible impression on the novelist and short-story writer Rhys Davies, born in Clydach Vale in 1903:

> For concerts, the men sat on upper tiers of scaffolding erected below the grand pipe organ, their abnormal air of obedience lending them a saturnine mien. The women, ranged on the lower tiers, all looked swollen in readiness for any challenge, and, at the conductor's signal to rise to their feet, they were a concourse of dark swans mounting in ominous disturbance of the air. Above them, the male ranks stood poised more rigidly, even darker guardians of the empyrean spaces. Our chapels were too confined for the ensuing mighty harmonies, ears too miniature for such impassioned shatterings. The walls contracted closer on a dense audience stifling in best clothes, odour of mothballs, and sense of occasion.[12]

There was no full-blown oratorio in the Rhondda at Christmas 1900, at least if we discount for this purpose the second sprouting of cantatas and small-scale oratorios like Sullivan's *Prodigal Son* at Bethania, Tonypandy, G. F. Root's *Belshazzar's Feast* at Penygraig by Salem,

Williamstown, and T. Mee Patterson's *A Day with the Lord* at Bethania, Treorchy.[13] But the year 1901 pointedly opened with the unveiling by Dr Roland Rogers of Bangor of a new three-manual organ at Noddfa Chapel, Treorchy, a magnificent instrument for the immediate benefit of Noddfa's new organist J. T. Jones, LRAM, accompanist to the Royal Treorchy Male Choir which was conducted by William Thomas, who was also conductor of Noddfa Choral Society.[14] J. T. Jones would soon be soliciting pupils and concert engagements from his home at Gaffers Row, Cwmparc, while Noddfa Choral Society geared itself to becoming the premier non-competitive choral society in Wales, a position it held for the next four decades. Even quicker off the mark was another local musician, W. T. David, organist of Ebenezer, Tonypandy, who made his début conducting the chapel choir of 150 and an orchestra formed by E. J. Roberts of Cardiff, in *Judas Maccabaeus*.

The alarm had been sounded. Within the next eight weeks M. O. Jones's Treherbert Choral Society put on *Hymn of Praise*, and Tom John's Llwynypia choristers followed up the previous year's triumphant *Jephtha* with another *Lobgesang*.[15] It was not a coincidence that this was the test piece at that year's (1901) National Eisteddfod at Merthyr, for which the entire work had to be mastered by the ten competing choirs, three of which came from the Rhondda. Thus Christmas 1901 saw the usual crop of cantatas (who now remembers J. Astor Broad's *Joseph*; or *Amos, the Cripple of Capernaum?*) but also, now, oratorio. Noddfa, whose seating capacity of 1,450 made it the second-largest 'sacred edifice' (that is, a Nonconformist chapel) in Wales, was full to overflowing for three performances of *Messiah* while the indefatigable Salem Choral Society brought in Harry Evans of Dowlais as guest conductor of 'Haydn's most beautiful work, "Creation" ' and Mendelssohn's *Walpurgisnacht* in Llwynypia. A tradition of large-scale massively attended oratorio performances was established, as Noddfa's programme (until 1906 conducted by William Thomas, from 1907 by J. T. Jones) for the rest of the decade indicates:

1901   *Messiah*
1902   *Messiah, Elijah*
1903   *Emmanuel* (Joseph Parry), *Elijah*
1904   *Samson, Hymn of Praise, Captivity* (D. Emlyn Evans)
1905   *Messiah, Hymn of Praise, Judith* (C. H. H. Parry)
1906   *Light of Life, Elijah, Last Judgement* (Spohr)
1907   *Redemption* (Gounod), *Hymn of Praise, Light of Life*
1908   *Redemption, St Paul, Last Judgement*

1909 *Messiah, St Paul, Rejoice in the Lord* (David Evans)
1910 *St Matthew Passion, Hymn of Praise*

At Ebenezer, Tonypandy (Rhondda's 'Temple of Music') W. T. David conducted the following:

1901 *Judas Maccabaeus*
1902 *Samson*
1903 *Light of the World*
1904 *Messiah*
1905 *Captivity*
1906 *The Seasons* (Haydn)
1907 *Daughter of Jairus* (Stainer), *Psalm 42* (Mendelssohn)
1908 *Gate of Life* (Leoni), *Alexander's Feast* (Handel)

At Salem, Porth, Rhys Evans's Porth Harmonic Society could boast a comparable record: between 1903 and 1911 they did *Messiah* and *The Creation* twice, *Elijah*, *Hymn of Praise*, Rossini's *Stabat Mater*, *Last Judgement*, Joseph Parry's *Saul of Tarsus* and Beethoven's *Mount of Olives*. In 1912 they tackled both the Mozart *Requiem* and *Hiawatha's Departure* by Coleridge-Taylor. Salem, Llwynypia's annual offerings further varied the menu, with Schubert's *Song of Miriam*, Sterndale Bennett's *May Queen* and John Ambrose Lloyd's *Gweddi Habacuc*.

This constitutes a remarkable catalogue of amateur achievement by any standard, despite the absence of Dvorak, Brahms, Verdi and Elgar, who can be seen to be making inroads into even the Welsh oratorio tradition by 1914: the Tabernacle, Morriston, did Dvorak's *Stabat Mater* in 1907, and Brahms's *Requiem* was performed twice in the same month by two separate choral societies, one of them a chapel choir, in Swansea in 1909. The infrequency of works by Welsh composers, and none by the prolific David Jenkins, is also striking, but this is surely outweighed by the appearance among such predictable if challenging fare of Bach's *St Matthew Passion*, a colossal hurdle for even a professional choir.

Oratorio, after an apparently slow start, had become a tradition in the Rhondda by the eve of the First World War. But only apparently. While the valley's weekly newspaper provides a useful guide we would do well not to be deceived by its own preoccupation with the newness of the present, for the Rhondda had an extensive musical prehistory. Despite all the assertions to the contrary, oratorio did not need to be introduced in 1900: it was already well established.

2. Ocean Deep

Parish records indicate that the Rhondda was not without music even in the eighteenth century, but the singing teacher employed there in 1752[16] can scarcely be credited with the musical accomplishments which began in the area a century later in the decade which saw the first coal-laden wagons trundle out of the Bute Colliery, Treherbert, in 1855, and the beginnings of Rhondda's pell-mell demographic growth from less than a thousand (951) in 1851 to almost 17,000 (16,914) in 1871 and to 152,000 by 1911. Thereby the two Rhondda valleys outstripped relatively and absolutely the slower growth of Merthyr from 52,000 to 81,000 between 1871 and 1911, and of Aberdare from 36,000 to 50,000 in the same period. The early immigrants were male, young, mostly Welsh-speaking Nonconformists from rural west Wales where the effects of the 1859 Revival could still be felt, and short-distance migrants from the neighbouring older industrial valleys of the Cynon (Aberdare) and Taf (Merthyr) with their traditions of temperance choralism, eisteddfod rivalry and, from the 1860s, familiarity with the tonic sol-fa notation. All these factors potently influenced the nature and development of Rhondda music for the next hundred years, irrespective of changing patterns of immigration, and, after the First World War, rapid Anglicization: before it, in 1911 half the Rhondda's 152,781 population was still Welsh-speaking (76,796).[17]

In the links with the older industrial areas of east Glamorgan are to be found the beginnings of Rhondda choralism. The Cymmer district of Porth, for instance, had a musical history considerably pre-dating the choral activities of Rhys Evans's Porth Harmonic Society in the 1900s. Cymmer choristers participated regularly in the annual festivals of the Gwent and Glamorgan Temperance Choral Union from its inception in 1854 to the 1870s, and special trains (*cerbydau arbennig*) ran from Cymmer to the 1861 festival in Hermon, Dowlais, where Ieuan Gwyllt conducted five to six thousand choristers from nine different choirs.[18] These were not competitive affairs; rather, choirs prepared choruses to be sung by massed voices (in 1862 these numbered nearly 700, including two Cymmer choirs; in 1869, 800) and others to be sung by individual choirs: in 1867 the Porth Choir (Côr y Porth) individually sang Verdi's 'Hail us, ye Free'.[19] They were occasions which provided not only opportunity for travel and sociability, but also a valuable musical education for the fledgeling Rhondda choristers hearing seasoned choirs from the longer-settled chorally mature districts of Merthyr, Dowlais,

Rhymney and Tredegar.[20] Rhondda choralism was still in the learning stage: significantly, there were no Rhondda entrants when choral competitions first became a feature of the National Eisteddfod in the 1860s.[21]

It is in that decade, however, that an emerging infrastructure of local eisteddfodau can be discerned: at Dinas in 1862, where the Porth choir made its first appearance at the Soar eisteddfod, at Treorchy in 1867,[22] at Treherbert in 1869, and then at Ferndale in 1870 and Blaenllechau and Tonypandy in 1872.[23] The Tonypandy eisteddfod, soon to be accorded the privileged status of semi-national, became a two-day affair in 1874 when the guest adjudicator Joseph Barnby, conductor of the Royal Choral Society, lavished excessive praise on the choirs he heard there, awarding the £600 prize, a colossal sum, to Aberdare (conducted by Hywel Cynon) for 'Thanks be to God', with a Rhondda choir second.[24] By 1884 annual Christmas eisteddfodau were held at Porth, Tonypandy and Treherbert, thereby covering lower, mid- and upper Rhondda, and were keenly awaited.[25] This competitive spirit was mobilized by the extension of the Taff Vale Railway's passenger service from Porth to Ystrad in 1862, and up to Treherbert the following year. The Rhondda Fach branch was constructed in 1862, eventually reaching Maerdy in 1877, while the Rhondda and Swansea Bay Railway Company was established in 1882 to give the hill districts a prospect of the sea: now the whole of Glamorgan was prey to the Rhondda's competitive choristers.[26]

The thirteenth of April 1871 is a milestone date in the history of Rhondda music for on that day Caradog conducted the first oratorio heard there, Louis Spohr's *Last Judgement* in Treherbert, to the accompaniment of Mr Crawshay's string band, two flutes and a harmonium. In 1875 he did *The Creation*, again with instrumental support, and in 1882 further extended the upper valley's acquaintance with Haydn by conducting the Libanus Chapel Choir and String Band in the Third ('Imperial') Mass in Treherbert Public Hall.[27] It is worth noting that orchestral music was sufficiently advanced for Treherbert to enter the Cardiff National in 1883 and play the overture to *Masaniello*, even if they came third.[28] By then Tonypandy had heard *Judas Maccabaeus* (1878) and *St Paul* (1879) conducted by Buallt Jones, who died there aged thirty-eight later that year, one of a generation of incomers who spearheaded the Rhondda's choral forward march.[29] Just as Caradog came from the adjacent Cynon Valley to settle in Treorchy in 1870, moving to Treherbert in 1876, D. T. Prosser ('Eos Cynlais', also known as Prosser Bach, 1844–1904), represented another established choral bastion, the

Upper Swansea Valley. Born in Ystradgynlais he had been deputy to Ivander and conducted a choir of his own in Cwmgïedd aged seventeen, a few years before Daniel Protheroe was born there in 1866. He moved first to the choral hothouse of Dowlais, then, in 1875, to employment at Cwmparc Colliery where he became a precentor (*codwr canu*) at Bethlehem, Treorchy, and founder of the Rhondda Philharmonic Choir. He took all 130 of them, their ranks stiffened by another seventy from Merthyr, to the Birkenhead National Eisteddfod in 1878, where Sir George Macfarren, Joseph Parry and John Thomas (Pencerdd Gwalia) gave the prize to the Eryri Choir from the Snowdonia district, who promptly distributed mourning cards – a practice also adopted by football supporters – lamenting the departed glory of the south Wales choirs from Merthyr and Aberdare as well as Rhondda, who came third, after Aberdare.[30] Prosser Bach would be back, to beat another four south Wales choirs, each 150–200 voices strong on 'Ye Nations' from *Hymn of Praise* and D. Emlyn Evans's 'Haleliwia Amen' at Merthyr in 1881, and, sweeter still, at Brecon in 1889, when his Rhondda Philharmonic and Taliesin Hopkins's Cymmer and Porth took the first two placings relegating their two Dowlais rivals – *two* Dowlais choirs of nearly two hundred singers each – to third and fourth. Overall the Rhondda 'Phil' lost more times than it won: it was unsuccessful at six Nationals, and Prosser's last appearance was at Merthyr in 1901 when he failed to repeat his victory of twenty years before. It was the Brecon National, his greatest triumph, that announced Rhondda's choral coming-of-age, for there also William Thomas's Treorchy and Tom Stephens's Ton-based Rhondda Gleemen took the first two prizes in the competition for male choirs.

The Rhondda's major choral figures in its golden age followed in the footsteps of Caradog, Cynlais and Buallt Jones: they all came from outside. Taliesin Hopkins (1859–1906) would always be associated with Cymmer, where he lived from the age of twenty, but he was born in Mountain Ash, and sang in Caradog's choir before moving to the Rhondda in 1878 to become a weigher at Insole's Cymmer Collieries and precentor at Capel y Cymmer Independents' chapel. Having first tasted success at Trealaw eisteddfod on Good Friday 1879, by the late 1880s he was regarded as a formidable eisteddfod competitor, winning over a dozen major competitions between Christmas at Porth 1887 and Caerphilly's Whitsun semi-national in 1891 including the Brecon National in 1889. The men in his choir formed their own male-voice party, and Tal led them to victory over the redoubtable Moelwyn choir of

Blaenau Ffestiniog in the Llandudno National Eisteddfod of 1896.[31] When he conducted his chapel choir in the numerous oratorios they performed together he did so with full orchestra; a string instrumentalist himself, this versatile self-taught musician was also a drum-and-fife conductor.

By geographic contrast, M. O. Jones (1842–1908), who lived the last forty-six years of his life in Treherbert, was a native of Llandinorwig in the Caernarfonshire quarry districts. Trained as a teacher at Borough Road, London, he taught only briefly in his native Carneddi before leaving for Treherbert in 1862. He thus witnessed in microcosm the dramatic growth of the Rhondda: when he arrived in Treherbert the village's population was about 800; by 1897 it was near 10,000 and from 1862, as the *Rhondda Leader* noted on his death, 'the new schoolmaster and the new village grew together'[37] – and, it might have added, so did Rhondda choralism. Like Tal Hopkins and Prosser Bach, M. O. Jones was a precentor, from 1868 until his death, at Carmel, Treherbert, where he reformed the psalmody by insisting on an anthem being sung every Sunday evening, and frequently a chorus as well, a practice he imported from the Carneddi; 'during the decade 1840-50', he wrote, 'there were more congregational choirs in the populous districts of North Wales, especially Caernarfonshire, than in South Wales.'[33] Like Tal Hopkins he too was able to form a male party from his Carmel choir. Beyond that he was a teacher of sol-fa, having learned it for himself; he was also a composer of anthems, part-songs and hymn-tunes, as well as being a literary figure of some importance. As his papers abundantly testify, his interests ran from the development of the Rhondda coal industry to local antiquities (a *History of the Parish of Ystradyfodwg*), literature (*Llên Gwerin Cymru* – Welsh folk literature) and musical biography.[34]

Historically, what Ieuan Ddu was to Merthyr M. O. Jones was to the Rhondda: in September 1876 his choir of 160 gave the first complete performance of *Messiah* for a Rhondda audience to hear. Like all successful conductors he had to take the rough with the smooth: his Treherbert choir was the occasion of a minor riot at a Christmas eisteddfod at Merthyr's Drill Hall in 1880 where, clearly the victors after singing 'The Heavens are Telling', they were prevented by 'mob law' from singing their second piece.

A robust industrial society fuelled by the labour and social requirements of a young, often single male population – Rhondda, Dr Chris Williams reminds us, 'was both a coal society and a man's world'[35] – was fertile soil for male choirs, as it would remain into the second half of the next century. What Tom Stephens (1856–1906) achieved was to bring Rhondda male choralism to the attention of a world that knew of the valley's steam coal but little else. He again was an in-migrant from two musically active centres, Aberdare directly, but originally from Brynaman further west. When Caradog relinquished the leadership of the Aberdare Choral Union to move to Treorchy, his mantle fell jointly on Rees Evans and Tom Stephens, who had sung alto at the Crystal Palace on both occasions (1872, 1873) of Caradog's triumph. In 1877 Stephens moved to the Rhondda when he was appointed precentor at Bethesda, Ton Pentre, and he was shortly persuaded to take on the leadership of the newly founded thirty-strong Rhondda Glee Society upon whom he promptly imposed the strict regime under which during the hour's choir practice no one but the conductor was to speak.

After several semi-national successes at Porth and Bridgend, the Rhondda Glee went to the Cardiff National in 1883 and won out of seventeen choirs, impelling the *Daily Telegraph*'s correspondent to observe that he 'did not expect to hear better singing in London than that of these miners from the Rhondda. Power and delivery, precision and artistic freedom were conspicuous to a degree which filled strangers with amazement.' At the 1887 London National Eisteddfod they beat nine other choirs to share first prize with John North's formidable Huddersfield organization, in a competition for fifty to seventy male voices in which the test pieces were Arthur Sullivan's 'The Beleaguered' and David Jenkins's 'Valiant Warriors'. Such was the continued success of the Rhondda Gleemen that by 1900 no other musical society in Wales had raised so much money for good causes: they were virtually a charitable organization. It was to Tom Stephens's Glee Party that 'the present popularity of male voice choral singing in Wales is traceable', according to one tribute on his death in January 1906 in Llantwit Faerdref. At his funeral the mile-long cortège of this collier-publican-conductor included every notable musician in the three valleys of the Rhondda, Cynon and Taf: Dan Davies, Harry Evans and E. T. Davies from Merthyr; W. J. Evans and Arkite Phillips from Aberdare; William Thomas and Percie Smith from the Rhondda.[36]

While his fame rested on his many local and national eisteddfod triumphs, the one that stood out above all others was achieved four thousand miles away. The winners at the 1893 Pontypridd National would, it was decided, represent Wales at the World's Fair Eisteddfod in Chicago later that year. Suitably bellicose renditions of David Jenkins's 'The War Horse' and the French composer Ambroise Thomas's 'The

*9. Tom Stephens (1865–1906) led the Rhondda Gleemen
to victory at the Chicago World's Fair in 1893.*

Tyrol' gave them victory over William Thomas's Treorchy choir. Apparently Stephens, landlord of the Blacksmith's Arms, Treherbert, had received first-hand information about the yodelling techniques of the Tyrolean mountains from a brewery traveller who had been there, and the introduction of this piece of realism in the singing of Ambroise Thomas's test piece was the turning-point of the competition, and won the Gleemen their transatlantic ticket.[37]

They had already visited the USA in 1888–9, singing a phenomenal 140 concerts over a period of six months. In 1893 the violent hauliers' strike of that year, which had required 1,000 soldiers to occupy the coalfield, enabled Stephens to assemble his choir for practice afternoon and evening, certainly more frequently than the usual three times weekly. Chicagoans, with bitter memories of their own strikes of 1877 and 1886 and the tensions that would lead to the Pullman strike already accumulating, were hardly in the mood to greet Tom Stephens's choristers as strikers but as musical emollients, which fortunately they did. After giving Caradog, twenty years after his Crystal Palace triumphs, a reception worthy of the president himself, the audience of 2,500 was transfixed by the male-choir competition between choirs from Pittsburg, Edwardsville and Wilkesbarre (Pa.), the Salt Lake City Tabernacle and Iowa, all with Welsh connections, and the two Welsh choirs, Edward Broome's Penrhyn choir from Bethesda, who had raised £1,000 for the trip including a £300 donation from Lord Penrhyn, and Tom Stephens's Gleemen. They had travelled together packed like herring in a barrel on the way out and would be hardly more comfortable on the cattle boat that took them home. They were also clearly the two best choirs, and the prize money lay between them.

The 'Windy City' lived up to its reputation by playing havoc with the copy of the Penrhyn accompanist (though the Rhondda choir preferred to believe the Penrhyn soloist flattened in Joseph Parry's 'Pilgrims Chorus') enabling the Gleemen to snatch the prize. It was the greatest choral victory since that achieved by Caradog, who was himself back at Pontypridd station in time to join the ecstatic reception given the choristers on their return.[38]

Four years later, on 23 February 1898, they sang in front of the Queen at Windsor, an honour already accorded to another party of Chicago prizewinners, Clara (mother of Ivor) Novello Davies's Welsh Ladies' Choir. In their tails and white gloves the 50-odd male choristers may have been the most sartorially elegant miners ever seen at Windsor Castle[39] or anywhere else, but they were not the first to appear there, or to be entitled to attach the prefix 'Royal' to their name. This distinction had already befallen their great rivals from Treorchy, merely in their Sunday best, and their conductor William Thomas.

The intense rivalry between these two choirs – as keenly fought as between any neighbouring football teams, Tom Stephens's territory being Ystrad and Ton against William Thomas's Treorchy and Pentre – dominated Rhondda music for two decades.[40] William Thomas, born in Mountain Ash in 1851, was conducting a choir there at the age of eighteen, and, like so many of the Welsh musicians who came to prominence in the late nineteenth century, was a member of the South Wales Choral Union that sang at the Crystal Palace. In 1873 he moved to Treorchy and became choirmaster of Noddfa Baptist Chapel.[41] He was precentor at Noddfa, schools attendance officer and manager of the local co-operative when he was invited to lead the fifty-strong Ocean colliers who naturally met to rehearse in the long room of the Red Cow in Treorchy. William Thomas would rise to a position of influence and authority in the Ocean Collieries, which were sufficiently strong numerically and vocally – they employed 8,000 men in eleven collieries – to hold their own eisteddfod (to mark the coming of age of 'the young squire of Llandinam', David Davies) to which each of the eleven collieries sent a choir.[42] William Thomas, a zealous Baptist and temperance advocate, agreed to their request if they came out of the Red Cow and into the schoolroom, which in 1885 they did, and where they still are.

Their first competitive victory was on 'Comrades in Arms' at St Fagans near Cardiff, as a result of which Thomas and his choir were embraced by the Glamorgan aristocracy in the persons of the Earl and Countess of Dunraven Castle, whose links with royalty and useful patronage (the Earl paid their expenses to Windsor) secured their coveted command performance in 1895. Treorchy were the winners the first time a prize of £25 was offered in a male-choir competition in Wales, and became national winners on several occasions, notably at Brecon in 1889 with 'The Young Musicians' (Knüchen) and Tom Price's 'Seren Hwyrol' (The Evening Star). An epic five-hour contest in 1891 at Swansea, featuring ten choirs attacking Joseph Parry's 'Pilgrims' and Laurent de Rille's 'Destruction of Gaza' saw Treorchy yield, not for the first time, to T. Glyndwr Richards's Pontycymmer Choir.

After also conceding to Tom Stephens at Pontypridd in 1893, Treorchy returned to winning ways at Llanelli two years later, when the prize was an unprecedented (for such choirs) £60. Although it was a smaller field, with only three other choirs competing on Joseph Parry's 'The Druids' and Limnander's 'Safe in Port', the four adjudicators – Joseph Barnby, R. C. Jenkins (Llanelli), David Jenkins and Joseph Parry – each independently of the other wrote down 'wonderful' and awarded William Thomas's choir a staggering hundred out of a hundred.[43] They were the first Welsh choir to travel widely within the United Kingdom, invited to the annual dinner of the Drapers' Company in the presence of the Duke of Cambridge, to Edinburgh, to Bristol's Colston Hall, and five times to Dunraven Castle. Specializing in a robust style of singing which a later conductor of Treorchy Male Choir, John Haydn Davies, was to uphold in the 1950s and 1960s, in a six-month period from October 1895 they performed sixty-one concerts in which they raised £2,270 to help clear chapel debts as well as making £2,093 for themselves.

Respectability was the keynote of their visit to Windsor Castle on

10. *After their Command Performance at Windsor Castle in 1895, William Thomas's Treorchy choristers were entitled to call themselves the Treorchy Royal Welsh Choir. Reduced in size they toured the USA in 1906–7 and undertook a 50,000-mile world tour in 1908–9.*

29 November 1895.[44] The party of seventy-five received strict instructions before leaving as to correct behaviour and appropriate dress. Although there was a modest variety of texture, cut and style in their Sunday-best suits that ranged from light grey to brown, dark blue and black, there was a responsible air about the whole choir. 'As a precaution against over-exuberance, it should be borne in mind that among this choir are several very young men and mere lads, every one of them belonging to the working classes', and, anxious lest any semblance of bad taste be shown, the conductor travelled with one coach while the non-singing secretary, W. P. Thomas, accompanied the other. 'W.P.' (1861–1954) was not merely a prominent member of Noddfa chapel, he was also a clerk at the Ocean Collieries where most of the choir were employed; he rose to become secretary and a director of the company, and became an influential though also controversial figure in local politics; his photograph appears before, and larger than, that of even the conductor in the commemorative brochure published soon after the Windsor event. The Treorchy choir axis, and W. P. Thomas's own career, turned on a Noddfa–Ocean pivot.[45] The Revd William Morris, minister of the

chapel, and Mr A. S. Tallis, deputy agent of the Ocean, had delivered 'interesting and inspiring speeches' to the choristers on the eve of their departure, motivated by 'a basic benevolence arising from a sympathy with the plight of the industrial worker, a humanitarian concern reinforced by practical considerations of social stability'.

The audience of around sixty consisted of several members of the royal family, assorted lords and ladies and members of the royal household, including the Queen's German librarian and her Welsh-speaking head gardener Owen Thomas, who had been in the royal employ for the last thirty-five years. Also on hand was Sir James Reid, the Queen's physician, possibly a wise precaution given the distinctly warlike musical fare being provided, from 'The Men of Harlech' and Joseph Parry's 'Druids' to Ambroise Thomas's 'The Tyrol'. These were alleviated by more contemplative items like the late Prince Consort's composition 'Gotha' sung to Welsh words, and a Welsh hymn. Informed by Prince Henry of Battenberg that the Queen wished to hear another chorus, William Thomas made no concessions to any wish for a soft and soporific number, but led the choir's charge into one of the popular male choruses of the time, 'The Destruction of Gaza', from the same stable as 'Martyrs of the Arena'. On being informed by William Thomas that the composer was Laurent de Rille, the Queen asked, 'Is he a Welshman?', to which Thomas replied he was sorry to say he was a Frenchman, at which she laughed heartily and the ladies of the Court 'joined with alacrity'.

At least the royal party appeared pleased and interested – for the most part. The Duke of Saxe-Coburg ('who himself is a distinguished musician and a passionate violinist') showed his appreciation of the music by talking earnestly to his sister, Princess Louise, all through it, and further confirmed his essential non-musicality by waving his princely right hand to keep time. It was the Duke who, on the Queen's behalf, asked for 'Y Delyn Aur' (The Golden Harp) by pointing to the piece on the programme, whereupon the choir entered into the old Welsh hymn with spirit and gave it a vigorous rendition. Much play was made of the encounter 'between a Rhondda school attendance-officer and the Queen-Empress', but quizzed later as to which of the two he feared the more, the Queen or William Jenkins, Ystradfechan, director and general manager of the Ocean Coal Company, William Thomas had no doubt it was the latter.[46]

Victoria's interest in Welsh music and song dated, it was believed, from her visit to Merioneth in 1889 when she was regaled with a selection of Welsh airs by a choir from Llandderfel and district. During the next decade that interest was well catered for, by the two Rhondda male choirs, the Welsh Ladies' Choir who sang at Osborne, on the Isle of Wight, in February 1894, and in 1899 by John Williams's Eryri Choir of Dinorwig quarrymen. By then the programme was required to be submitted in advance, with the result that Gounod's 'Soldiers' Chorus' in the depths of the war in South Africa 'did not commend itself to the royal taste' and was by request eliminated from the programme; Saintis's 'On the Ramparts' was in it, but this too was left unperformed at the request of the Prince of Wales.[47] The programme was further curtailed when the Prince, in the absence of his mother, requested the omission of 'Martyrs', this time owing to the lateness of the hour: a concert timed to take place between ten and eleven in the evening was admittedly an oddity to working people unfamiliar with the social habits of the upper classes, but hardly constituted a problem to choristers used to eisteddfodau that ran on well past midnight. At the concert given by the Eryri Choir the German Emperor had remarked in conversation with John Williams that their singing was more after the German than the English style inasmuch as they 'opened their mouths and sang out'. At the same time, the Empress thought many of the Welsh words sung were similar to those found in Danish, while, not to be outdone, the Prince of Wales thought they resembled Swedish.[48] Irrespective of the bizarre responses of their imperial auditors the point was that the Eryri quarrymen, like the Rhondda colliers before them, had 'behaved like gentlemen and sung like angels'.[49]

After decades of calumny and prejudice regarding the Welsh and their language, their reputation, partially restored by the Crystal Palace victories of 1872 and 1873, was now further enhanced. The coalfield and slate districts were the sites of more than industrial conflict. Henceforth William Thomas's Treorchy choir was entitled to prefix the designation 'Royal' to its name, to the measured satisfaction of *Y Faner*: 'As a nation we value this honour greatly. No doubt it counts for little in itself, but it is more than our nation is accustomed to from the royal family.'[50]

The Royal Treorchy were the toast of Wales, and from Windsor they proceeded to conquer the world – though at some cost. In order to be able to fit into small halls and to tour abroad, William Thomas deliberately set about a ruthless reduction of his hundred-strong choir to about twenty-five; and the former Treorchy Male Voice Choir fell into decline until its post-Second World War revival, while the Royal rump established for itself a new but reduced identity. Seventeen of them visited the Welsh settlements in North America in 1906–7, to an ecstatic welcome – a crowd of a thousand was waiting for them when they arrived

in Scranton at midnight – and an equally cordial critical reception: the
New York World praised their 'exceptional tone, blending and clear
enunciation', the *Philadelphia Press* compared them to an orchestra, while
'such fine pianissimos, such shading and working up to grand climaxes
(had) never been heard before' by the scribe from Milwaukee.[51]

Then in 1908–9 William Thomas took twenty-one of his choristers on
a world tour, an immense 50,000-mile undertaking, paying their way
with a concert schedule of 310 engagements: they began on the SS
Pericles on the way out and kept singing for the next fourteen months.
Their performances drew audiences of over 420,000, including hundreds
of choirs: fifty-five choirs turned up to listen to them in Sydney, to hear
for themselves what had overwhelmed the *Ballarat Star*: 'the purity of
tone, the exquisite harmony, the mellowness, the delicacy of the gradation, the accuracy of the attack, the colour of the enunciation and robust
and reverberating resonance', all of which 'simply surpassed the
conception of the Australian citizen'. It was the same in South Africa. To
the Transvaal critic, who had heard the finest choirs of Great Britain in
the previous quarter of a century, 'the unassuming Welshmen are miles
ahead of everybody else'. In fact 'the Rand has gone mad over the Royal
Welsh Male Choir. Halls are filled to overflowing and what a feast they
had. Such precision, such volume, such grandly perfect harmony . . .
there are no rivals to this superb combination. They stand alone.'[52]

3. Sliding Scales

It was in the more confined space and altogether grimmer environment
of the Rhondda itself that men like Tom Stephens and William Thomas
had laid the foundations of their wider fame. It was on an accumulated
capital of eisteddfodau, singing festivals and oratorio concerts that they
drew their cheques. Invigorating, enriching, enlarging and enabling as it
was, it was a musical culture that had disabling limitations: the predict-
ability and narrowness of the repertoire, the frequent parochialism, the
obsessive prize-hunting. Taliesin Hopkins's Cymmer United won four
first prizes in two days at Christmas 1899, singing 'Worthy is the Lamb'
on each occasion.[53] Tom Thomas, a baritone from Ynys-hir and member
of the Royal Welsh Choir, in 1903 provoked an indignant and protracted
local correspondence after attacking 'the moral tone of our choral
societies' and questioning the integrity of conductors 'and others who
take a leading part in our choirs'. The atmosphere in some of the choirs

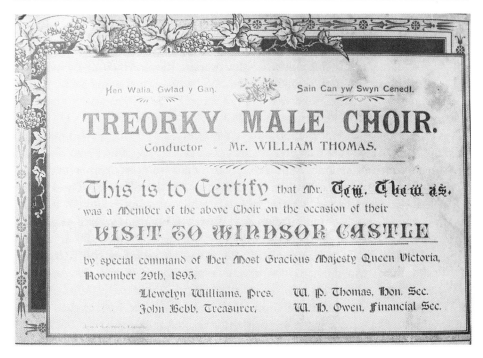

Hen Walia, Gwlad y Gan.

Sain Can yw Swyn Cenedl.

TREORKY MALE CHOIR.

Conductor · Mr. WILLIAM THOMAS.

This is to Certify that Mr. Tom Thomas,
was a Member of the above Choir on the occasion of their

VISIT TO WINDSOR CASTLE

by special command of Her Most Gracious Majesty Queen Victoria,
November 29th, 1895.

Llewelyn Williams, Pres.   W. P. Thomas, Hon. Sec.
John Bebb, Treasurer,   W. H. Owen, Financial Sec.

11. Tom Thomas (1872–1939) sang one of the solo verses of 'Hen Wlad fy Nhadau' on this royal occasion. An Ynys-hir collier in 1895, he later went on to study and teach singing professionally.

in which he had sung was, he claimed, 'very foul' and their leaders egomaniacs. For this state of affairs he largely blamed the chapels, since Nonconformity, he believed, was inimical to the musical art, the few excellent performances of classical works 'owing more to the zeal and sacrifice of a few enthusiasts than to the chapel authorities' whose only interest was in raising money. Eisteddfodau, with their hideous parade of the same test pieces, were 'a prohibition of the (musical) art, more in keeping with the ethics of Beer Clubs'.[54]

That this combustible, competitive atmosphere bred pettiness, vindictiveness and, on occasion, violence there can be no doubt: 'the eisteddfod', noted one Rhondda observer, 'will soon vie with football and the prize ring for disorderly scenes and rowdyism'.[55] Three vocally accomplished members of the Cymmer choir, all Porth colliers, sued the conductor of the Mid-Rhondda male-voice party for alleged breach of contract when he reneged on a promise to pay them 15*s.* (75p) each to sing top tenor at the Mountain Ash National Eisteddfod (1905) and another at Neath. Engaged, as they believed, on the understanding they attended two practices a week, the Porth 'professionals' were dismissed for failing to attend a tenor part-practice from which they believed themselves exempt. Judge Gwilym Williams, who having sung under Caradog thirty years earlier was not entirely unversed in these matters, believed they were exempt too and found in their favour.[56]

Another Rhondda choir, the Cambrian Male Voice Party, ran into difficulty in 1906 because of their conductor's ethically principled but competitively suicidal refusal to buy in singers to prop up an ailing tenor section, which resulted in the six-year-old choir being wound up.[57] Sought-after choristers were paid large sums for singing, and got all their expenses paid, a monetization that William Thomas regretted as under-mining what he liked to recall as the pristine amateur ethic that once prevailed in Welsh choral circles. Recalling a time 'when choristers were proud to take part in a competition and would attend the practices regularly for months previously', he lamented that 'now [1902] things have changed and many choristers, especially those with slightly more than average ability, will not attend . . . unless conveyed in brakes, in addition to which they require to be paid for their services on the day of the eisteddfod'.[58]

We can see, then, that it was not merely among sportsmen that professionalism was rampant in the Rhondda.[59] Indeed, if music was encouraged as an antidote to the less edifying attractions of spectator sport, these hopes foundered on the resolutely unreformed behaviour of its working-class participants. Eisteddfodau in particular fostered and nourished a vigorously competitive element which in turn encouraged the same unruly behaviour as the contests for sporting titles, cups, championships and prizes: the same intense rivalries expressed by dis-order among supporters and spectators; the distribution, as we have seen, of mourning cards to vanquished opponents; the same expression of village tribalism, civic pride and valley patriotism in noisy street receptions for victorious choirs as for bands and football teams; the hiring of outsiders to enhance the possibility of victory; the gambling, the excursions, the opportunity to travel further than the next valley; and the recurrent mayhem and rowdiness, like, for instance, the 'uproar' that ensued at an eisteddfod in 1906 at the Workmen's Hall, Ton Pentre, when the two policemen engaged to keep order during the day were required to safeguard the adjudicators who had awarded the prize in a competi-tion for choirs over sixty voices to a choir under that number (and thus more amenable to discipline and control), an incident that escalated into a full-blown legal wrangle as Treorchy Music Lovers took Tonyrefail Mixed Choir to the county court at Ystrad.[60]

Communities 'moved in rhythmic sympathy with the choirs'[61] and there was a musical 'season' as there was a sporting one. The oratorio season, for instance, peaked at Christmas and Easter, while the eisteddfodic season overlapped it at both ends by running from October to Whitsun, when the popular semi-nationals at Porth, Mountain Ash, Bridgend and Abergavenny were held. The National Eisteddfod in August or September was a high point in itself, the chief choral competitions held whenever possible on a Bank Holiday (established by Parliament in 1871) which enabled entire communities to accompany their choral gladiators to the vocal arena. Oratorio concerts, on the other hand, believed to be undergoing 'a regular renaissance' in the Rhondda in the early years of the twentieth century, were an opportunity for the assertion of community of interest between the respectable working class and their elected representatives: it was noteworthy at the performance of *Messiah* at Ebenezer, Tonypandy, in 1904 not only that the audience included district and county councillors and tradespeople, but that a large proportion of those present were following the performance with copies of the work in their hands. Nor were they reticent in appraising the vocal fare on offer: disappointment was expressed at the below-par performance at Ebenezer of one metropolitan soloist, when 'quite half a dozen tenors of our little Principality . . . would have made an infinitely better show than this London tenor.'[62]

Rhondda audiences may not have had wide musical horizons, but they were self-aware and critically minded. Not even William Thomas was immune. At Christmas 1906 the annual Noddfa oratorio was conducted for the first time by the thirty-year-old J. T. Jones, the chapel organist who was by now a qualified musician and FRCO, an index of Rhondda's musical growth being that where 'less than ten years ago the valley did not possess a single pipe organ', by 1900 there were fifteen in various churches and chapels.[63] The 'book' was Elgar's *Light of Life*, sufficiently unfamiliar to keep attendance down but proof that the day of the sol-fa conductor for important modern works was over, since an enterprise of this kind required a wide knowledge of music and techniques of orchestration. A revelation to the audience, the performance was hailed as a triumph for the choir and – a none too subtle dig at J.T.'s predecessor, William Thomas – to have 'considerably surpassed anything of this kind ever given in the Valley'. The writer was delighted to see the work being conducted from a full score ('the only proper way') and 'Mr

Jones not only had the choir in hand but was able to keep the orchestra moving along without any of the scrappy and uneven playing we have been accustomed to in the Valley'.[64]

This was striking testimony, too, to the dramatic progress made in the Rhondda by orchestral music in only a few years, for in 1899 it could be stated that while the Rhondda abounded in singers, instrumental music was at a discount – 'the orchestral concert is a luxury in the Rhondda Valley', it was noted at the turn of the century.[65] The announcement that the Pontypridd Orchestral Society was to give a concert in the Rhondda was greeted in terms suggesting this was indeed a novelty, though the element of innovation lay in the fact that this was a full orchestra, for a string band was already in existence conducted by A. A. Leeke of Trealaw.[66] Calling themselves the Mid-Rhondda Orchestra, consisting entirely of working men who bought their own instruments, they shared first prize with the longer-established Merthyr orchestra at the National Eisteddfod in 1901 and made the journey north to secure a walk-over at Bangor in 1902 to 'win' for the second successive year.

The Pontypridd Orchestra which gave the first-ever full orchestral concert in Pentre in May 1902, playing a selection from the Savoy operas, the overture to *The Magic Flute* and the first movement of Schubert's B minor Symphony, was conducted by a Rhondda resident, Percie Smith, who had been born in Dover in 1870, moved to the Rhondda in 1890, married the daughter of William Abraham ('Mabon') and been accompanist and deputy conductor of Tom Stephens's Rhondda Glee party.[67] When, inspired by the Pontypridd example, a group of enthusiastic instrumentalists in Ynys-hir formed themselves into an orchestral society in December 1902, their natural choice as conductor was Percie Smith, under whom they gave their first public performance at a local chapel the following April. Thus emboldened they decided to compete at the Rhyl National Eisteddfod in 1904, and won; they came second at Mountain Ash in 1905 and won again in 1906 at Caernarfon where the two Rhondda orchestras were the only contestants. They did not compete again but this shows what the eisteddfod could do as a stimulant and focus for musical enthusiasm. Smith's Pentre-based society was a different organization from Leeke's Mid-Rhondda orchestra, their rivalry characteristic of Rhondda and Welsh musical life of the period. Smith himself was in no doubt as to the significance of Rhondda orchestralism after the Rhyl victory of 1904: choral music, he claimed, had had its sway – 'we shall have to look to the Orchestral Society in future as the champions of our prestige.'[68]

It certainly put paid to the condescending notion that working men – or women, Smith's orchestra of fifty, mostly colliers, included six women – lacked the sensitivity or digital dexterity to play string (as opposed to brass) instruments because of calloused or thickened fingers. The Rhondda's Orchestral 'colliers with fingers deft . . . and elastic'[69] signalled a salutary riposte to *The Times*'s contemptuous claim (18 October 1902): 'that the working man should learn to suit his stubborn fingers to the violin, at any rate with any success, is hardly to be expected.' Similarly disproved was the claim that the amateur orchestra was primarily a middle-class institution: there was a far greater working-class presence in amateur orchestras than has been assumed, and Rhondda musical history, like that of Aberdare and Merthyr, indicates that virtually exclusive working-class orchestral institutions followed soon after their emergence in England in the 1880s.[70]

By 1910 Smith was routinely giving pre-concert introductory talks on the programme his orchestra was about to play, identifying for the audience the themes to look out for in symphonies by Beethoven ('Eroica'), Mendelssohn ('Italian') and Schubert ('Unfinished') while in 1911 he conducted Dvorak's 'From the New World', Sibelius's 'Finlandia' and Second Symphony, and Mendelssohn's Violin Concerto.[71] The soloist was Alexander Mason Thomas ('ap Tydfil') one of a small group of exceptional instrumentalists – A. M. Setter and Haydn Gunter were others – to emerge in the Rhondda in the period 1900–14. Ap Tydfil took his violin from Pentre to the Leipzig Conservatoire, won first prize at the Rhyl National Eisteddfod, and died aged thirty-one in 1911.[72] Even chamber music held no terrors for the receptive, if it was properly packaged. In 1903 'a grand piano and violin recital' took place at Ferndale under the auspices of Horeb Welsh Baptist chapel, Tylorstown, when Setter gave piano solos and accompanied the viola of Haydn Gunter of Ynys-hir who spoke German as well as Welsh, numbered Judge Gwilym Williams, the bishop of Swansea and the dean of St David's among his patrons, and prior to his London début gave a solo concert at the Workmen's Hall in Ton Pentre in 1906 that was described with circumspection as 'classical and educative'.[73] Five years earlier a Tonypandy audience had subjected itself to a rigidly classical programme of three Mozart quartets and Schubert's 'Death and the Maiden', which was reckoned to represent 'a severe test to the musical taste of the audience'.[74]

For this was a society with an insatiable thirst for self-improvement and education. As well as its weekly choir practice, the Alaw male-voice party of Trealaw held a class every Thursday in the theory of tonic sol-fa;[75] and prior to conducting the symphony which introduces the *Hymn of Praise*,[75] Sol Watkins explained the different instruments to an appreciative audience at Bethany English Baptist Chapel, Treherbert.[76] Rhondda's musical life was diverse and pluralistic, and its various strands were remarkably intertwined in the baby son of Mr and Mrs Edward Lister, an engine-driver at the Ynysfeio Colliery, Treherbert. Little Ivor Lister, 'a Rhondda musical prodigy', developed an ability to hum before he could talk. By two years and seven months he was able to include in his selection portions of no fewer than fifteen songs including 'The Belle of New York', the 'Soldiers' Chorus', 'Put me amongst the Girls' and the graveside hymn-tune 'Crugybar'.[77]

4. *Raucous Glitter*

Rhondda musical life, by whatever criteria we adopt – participation, audience size, frequency, ubiquity, press coverage, external perception, – and for all the counter-attractions of rival leisure forms, was dominated by the hymn-singing festival (whose language was Welsh), the oratorio concerts (whose language was English) and the eisteddfod (in either language, or, more commonly, both). These coexisted with other not necessarily alternative diversions across the spectrum of popular cultural activities, from organized sport to opera. The Rhondda's population had doubled in a decade to 55,632 by 1881; its continuing upward trajectory (1891: 88,351; 1901: 113,735; 1911: 152,781) brought in its wake a wide range of associational forms from sports clubs to dramatic societies, and an unquenchable thirst for varieties of entertainment.

This was particularly marked in the centres of demographic concentration like Mid-Rhondda, a conglomerate of Tonypandy, Trealaw, Penygraig, Clydach Vale and Llwynypia that by 1911 had a population density ten times the national average.[78] From the 1890s the Theatre Royal, Tonypandy, was a favourite venue of touring companies who followed each other in weekly succession, assembling and dismantling their scenery with bewildering speed: in the first weeks of 1900 it was visited by Frank Barton's company, Foster and Arthur Schaller's company and Matt Wilkinson's company, in March alone by the Ben Greet company (doing *The Belle of New York* from which Master Lister took his cue), Herbert Barr's No. 1 company, Miss Winifred Maude's company, Miss Ida Millais's company and Mr Charles March's No. 1

company.[79] This hectic programme owed much to the entrepreneurial flair of the Theatre Royal's go-ahead lessee and manager Sam Duckworth, who opened the Lyceum in Pentre in 1902 the very month that the local paper had bemoaned 'the need of popular and innocent amusements . . . in the Rhondda, a district which teems with a huge population, a large percentage of whom belong to the lodger class and who, after they have finished their laborious day's work, have nowhere to go'.[80]

In 1903 large crowds were in attendance nightly at the Tonypandy Hippodrome to see the forty-four Dahomey Amazons whose military drills and weird shouts reportedly 'threw an interesting light on West Africa'. Well-disciplined and precisely choreographed, they could certainly show Welsh choirs, that took anything up to twenty minutes to form up, a few tricks in stage management.[81] In the first week of August the same year Harry Lonsdale's No. 1 company was at the Theatre Royal, Tonypandy, Mr T. Morton Powell's at the Lyceum, Mr Ernest R. Abbot's at the Porth Opera House.[82]

Such fare was complementary rather than inimical to the persistent attraction of competitive music, to the simultaneously reported activities like Mid-Rhondda's Philharmonic's victory, worth £100, at Mountain Ash semi-national on 'Rise up, Arise' from *St Paul*, the Cory Workmen's Band's winning account of *Don Pasquale* at the same venue, and the Mid-Rhondda male voice party's victory at Senghennydd. During the busy April week that saw three travelling companies in Porth and Tonypandy, Bethel Welsh Baptist, Cwmparc, gave two well-supported performances of J. Astor Broad's cantata *Ruth and the Moabites*, a form of entertainment too easily dismissed unless we remind ourselves that it was these cantatas (small-scale secular oratorios) and operettas that fuelled the aspiration for grander oratorio and opera. They were often performed by male parties, with female support. In April 1900, for instance, while William Thomas's Royal Treorchy staged Prout's *Damon and Phintias* in Pentre, the Treherbert male-voice party did T. Mee Pattison's *Sherwood's Queen* 'in character', an early form of virtual reality that could be taken too far when in 1911 the thespians of Hermon Tonypandy brought a donkey and sheep on stage in their Oberammergau-like production of *Joseph* at the Old Hippodrome.[83] The Porth and Cymmer male-voice party had a notable record in this department with *Il Trovatore* (1897), David Jenkins's *David and Goliath* (1898) and the ever-popular *Blodwen* (1899) with orchestra and chorus – indeed, 'a finer chorus has seldom been heard in opera',[84] in Mid-Rhondda or, presumably, Milan.

Soon the Porth Opera House and Treherbert Opera House, as well as
Tonypandy's Lyceum, Hippodrome and Theatre Royal, were staging the
kind of productions which lived up to those venues' grand titles. In 1903
the Neilson Opera Company visited Treherbert with *Maritana*, *The
Bohemian Girl*, *The Daughter of the Regiment*, *Faust* and *Il Trovatore*.
D'Oyly Carte, the Gilbert and Sullivan specialists, paid their first visit to
the Rhondda in January 1905, precipitating the formation of the Ferndale Harmonic Society at the end of the following year, so that early
in 1907 'the chief voices of the locality' launched into *Maritana* in
character. In June 1908 the Ferndale company held an operatic ballad
concert with professional singers brought in to do numbers from grand
opera.[85] In 1911 the Workmen's Hall in Ferndale was the venue for
Merrie England, the kind of cramped location which was still staging
operatic productions in the 1950s, despite the fact – no doubt with an
eye to a focal civic edifice like the recently opened Hanley Town Hall in
the Potteries which could seat 2,500 – that the need had been identified
as early as 1902 for three or four public halls in the Rhondda (the
requirement was seen as particularly severe in Mid-Rhondda) capable of
holding three to four thousand.[86]

Opera, which in the nineteenth century had been associated in the
Nonconformist mind with the theatre and sensuality, contributed
significantly to the secularization of the repertoire. It reached its take-off
into self-sustained growth in May 1909 with the production at Tonypandy's Theatre Royal of *The Pirates of Penzance* by the Mid-Rhondda
Operatic Society, the first production drawing entirely on local resources
without any professional or outside help.[87] It was an accomplishment – 'a
red letter week in the history of Rhondda progressivism' – made possible
by the convergence of orchestral playing (David Lloyd was also conductor of the Tonypandy Orchestral Society founded in 1907) and the
sheer abundance of vocal material in a society that prized and promoted
it, with national eisteddfod success seen as the pinnacle of achievement.
It was a peak scaled by 1914 by Rhondda singers like Ivor Foster, Todd
Jones, Bessie Jones, Amy Evans and Tom Bonnell. When Bonnell won the
tenor solo at the 1909 National Eisteddfod, the *Rhondda Leader* glowed:
'A National Eisteddfod without a Rhondda victor is an impossibility. For
several years this Valley of coal and song, of sorrow and sunshine, has
sent its sons and daughters to do battle in the great Olympian lists of the
National gathering.'[88] Sons and daughters, for the Rhondda ladies'
choirs were numerous, individually and collectively: adjacent townships
at the top end of the valley could boast the 95-strong Cwmparc Ladies'

12. The Rhondda was not only a crucible of choralism and brass bands. Top, *the Cwmparc Drum and Fife Band in 1890;* bottom, *the Llwynypia Prize Flute Band, the UK champions in 1902.*

Choir, dressed all in white with red rosettes, Treherbert Ladies', and Treorchy Ladies'.[89]

The writer might have added bandsmen to his list: Cory Temperance of Pentre, Parc and Dare of Cwmparc, founded as a temperance band in 1896, and the Llwynypia Prize Flute Band that won the UK championships at Stalybridge in 1902 and the Irish Championships at Waterford in 1909.[90] These were the apex of a pyramid of bands whose base extended the length of both valleys. Treherbert, Cwmparc, Tonyrefail, Maerdy and Ferndale were familiar names in brass-band circles at the turn of the century; ever present at times of ritual celebration, they were sometimes accompanists to social protest. It was the Cwmparc band that headed a 'white-shirting' procession at Clydach Vale in 1911, when a protracted stoppage at the Gelli colliery over a price-list dispute led non-unionists to be paraded through the streets by a thousand workmen with the Federation banner and white shirts on poles; we would be ill-advised, for all that, to see bands as fully fledged cultural adjuncts of organized labour.[91]

A prize-winning band that attained national prominence in these years on account of a competition record that could boast victories over renowned opponents like Irwell Springs, Black Dyke Mills and Wingates was Ferndale, established in 1898. Its code of behaviour resonated with overtones of moral reform. According to its by-laws every member 'must be attentive and obedient at practices, no improper language shall be used and every respect must be given to the bandmaster'. No refreshments of any kind were to be allowed in the band area during practices, and members not playing were requested to maintain perfect silence and order, to keep their seats, and not to smoke. Away from home they were expected to be 'gentlemanly, courteous and civil'.[92]

The writer of 1909 had spoken too of 'sorrow and sunshine', for life in these coal-stricken communities pulsed to the macabre but unpredictable rhythm of mining fatalities, disablement and death underground. They might strike individually, as when a fourteen-year-old boy who had begun work only five months previously was killed in the presence of his father by a falling stone at the Abergorki colliery,[93] or in catastrophic clusters that reduced even religious revivals to inconsequence. In March 1905 Cambrian No. 1 colliery extinguished thirty-three lives in an explosion at Clydach Vale; in July the National No. 2 at Wattstown killed 119 men and boys, 55 of whom were under twenty years of age. The chorus 'Surely He hath Borne our Griefs' was always sung with intensity of conviction in the coalfield; at Christmas 1905 it acquired a particular poignancy at that year's Noddfa *Messiah*.[94]

The Noddfa oratorio series, through that gift for organization and boosterism at which W. P. Thomas was so adept, became the 'Rhondda Musical Festival'. It is true that by 1910 social developments – continuing inward migration, linguistic and religious change – were weakening the 'firm grip' that performances of this kind exercised when the 'inhabitants of Mid-Rhondda . . . used to crowd to Aberdare, Merthyr and various other places to hear such entertainments, but today . . . the masses were running in another direction'.[95] In the Upper Rhondda, nevertheless, the Noddfa concerts retained their standing as the chief musical event of the year well into the 1930s.[96] The Noddfa choir could always be relied upon to provide more than a correct rendering of the notes; to one critic aware of rival performances lower down the valley where Rhys Evans's Porth Harmonic held sway at Salem, the difference between performances at Noddfa and those elsewhere turned on 'the degree of intelligence attained' as well as 'a volume of tone commensurate with the size of the choirs'. Although the Noddfa choir was down in numbers (in 1911) 'it [was] remarkable what a big tone some small choruses produce and what small one proceeds from some large choruses', a palpable jab at the 180-strong Porth Harmonic's recent rendering of *Mount of Olives* and Haydn's *Spring* (their thirty-second in an unbroken sequence of annual concerts).[97]

Beethoven and Haydn had traditionally come lower in the pecking order than Handel and Mendelssohn. Bach hardly featured at all, until 1910, a year of angst and suffering for the Rhondda, when J. T. Jones's Noddfa choir back to full strength at around 150 did the *Passion according to St Matthew* with renowned soloists Carrie Lancelyn, Frank Mullings and Norman Allin. This first performance in south Wales was seriously marred by the stir of a restless audience leaving their seats. A local critic shared their doubts, for while both Bach and Handel had much in common – dramatic double-choruses, expressive solos, wonderful choruses – and although Bach's gift of melody was perhaps the greater, nevertheless 'he had left very few tunes such as singers love and would sing if he had written them'. Conceding that the choruses were 'magnificent monuments of musical art', what militated against the popularity of the Passions was the large amount of recitative. 'Unless the narrator was thoroughly imbued with the story he has to tell, thoroughly trained in this difficult branch of his art, and possessed of a fine voice, the audience loses interest . . . and vows to give Bach a wide berth in future.'[98]

For all his wrong-headedness, the critic, whose exacting standards Frank Mullings fortunately met at Noddfa in 1910, knew his Bach, and his Welsh audience. He rejected the singing of the chorales by the congregation on 'both artistic and practical considerations . . . the harmonising is too subtle and the harmonies are often modified and embellished in a way that precludes the idea that they were intended for the congregation'. It was a lesson which Henry Walford Davies, in 1919 controversially appointed professor of music at Aberystwyth and director of the Welsh National Council for Music, learned the hard way when he attempted, and failed, to secure a restless audience's participation in the chorales at one of the Mold National Eisteddfod concerts in 1923 and his appeal to them was met with a fervent rendition of 'Hen Wlad fy Nhadau' from the back of the pavilion.[99] It was not so much the traumatic events at Tonypandy in 1910 that disposed many that year 'to give Bach a wide berth' as secularization and the more alluring popular cultural forms of the skating-rink (the Pavilion opened at Tonypandy the same year, to join the Pentre Olympia in catering for the new fad), the myriorama, eventograph and electric bioscope which in Dai Smith's chiaroscuro characterization 'all added to the raucous glitter of a spectating world which was undermining the more sober pursuits of Nonconformist *Weltanschauung*'.[100]

Yet there was still a typically colourful musical palette on offer from which Rhondda music lovers could choose to lighten the physical drabness of their environment. January saw *Messiah* in Pontygwaith, February the first Rhondda performance by the Cymmer Musical Society of Elgar's *King Olaf*, and at Siloam, Maerdy, of Eos Bradwen's Welsh cantata *Owain Glyndwr*, a sure indication that an older dispensation would not meekly yield to the commercialized imperatives of the new. Zoar, Penygraig, did the *Hymn of Praise* and in March Ebenezer, Tonypandy, staged their tenth annual concert at Judge's Hall, opened the previous year, the programme consisting of Mendelssohn's 'Hear My Prayer' and Elgar's *Banner of St George* with Rhondda's own Todd Jones and Bessie Jones as soloists. The same month the 120 choristers of Libanus, Treherbert, did *Judas Maccabaeus*. At Easter several operettas appeared in local chapels, *The Prince and the Pedlar* at Seion, Ynys-hir, *The Great Light* at Bethel, Trealaw, *Ruth* at Carmel, Treherbert, followed in May by C. V. Stanford's *The Revenge* and the *Hymn of Praise*, a nice balance of the dramatic and the devotional, by Maerdy United Choir. In October, a month before rioters made hay in Tonypandy High Street, Porth and Cymmer Amateur Operatics did G. F. Root's *The Haymakers*, and at Christmas, the same nights (26 and 27 December) as Noddfa's *Passion*, Rhys Evans's Porth Harmonic sought to apply balm to the community's wounds with the perennial *Messiah*.

To dwell on these activities in such fine detail is not to indulge in 'thick description' for its own sake; on the contrary, this is a litany of all that was best in Victorian and Edwardian Wales's musical life. The grimness of the environment and endemic material deprivation may even have engendered a vigorous community existence as poor housing drove many men (though fewer women) to seek their satisfaction outside the home. Organizations which began through their association with specific institutions, like Treorchy male choir's roots in the Ocean collieries, became identified with the whole community. Elements of this communal musical culture would survive into the second half of the twentieth century, but it would never again attain the hegemonic and empowering role it enjoyed in its golden era when, democratic and disciplined, parochial and progressive, it had been a central feature of people's existence, transcending their work, their politics and even their poverty.

7

'Disastrous Vehemence': Welsh Choralism in Crisis

ഇ

1. Liverpool 1900 and Other Massacres

Golden ages are generally retrospective constructions. The years between 1870 and the First World War were the high noon of Welsh choralism, but just as empires at their zenith contain the seeds of their own decline, so in the years around 1900 enlightened and critically minded Welsh musicians were concerned for the future and entertaining grave doubts about the current state of music in Wales. This unease was shown to be fully justified by a series of crushing defeats suffered in the competitive arena that threw Welsh choralism into a prolonged spasm of self-doubt and crisis.

Despite a welter of contemporary comment on this predicament, no one linked it to the accompanying crisis of Nonconformity, though there had been a gradual decline in chapel membership since the 1880s which the religious Revival of 1904–5 only temporarily arrested. Just as the driving energies of the nineteenth-century Welsh moral economy – temperance and religion – had lost their force, so had Nonconformity lost its evangelical propulsion, becoming 'comfortable, settled, part of established society, institutionalised and rather complacent'.[1] That Welsh choirs had been lulled into a similarly dangerous complacency was dramatically highlighted in the early 1900s by a plummeting change in the climate as gauged by the Welsh choral barometer, the National Eisteddfod.

For at least ten years before the turn of the century there had been reservations voiced about the technical deficiencies and general lack of progress in Welsh singing. At Rhyl in 1892 it was a matter of comment that while the highest point of excellence, indeed one of the finest accounts heard at any recent eisteddfod, was the singing of an unaccompanied part-song (J. H. Roberts's 'Rest, Soldier, Rest') by a choir from Birkenhead, it was Dowlais's performance that had been the least satisfactory. One correspondent wrote:

In heavy choruses where the *forte* predominates these Glamorganshire vocalists are capable of producing very good effects; but in *mezza voce* and *piano* pieces the necessary firm gradation of tone seems to be beyond their power; a *piano* tone, if attempted, becomes an ineffective whisper without quality or expression and with no sympathy between the various parts.[2]

Even earlier George Macfarren, principal of the Royal Academy of Music, had expressed similar doubts when, adjudicating at Cardiff in 1883, he awarded the palm to the Penrhyn Quarries Choral Union conducted by Dr Roland Rogers, a professional musician, organist and choirmaster at Bangor Cathedral. Too many Welsh choirs, opined Macfarren, suffered from 'excessive ardour' and it was the defeated Llanelli, Dowlais and two Rhondda choirs who were the specific targets of his lancing observation that 'noise is not power', an assertion he rested on a list of technical misdemeanours regarding intonation, breathing and phrasing.[3]

'Why had the South Wales choirs failed?' the music correspondent of the *Daily Telegraph* wanted to know, and his conclusion was that they were not trained by educated musicians but solely by their working-class conductors. Generally speaking, as is the conductor so is the choir thought that correspondent, Joseph Bennett, who believed the problem with the Dowlais choir was that their conductor Dan Davies's business was 'something to do with pigs'. A further perceived handicap was that of boy altos (soon to be abandoned) who forced up the pitch; but essentially it was an ethnic trait, the sheer excitability of the south Wales choirs who at Cardiff in 1883 sang 'with unrestrained and as it proved disastrous vehemence'. The natural emotionalism of the Welsh, so ran this argument, needed to be kept in check by strict discipline, otherwise 'their entire organization explodes   through the force of its internal force, and the result is a heap of fragments'.[4] Macfarren's caution against the prevalent belief in Welsh choral circles that the best music simply meant the greatest noise proved prophetic: it was, as we have seen, the undoing of Dan Davies's Dowlais and Merthyr choirs, while the ability of the technically accomplished Harry Evans to absorb it made him one of Britain's finest conductors in the early 1900s.

In a canvass of views taken in 1902 to assess the current situation Evans was characteristically clear-eyed as to the past shortcomings, current condition and further prospects for Welsh choral singing which for too long had been living in 'a fool's paradise'. The Welsh had been the victims of extravagant praise from inside and outside (like Joseph Barnby's encomium to the 'choral magnificence' he had heard at Llanelli in 1895) which had bred complacency, whereas in fact 'the standard of Welsh singing was not right'; there was too much enthusiasm at the expense of technique, and too little attention to detail. Where English choirs excelled in accuracy, purity of tone, intelligent phrasing and 'a potent restraint', Welsh singing, as even Barnby conceded, was 'all hill and dale and no level plain'.[5]

This contrast in styles was illustrated by the visit of the Bristol Glee-men to Newport in 1898. Their programme eschewed the noisy dramatic pieces so beloved of Welsh male choirs and their audiences. The compositions sung by the Bristolians were of a different character, 'and their art . . . of another kind'. They did not attempt showy pieces; the fire, the force, the marked contrasts of light and shade which characterized Welsh choirs were absent, but for all that, or because of it, they sang 'with delicacy, self-restraint and artistic expression'. While the English choir seemed temperamentally incapable of the fiery vigour of the Welsh – 'though through music we may reach a fleeting paradise, it is certain that the Bristol Gleemen will never take that kingdom of heaven by violence' – it was equally true that 'we never heard a Welsh male voice party with the refinement and the truly artistic restraint and finish of the Gleemen'. It was possible, this writer believed, to like both, and even to prefer 'the trumpet's war note to the appealing strains of the cello', but in practice diverse ideals and differences of temperament led to different results.[6]

The nature versus nurture debate as to whether styles of singing were determined by inherent emotional differences or by related standards of musicianship, anticipated by the furore over the verdicts at Llandudno (1896) and Newport (1897), reached an unprecedented intensity at the Liverpool National Eisteddfod in 1900 when English choirs virtually swept the board: the chief choral competition was won by the Potteries and District, the second choral shared between Blackpool and Talke (Staffordshire), and the winning ladies' choir was also from Blackpool. This set the tone for the decade, with Staffordshire choirs winning the chief choral six times between 1900 and 1910; in 1902 at Bangor six of the nine choirs were English, and they took the first three prizes; three of the four choirs at Rhyl in 1904 were again from the English Midlands, and at Colwyn Bay in 1910 Herbert Whittaker's victorious North Staffs and William Tattersall's Southport between them sandwiched Dan Owen's vaunted Rhymney choir into second place. It was the Liverpool massacre ('cyflafan Llynlleifiad') that, to David Jenkins, confirmed what

Y Cerddor (i.e. himself) had been saying for years: Welsh choirs, for too long sunk in a complacency rimmed with bombast, were paying the price of confining themselves to the same narrow range of test pieces.

For the Merthyr National Eisteddfod the following year (1901) the *Hymn of Praise* was to be learned in its entirety, with the adjudicators selecting any three choruses for competition. No self-respecting Welsh choir was a stranger to the *Lobgesang*, and most of them learned it by ear and wholly mechanically, a method which intrigued and horrified English observers in equal measure. At Merthyr in 1881 John Spencer Curwen was clearly impressed that Welsh choirs could sing long and difficult choruses 'wholly from memory'. At Cardiff two years later Sir George Macfarren drew attention to the fact (pointed out to him, for he was blind) that in all the choral competitions copies were hardly used, 'and many looked not at those they held. This implies memory but memory is not musicianship.' Harry Evans's experience confirmed this, reckoning that as a general rule few women among Welsh choristers could read, and only half the men, and those mostly sol-fa readers.[7]

For a work so familiar and accessible, the Merthyr chief choral attracted ten choirs, one of the largest fields ever, but it was James Whewell's North Staffordshire choir that snatched it from beneath the noses of the Welsh. That year English choirs, mixed and men's from Blackpool, St Helens and Wigan, were also victorious at Corwen and other major competitions in north Wales, thus serving only to reinforce the sense of Welsh choral decline which was a cause of mounting concern to the monthly journal *Y Cerddor*.

It had already identified several deficiencies.[8] One was that choirs had become fossilized, trapped in a time warp and endlessly singing the same works and seeking ever more bizarre ways of introducing novelties into the already overfamiliar, such as beginning 'Worthy is the Lamb' very loudly (*ff*) and on the words 'that was slain' suddenly reducing the volume to a double *piano* (*pp*), a stroke at which south Wales audiences – south Walians being perceived as the most persistent offenders in this as in most other respects – looked at each other with wonderment as if they had just heard the most brilliant piece of musicianship conceivable. By the bottom of the page the effect, such as it was, was destroyed by a loss of pitch. Going out of tune was another weakness of Welsh choirs: when, it was rhetorically asked, did an English choir last go out of tune? This propensity was not helped, it was alleged, by the Welsh, especially south Welsh, fondness for a tremolo or vibration in the voice, a disposition encouraged and commended by third-rate adjudicators who were often as ill-informed as the choristers themselves. 'The abominable tremolo' was adjudged by Dr Varley Roberts, one of the Liverpool adjudicators, to be 'the curse of the Principality'.[9] Then again, too many Welsh choirs were scratch affairs, formed only for competition purposes and then promptly disbanding until the next challenge presented itself. This was true of even the best-known and competitively successful Welsh choirs. What Wales lacked was choral societies that practised regularly, something Harry Evans aimed at in Dowlais and Merthyr, and then in Liverpool.

English adjudicators had long since complained of 'the tinkling piano' which almost inevitably, it seemed, accompanied all choral renderings. As part of his campaign to raise standards the critic, composer and music-journalist D. Emlyn Evans made sure that his readers knew what was happening at English festivals. At the 1907 Blackpool competitive festival, for instance, the test pieces were by Scarlatti, Arensky, Cornelius, Brahms, Tchaikovsky, Bantock and MacDowell, all to be sung unaccompanied, whereas of the nine pieces announced for the following year's National Eisteddfod at Llangollen, seven were by Welsh composers and only two were unaccompanied.[10] Less accompanied singing, it was argued, would expose deficiencies that might be remedied by more attention to voice production. English adjudicators since the 1880s had complained of the tendency of Welsh tenors to force the sound up from the chest, leading to a harsh, strangulated tone, though sopranos and basses were guilty of unnatural vocal production too. Singing was frequently out of tune in south Wales singing festivals, according to David Jenkins, who as a *cymanfa ganu* conductor claimed to hear too many tenors flattening and too many women producing a thick sound, as if there was dust in their throats.[11]

Welsh musicians, and choral conductors in particular, therefore ignored at their peril a rising wave of criticism emanating as much from informed and educated voices in Wales as from allegedly ill-informed London critics. It was 'quite evident' to *The School Music Review* that following the Liverpool débâcle Welsh choirs would henceforth have to raise their methods of choir training if they hoped to compete successfully against the best English organizations. It might benefit choirs in Wales if some of the crack English festival choirs, say Sheffield or Leeds, could be engaged for concerts, or perhaps leading English conductors invited to rehearse Welsh choirs, who also needed to attend more seriously to reading at sight 'and thus get up a work in half a dozen rehearsals as the North Staffs did, instead of wearing themselves out with endless rehearsals'.[12]

The *Musical Herald* in 1902 handily summarized the charge sheet: Welsh choirs had not progressed from where they stood thirty years ago because of poor organization and over-reliance on singing by ear and on the piano. The great English attribute was self-control, and Welsh choirs needed to follow suit; *'forte* does not mean shouting nor *piano* an indistinct whisper',[13] and English choirs triumphed because their more disciplined habits (inculcated by trained musicians) compensated for their being endowed with less naturally fine voices than the Welsh.

How did the Welsh respond? Some thought the answer was to amalgamate local rivals and pool their resources to form a united district choir: better one lion than any number of wolves. This was the metaphor adopted by the *Musical Herald*'s special correspondent at the Merthyr National Eisteddfod of 1901: 'A whole district of England united in one leonine effort . . . secured the prize [North Staffordshire in the chief choral] . . . There was a whole pack of Welsh choirs, almost all from one district, and they missed their prey.'[14] Rhymney, one of the bastions of Welsh choralism, was a case in point. It had a population of 10,000 and two large choirs at loggerheads with each other: John Price's Rhymney United would rather beat Dan Owen's rival Rhymney Gwent than any English opponent, though Whewell's Talke choir singly represented an area of half a million people in north Staffordshire. Or was it a matter of alighting on the best conductor? Perhaps the Boer War provided a timely analogy: Wales had enough vocal talent just as she had sufficient soldiers in South Africa: it was quality officers that were lacking.[15]

An entirely different argument was advanced by others. Wales, on this reckoning, lagged behind not through failing to emulate English standards but by neglecting Welsh music.[16] While *Messiah* and *Elijah* could safely be put out to graze, the Welsh were too sheepish about their own compositions, an alleged self-effacement that unwittingly fuelled a wider movement to Anglicize the eisteddfod. It was felt, too, that Welsh choirs suffered under a liability when forced to sing in English, but this *canard* had been disproved by Dowlais's winning performance at Liverpool in 1900.

D. Emlyn Evans took a longer, less partisan view. He could point to Huddersfield's shared first prize in both mixed and male competitions at the London National in 1887 as evidence that the Saxon invasion was not unprecedented, but he acknowledged that the threat had intensified in recent years. Welsh choirs' nemesis loomed and Talke would exact a heavy penalty for their neglect, inertia and complacency. It was actually Emlyn Evans who urged Talke to compete at the National Eisteddfod after awarding them the prize on their first appearance at a Christmas meeting at Chester in 1900. Neither vocal power nor large prizes determined musical quality, for although at Cardiff in 1899 attention had been focused on the chief choral and on the numerous male choirs' interpretation of Joseph Parry's new composition 'Jesus of Nazareth', by far the most instructive and musically significant event was the second choral competition, won by Talke for a prize only a third of that offered in the senior contest. Neither Emlyn Evans nor his editorial colleague David Jenkins believed in a national style, only in good, as opposed to bad, singing, which was why Ben Davies and Ffrangcon Davies were so appreciated in England. The good music would be forthcoming once the lesson was absorbed that 'what conductors needed was more brain and less of the baton business'.[17]

Following the national heart-searching triggered by the set-backs of 1900 and 1901, the events of 1902 offered no relief either. The New Year saw Talke in commanding mood, beating nine choirs in the mixed and male sections in the Chester eisteddfod. At the Bangor National later in the year 'the Welsh choirs were hopelessly beaten', according to the *Manchester Guardian*, which had good reason to crow. In the chief choral competition for choirs of between 130 and 150 voices, the test pieces were 'Come let us Sing' (Mendelessohn), 'I Wrestle and Pray' (Bach) and 'The Storm' (Roland Rogers). Nine choirs competed for the £150 first prize, and the first three places were taken by English choirs, with James Whewell's North Staffs again heading the table. Fifteen male choirs sang 'The Word went Forth' (more Mendelssohn) and Arthur Sullivan's 'The Long Day Closes' in a contest won, to the *Guardian*'s glee, by the Manchester Orpheus. Blackpool Ladies won their competition against six others, and in the brass section even Nantlle had to share with Batley, both bands conducted by the celebrated Alex Owen. It was the most traumatic capitulation to English forces since the reign of Edward I.

The sustained Welsh failures at Bangor chimed with, and could be partly explained by, the adverse effects of the paralysing Penrhyn strike in the Caernarfonshire quarrying districts between 1900 and 1903. The Penrhyn choir divided itself into a ladies' and two male parties, which between January 1901 and August 1903 went on eleven fund-raising tours that took them to Scotland and every single county in England and Wales. They raised £33,461 in all, though the deduction of crippling expenses left them with a mere £8,303 residue for their hard-pressed communities.[18] To some extent, therefore, the great triumph of English choirs was an optical illusion: their victories, Whewell's at Merthyr in

1901 apart, were achieved in a north Wales distracted by more pressing preoccupations. Again with the exception of Whewell, the English found north Wales more vulnerable to their incursions than the south, though the prospect of a confrontation between a Potteries choir and, in the early years of the twentieth century, south Wales's finest, Harry Evans's Dowlais and Merthyr Philharmonic, was mouth-watering indeed.

At Llanelli in 1903 everything was in place for just such a clash of titans, but the crack English choirs failed to take up the challenge, to intense disappointment as even English critics admitted ('Staffordshire would have found doughty opponents at Llanelli'). The Potteries' record at the premier Welsh festival was nevertheless a stinging rebuke to Cambria's choristers: under Whewell they won at Merthyr (1901), Bangor (1902), Rhyl (1904) and Caernarfon (1906). Whewell's background was not unlike that of many of his Welsh opponents. He had been a working collier himself at Talke until after a serious accident he became an insurance collector and his contacts with householders enabled him to form a choir.[19] 'Aberystwyth' was sung at his funeral when he died at the age of fifty-eight in November 1909.[20] In between, his musical career was not one that any Welsh conductor, bar Harry Evans, remotely approximated to, for he never once did *Messiah* with his Talke choir nor with the North Staffs society of which Talke was the nucleus. What he did perform were the works of Elgar, Bantock, Havergal Brian and Frederick Delius; in Wales before 1914 only Harry Evans, and possibly D. Vaughan Thomas and T. Hopkin Evans, were in that league. In 1903 Whewell imposed a ban on corsets for his female choristers (these were the days of tight lacing), and prepared to meet the Welsh again, but in the event, the Potteries failed to appear at 'Tinopolis', and Harry Evans's formidable phalanx of 200 beat seven others with two choruses from the first part of Mendelssohn's *St Paul*.

It is tempting – but misleading – to assert that in terms of competition with English choirs, Welsh dominance had not really been seriously challenged. After all, Waunfawr and Llanrug (Caernarfonshire) had beaten Blackpool in the second choral contest at Bangor, and the male choirs were still in the ascendant: had not Harry Evans's Dowlais salvaged Welsh pride with a stirring performance at Liverpool in 1900? The inaugural New Brighton Festival of 1901 had been a double triumph for Cadwaladr Roberts, whose Blaenau Ffestiniog choir had beaten Talke into second place in the chief choral, and his Moelwyn male choir beaten Manchester into second position and consigned Talke to joint-fifth with Wigan. The following year, however, Manchester turned the tables on Moelwyn, and Blaenau Ffestiniog had to give second best to St Helens. By 1903 there were no Welsh male-choir entrants, and the sole mixed-choir representatives, Waunfawr, were totally outclassed by Talke. This was to be the pattern of the New Brighton Festival, which combined the seaside holiday with choral singing, for the rest of the decade. The domination of English choirs led Welsh contestants to withdraw totally from 1904; there were hardly any Welsh representatives among the fifty-three choirs at that year's Morecambe Festival attended by four thousand people; and in 1911, although the test piece was by David Jenkins, Harry Evans was one of the adjudicators, and most of the audience was Welsh, there was not one Welsh choir among the eleven at New Brighton.[21]

2. 'The Great Eisteddfod of Cwmscwt and Glorious Troedrhiwfuwch'

The twin *bêtes noires* of Welsh male choirs in these years were J. C. Clarke's Southport and the Manchester Orpheus of Walter Nesbitt, who won the International Male Voice Choir competition at Cardiff on Boxing Day 1903. The test pieces sung by the seventeen competing choirs at Cardiff were two compositions entirely representative of the contribution of French composers, writing for their own *orphéonistes*, to the male choral repertoire, Dard-Janin's 'King of Worlds' (revived as a test piece at the National Eisteddfod in 1982) and de Rille's 'Song of the Crusaders', a piece designed both to create interest and give trouble, according to the *Western Mail* ('the diminished fifth in bar eight is . . . to be dealt with cautiously').[22] The 75-year-old Laurent de Rille adjudicated and then conducted the combined first six placed choirs in a performance of the composition by which he was already well known in Wales, 'Martyrs of the Arena'.[23]

De Rille and his wife, 'a vivacious and fascinating lady of distingué appearance', were the guests of the mayor of Cardiff over Christmas, in preparation for the competition on Boxing Day. In awarding the prize to Manchester, ahead of Cardiff and Mountain Ash, the composer-adjudicator mollified his audience by declaring that even 'the smoke of the Rhondda could not eclipse the beauties of the fine arts' and that 'it was wonderful how men who exhausted themselves in the pursuit of hard employment such as mining regained their strength in the bright intellectual pursuit of music'. He was not in the hall to hear the massed rendition of 'Aberystwyth' in memory of the late Joseph Parry, but Madame de Rille 'was carried away with the prevailing enthusiasm, and although knowing neither the words nor the music she joined in the singing'.[24]

The prize however was carried away by Walter Nesbitt's Manchester Orpheus, a relatively recent (1897) foundation that made summertime trips to the seaside profitable as well as pleasurable, dominating the competitive festivals at Morecambe, Blackpool and New Brighton for several years in the early 1900s. Nesbitt was no more a Royal Academician than Whewell; he was a Manchester ironmonger, but the occupational profile of his choir suggests more of a lower-middle-class composition than that of contemporary Welsh choirs: seven teachers, three organists and an assortment of clerks and businessmen.[25] When Nesbitt won again at the Llangollen National in 1908, singing pieces by Welsh composers David Jenkins and J. H. Roberts – rarely can a society have had so much contemporary music thrown at it as Wales between 1870 and 1914, much of it hailed with enthusiasm at the time though eminently forgettable since – the difference in social composition, and its consequences, were not lost on the chief newspaper of Walter Nesbitt's own city:

> The Welsh choirs are virtually self-taught. Often they are isolated and far away from opportunities of gaining musical experience. The native conductors are not musically educated in the strict sense . . . And the choirs are democratic in a far stricter sense than are the English choirs. English bricklayers and iron puddlers and quarrymen do not sing and pick one from their number to lead them. When a picked body of educated and generally intellectual English singers with a skilled musician to teach them go to compete against choirs having comparatively so limited an outlook the terms are unequal. The surprise . . . was not that the Manchester Orpheus won but that the Welsh choirs did so well against them.[26]

Whether or not it constituted a crisis, the slippage among Welsh choirs was clear, and the reasons for it were becoming equally apparent. Chickens deficient in vocal technique were coming home to roost: in comparison with the regular Welsh songbird, the English chorister was more carefully selected, lived nearer large centres of population, was able to hear a more varied class of music, and was a better sight-reader. In 1881 a questionnaire issued by John Curwen to choral conductors at that year's National Eisteddfod seeking information about the proportion of music-readers revealed that in one choir of 250, about eighty could read (tonic sol-fa in almost every case), sixty-eight in another choir of 220, and only six in a third choir that was sixty-strong. A London correspondent noted the weakness of sight-reading at the 1887 eisteddfod: 'this important branch (of music) seems to be sadly neglected in Wales and the fact is to be much regretted.' Joseph Bennett observed the following year that not one of the sopranos could read either sol-fa or old notation, and even its own local paper, the *Llanelly Guardian*, recognized that the number of music-readers in R. C. Jenkins's winning choir at Swansea in 1891 was 'deplorably small', indicating little improvement on the position in 1856 when Ivander's choir at the Cwmafan eisteddfod had contained only three readers.[27]

Dr Roland Rogers (1847–1927) was organist and choirmaster at Bangor Cathedral from 1871 to 1892 (when he was succeeded by T. Westlake Morgan of Merthyr) and in that time acquired a reputation as a skilful choral trainer who won a hat trick of victories (1882–3–4) with his virtually entirely monoglot Penrhyn Choral Union, with whom he communicated by means of an interpreter and his baton. He also acquired celebrity, of a kind, for using women contraltos instead of boys. In a report he submitted in 1886,[28] Dr Rogers thought there were not 'ten out of every sixty' who could read music in either notation. This posed particular problems for the inner parts, for whom picking up the melody by ear was rarely an option; hence the resort to boy altos, ten of whom could read for every one female contralto. Rogers, on his Anglican atoll in a sea of Nonconformity, shared the Welsh concern that the half-broken voices of boy altos often spoiled an otherwise excellent ensemble; trying to sound manly, they would 'shout in the coarsest manner in the *forte* passages and the effect is most unpleasant'. He attributed the success of his own Penrhyn Choral Union to the fact that he had contraltos and men with falsetto voices to sing the alto part. Rogers was also a stickler for weeding out baritones from among the tenors. The slate and coal districts alike produced men with strong, thick and generally short necks who were capable of standing a much greater throat strain than the ordinary English tenor. These Welsh baritone-tenors could produce high notes from E to A but did so from neither head nor chest but simply by an enormous contraction of the throat. The quality of these notes, in Rogers's view, was 'decidedly bad' and whilst being of very doubtful ability in loud passages were practically useless in soft music, and the use of them exhausting to the performer.

As a chorus trainer of quarrymen Rogers knew that his 'real bass voices' were unsurpassed even by the Yorkshiremen he had heard at the

Leeds Festival, so that in Handel's 'Wretched Lovers', a chorus which gives ample opportunity for testing the stamina and tone quality of basses, 'the fine Yorkshire basses were no better, if as good, in either particular as the Bethesda quarrymen'.

Rogers was also highly critical of the prevalent Welsh style of conducting:

> It is by no means an uncommon occurrence in choral competitions . . .
> for the conductor of a competition choir to describe every figure short
> of a triangle with his legs, drive out both arms, alternately, as though he
> were boxing with an unseen adversary, or suddenly sinking to a calm,
> spread out both hands as though he were giving a paternal blessing all
> round; and then, after putting himself into a magnificent state of
> perspiration by these means, and his choir into a key sometimes a whole
> tone sharper than the one in which they began, get down from his place
> of conducting looking as thoroughly exhausted as a man who had run a
> mile race in five minutes.[29]

Rogers's particular objection to over-demonstrative conducting – shared by Joseph Bennett, a frequent observer of the Welsh scene who was often scathing about an 'excess of gesture' by conductors who 'flung themselves about like dancing dervishes' – had been confirmed at the Rhymney 1886 Whitsun eisteddfod, when choirs were driven out of tune by the histrionics of their conductors in 'The waters gather, they rush along' section of 'Thanks Be to God'. One conductor was so carried away that he was 'positively writhing about' even during passages of piano accompaniment only. Welsh singers as a whole, Bennett felt, required conductors who could 'check an excess of enthusiasm instead of increasing it'. Could he have had Dan Davies in mind?[30]

There was no love lost between Roland Rogers and 'Terrible Dan' after the 1892 Rhyl National Eisteddfod when the former had placed Birkenhead above Dowlais, whereupon the Invincibles' fiery conductor claimed that the Bangor musician was out of sympathy with the south Wales style of singing. The *Musical Herald*, in supporting Rogers, conceded that the south Walian was a 'fine vocal animal' but that there were desiderata beyond the mere possession of a magnificent voice, such as continuous practice, training, and a capacity to learn and to think. South Wales choirs especially – this was social prejudice as much as musical judgement – were resistant to advice: had they not already won at the 'great Eisteddfod of Cwmscwt and glorious Troedrhiwfuwch'?[31]

Moreover, the *Cerddor*'s endorsement of this view confirms that it was not merely an English attitude. Its editors, the forthright D. Emlyn Evans and the fastidious David Jenkins, torn between admiration for south Wales's choral wealth, which they knew at first hand as conductors at singing festivals and as adjudicators, and a distaste for its irredeemable vulgarity, constantly admonished that shouting, going out of tune and other results of insufficient training hardly recommended themselves to any properly qualified musician, as each of them was.

There were therefore early warning signs of the nemesis that awaited Dan Davies in 1896–7, a come-uppance reinforced by the agonized self-appraisal of the Welsh choral style following the succession of stunning victories by English choirs in the early 1900s. Precipitated by 'the Liverpool massacre', its origins lying in the technical deficiencies and temperamental flaws first identified in the 1880s, the perceived 'crisis' was resolved partly by the withdrawal of English choirs from the Welsh competitive arena and partly by a determined effort by leaders of Welsh musical opinion to raise standards by widening and secularizing the concert and, especially, the eisteddfod repertoire – for the latter determined the former – beyond oratorio choruses to chromatic modern works and unaccompanied part-songs. The choice, therefore, of Elgar's 'Challenge of Thor' as the choral test piece at Mountain Ash in 1905 marked a significant breakthrough, and the impetus would be maintained by a generation of enlightened, formally educated professional musicians, chiefly in vulgar Glamorgan – men like Harry Evans, E. T. Davies, Bryceson Treharne, D. C. Williams and W. J. Watkins, all of Merthyr, and from west Glamorgan composers and conductors of the standing of David Vaughan Thomas, T. Hopkin Evans and David Evans – who aimed now at a more challenging repertoire, better-informed criticism, and a higher standard of performance.

If it took consecutive defeats at the hands of James Whewell, J. C. Clarke and Walter Nesbitt to drive the lesson home, it was a message that the editors of Wales's foremost musical organ *Y Cerddor* had been seeking to convey since its inception in 1889.

8

Criticism and Composition in the Welsh Musical Renaissance

&

1. The Life and Times of 'Y Cerddor'

Regular musical criticism of the journalistic kind was a product of the eighteenth century, with London's periodical press providing a well-informed and international coverage of the musical life of Europe that only Paris could rival.[1] The Welsh press could hardly hope to emulate this standard, but between 1861 and 1939 there was not a single year when at least one, and sometimes two or three, Welsh-language journals devoted to musical matters appeared. Between 1852 and 1891 fourteen such periodicals were published, though only six survived longer than five years, and three beyond ten years.[2] These serials met a significant demand, for while the Welsh may have not been deeply interested in music they were passionate about singing; by the 1860s there were already frequent complaints that music had ousted poetry as the principal activity at eisteddfodau; and by the end of the century it was a commonplace 'that the crowds follow the choirs'.[3]

Just as the emergence of a Welsh choral tradition coincided with spectacular growth of population in the industrial areas, so did a Welsh musical press, for which the temperance choral unions, the strength of Nonconformity and the ɔol fa movement created a market, and the extension of the rail network, the removal of the last tax on paper in 1861 and the expanding competitive movement provided a favourable context. By the time *Y Cerddor* made its first appearance in 1889, a dozen previous publications had provided a wide spectrum of musical services, from articles on the history of western music, lessons in harmony and counterpoint, to reports on eisteddfodau, concerts and singing festivals, as well as compositional analysis, biographies of the great composers and printed vocal scores. Despite a raft of short-lived publications in the 1880s and 1890s in places like Merthyr, Llanelli and Pontarddulais, the two most significant publications were Ieuan Gwyllt's *Y Cerddor Cymreig*

13. The tireless David Emlyn Evans (1843–1913),
composer, critic, adjudicator, editor and determined reformer
of Welsh musical standards.

(The Welsh Musician), 1861–73, published in Merthyr and then Wrexham, a Welsh equivalent of *The Musical Times* (which first appeared in 1844), and *Y Cerddor* edited by D. Emlyn Evans and David Jenkins.

David Emlyn Evans was born in Penralltwen near Castellnewydd Emlyn (Newcastle Emlyn) in Carmarthenshire in September 1843, and died in Cemmaes, Montgomeryshire, where he had lived since 1894 with his wife, widow of the poet 'Mynyddog' (Richard Davies), in April 1913. In between he lived a prodigiously active life as composer, adjudicator, conductor, editor, critic, music historian and entrepreneur. Frequently irascible, especially in his last years which he spent in severe and immobilizing pain, he was one of the foremost figures in Welsh musical life in the period between the triumph at the Crystal Palace and the First World War. His career may be said to bear the imprint of every formative influence that shaped and identified late-nineteenth-century Wales.

He was, for one thing, self-taught, via the most popular of all Welsh music grammars, John Mills's *Gramadeg Cerddoriaeth* (Llanidloes, 1838), and the two parts of Thomas Williams's ('Hafrenydd') *Ceinion Cerddoriaeth* (Musical Gems, 1852) with its 220 hymn-tunes and seventy anthems and choruses. Emlyn pored over the choruses from *Messiah*, *Samson*, *Israel in Egypt*, *Judas Maccabaeus*, *The Creation*, *Elijah* and the *Dettingen Te Deum* as well as the anthems of contemporary Welsh and English composers. Formal lessons by a music teacher, Hughes of Llechryd a few miles away, gave him a firmer grounding in the old notation used by Mills and Hafrenydd, until in 1858, the year Ieuan Gwyllt went to Merthyr to edit *Y Gwladgarwr* (The Patriot) Emlyn travelled twenty miles to his nearest railway station at Carmarthen Junction and took the first train he had ever seen to Bridgend, where he also first saw a piano and became apprenticed to a draper.[4]

Experiencing life in industrial south Wales for the first time, he could not fail to be struck by the vibrant musical culture he encountered there: the atmosphere was 'charged with singing'[5] and he relished the frequency of oratorio and eisteddfod and hearing the anthems and glees which hitherto he had known only on the page. In Bridgend he sang his first public song, conducted his first choir and won his first prize for composition. He read voraciously and was inspired by Ieuan Gwyllt's column on music in *Y Gwladgarwr* to attend lectures the great man delivered at venues throughout Glamorgan. In time Emlyn Evans would fulfil Gwyllt's own role as reformer, editor, composer and musical grammarian, though his admiration for Gwyllt's achievement was to be less than enthusiastic. In 1863 he moved to Cheltenham where he worked as a shop assistant and received some music lessons and basic tuition on piano and organ. He became a commercial traveller in 1871, and in this capacity for the next twenty years he travelled the length and breadth of Wales, making contacts, observing the progress of music in the Principality, and allowing himself to be caught up in the vortex of south Wales music, becoming a committee member of Caradog's Choral Union, and being briefly touched by the still eddying ripples of temperance, as is suggested by the chorus he wrote in 1881, 'Ffô rhag y Cwpan' (Fly from the Goblet).

This was probably among the many compositions he wrote in hotels at the end of the day's business and by which he made a rapid name as a formidable eisteddfod competitor in composition, so that sixty-six of his pieces won prizes in competitions in Wales, England and the USA. He contributed to the awakening of interest in the 1860s in the part-song and glee but soon tired of this form as restricting, and by the 1870s he had become a fierce critic of the habit that had become endemic in every eisteddfod of awarding composition prizes for glees alone, when the robust vocal forces of such places as Aberdare, Merthyr, Dowlais, Rhymney and Ebbw Vale were crying out for sterner stuff. His *œuvre* eventually consisted of two cantatas with full orchestral accompaniment, settings of Psalms and a Te Deum, twenty-four anthems, thirty-six glees and part-songs, thirty-nine solos and duets, eighty hymn-tunes and various other pieces for children, and madrigals and arrangements of old Welsh airs.

Emlyn Evans made a significant contribution to raising critical standards by his joint editorship of first *Y Gerddorfa* (The Music Place), published between 1872 and 1881 in Pontypridd, then *Cronicl y Cerddor* (The Musician's Chronicle), published in Treherbert 1880–3, and from 1889 *Y Cerddor*. Like many of his generation, notably Joseph Parry whose achievement he respected but to whose self-promotion he remained resistant, he was influenced early by Spohr (briefly) and Mendelssohn (permanently), paying homage to the latter's *A Midsummer Night's Dream* with his own operetta *Y Tylwyth Teg* (The Fairies), described by Alaw Ddu (W. T. Rees) as 'an opera in Welsh (not acted)'. Mendelssohn's lighter choruses had been instrumental, Emlyn believed, in weaning Welsh choirs away from the strenuous sonority of Handel and Haydn, thus easing the way of the part-song, glee and madrigal as test pieces for large choirs, and on which he cut his own compositional teeth.

While living in Cheltenham and then Hereford he was a regular attender at the Three Choirs Festival, gaining thereby an exposure to a rich choral repertoire which, allied to his own studies of classical scores, made him a critic of Shavian asperity. He was a purist in the rigorous Ieuan Gwyllt mould when it came to maintaining standards; like his mentor, he strove to influence taste by, for example, including in *Y Cerddor* of June 1893 madrigals by Dowland and Morley. Gwyllt too would have approved of Emlyn Evans's steadfast refusal to conduct community singing to fill time at eisteddfodau, and he walked out of the pavilion at Llandudno in 1896 when the American Welsh contingent wanted massed singing of the hymn 'Crugybar' (in the event, conducted by Joseph Parry). He cared little, too, for the impression these spontaneous displays of harmonized congregational singing made on guest adjudicators like Dr McNaught, who was 'thrilled to tears' by the impromptu hymn-singing of the massive eisteddfod audience; since two of the hymn-tunes on that occasion were 'Crugybar' and 'Diadem',

Emlyn's distaste for the whole performance was intensified, as in his view these tunes failed on all counts to meet his exacting criteria of what constituted a good hymn-tune. He shared Ieuan Gwyllt's hostility to the inclusion in the several congregational hymn-books he was called upon to edit of 'corrupt' tunes like 'Lingham', 'Deemster', 'Helmsley' and 'Diadem', 'conglomerated particles', he believed, 'of third-rate glees . . . at once showy, weak and undevotional'. Compared with 'Diadem', he acidly observed, music-hall favourites like 'Ta-ra-ra-boom-de-ay' and 'We Knocked 'em in the Old Kent Road' were 'musical gems' (*perlau cerddorol*).[6] His own inclination was towards the sinewy classical style of John Ambrose Lloyd and Gwyllt himself above the melodic, identically alike tunes of Joseph Parry. His edition of *Y Caniedydd Cynnulleidfaol* (1895), the Welsh Independents' hymn-book, bears the influence of his strict standards, not least in the rejection of tunes of secular origin and of too many minor-key tunes to which he thought, with some justice, that the Welsh (and Joseph Parry particularly) were too partial.

He recognized the immense strides Wales had made chorally, instrumentally and in composition thanks to the revival of the eisteddfod from the late 1850s.[7] In this he was surely right. We have only to consider works which owed their origin to the eisteddfod: J. Ambrose Lloyd's *Gweddi Habacuc*, Owain Alaw's *Tywysog Cymru*, John Thomas (Pencerdd Gwalia)'s *Bride of Neath Valley*, as well as the voluminous output in part-songs, anthems, cantatas and solos of Gwilym Gwent, R. S. Hughes, and D. Pughe Evans, not to mention the entire *oeuvre* of Joseph Parry. To this ought to be added the significance of the eisteddfod evening concerts as a forum for the first performance of the more substantial of these compositions.

The so-called 'English musical renaissance' he viewed with suspicion; even Elgar was the victim of excessive praise, for Emlyn Evans could drop the occasional spectacular clanger. Equally misguided was his ringing assertion that Daniel Protheroe's symphonic poem *In the Cambrian Hills* was likely to be as significant a turning-point in Welsh music as Tanymarian's *Ystorm Tiberias* fifty years earlier,[8] in the event a turning-point that failed to turn.

When it came to promoting new Welsh music, he found north Wales's eisteddfodau more virtuous than those in the south: Parry's *Saul of Tarsus* was performed at Rhyl in 1892 and Llandudno in 1896, David Jenkins's *Dewi Sant* at Caernarfon in 1894 and Ffestiniog in 1898, his own *Captivity* at Rhyl in 1904. Once again, south Wales was cast in an inferior light, where the 'tyranny of the choirs and the monetary exigencies of the

committees' who chose the same narrow range of test pieces and sub-
standard adjudicators overrode all else. In north Wales, by contrast,

> it is a pleasure to adjudicate these people – quarrymen etc. – robust
> mentally and plain speaking themselves, they welcome directness and
> outspokenness in their judges. They also give more prominence to
> theory, sight-reading and literature generally than do those in our South
> Wales music fights.

Still, 'the South Walian was capable of great things if he deigned to drill
himself, or be drilled.'[9] Here was a pungent mix of social prejudice and
cultural superiority masquerading as informed criticism.

Never in anything other than delicate health for most of his life, he
became so wracked by pain from 1912 that he was forced to relinquish
both his joint editorship of *Y Cerddor*, which he had held since its
inception in 1889, and his position as music correspondent of the *South
Wales Weekly News*, for which he commented on Welsh musical affairs
from 1899. During these years he rode several hobby-horses with a
vigour which belied his indifferent health, clung tenaciously to some
critical standpoints, and changed his mind on others. Volatile and quick-
tempered, he bore unforgiving grudges and was a dangerous enemy. It is
by virtue of his criticism and journalism that he must be reckoned one of
the pivotal figures of the Welsh musical renaissance, for although he was a
prolific composer in a variety of vocal forms from the solo to the cantata,
he survives creatively only through two powerful congregational hymn-
tunes, the hypnotic, rhythmically repetitive minor-key 'Trewen',[10] which
was sung to the words 'Mi wn fod fy Mhrynwr yn Fyw' (I Know that my
Redeemer Liveth) at the funeral of Harry Evans in 1914, and the
majestic 'Eirinwg', both representative of the final flowering of the richly
harmonious four-part congregational singing that was such a public part
of Welsh devotional and social life in the years before 1914.

Similarly his baleful critical eye came to focus at some point on all the
issues that agitated contemporary Welsh musical life. An unwavering
defender of the National Eisteddfod and an opponent of Anglicizing
elements, like importing English professional artists to perform in the
evening concerts, he was no linguistic zealot[11] and regarded the insistence on the adjudication being delivered first in Welsh as 'mere puerility',
since the announcing of the actual verdict by the English-language
adjudicator only confirmed the inferiority of the Welsh. At Liverpool in
1900 the attempt was made by the stage compère (*arweinydd y dydd*) to

translate the Welsh adjudication sentence by sentence until a member of the audience shouted 'Stop that farce'. English had always been spoken freely from the Eisteddfod platform; it was now the bone of contention it would remain throughout the twentieth century, though Emlyn Evans shrewdly noted that 'it by no means appears that the protesters are always from among "the people", the most monoglot portion of an eisteddfod audience, the backbone of the institution and the real conservators of the language'.[12] He ignored protests of 'Cymraeg, Cymraeg' when he adjudicated English choirs in English, though there was no more zealous advocate of eschewing the pale Cymricization of English musical terms in favour of reviving the sturdy terminology of the Welsh music grammarians of the first half of the century, who spoke of *ehedgan* (fugue), *traethgan* (recitative), *côrgan* (chant), *erwydd* (staff), *allwedd* (clef), *llonnod* (sharp) and *lleddfnod* (flat) etc.[13] Events at the 1910 Colwyn Bay National Eisteddfod confirmed his sense of a Welsh linguistic inferiority complex when the Dublin Irish Ladies' Choir sang the Welsh test piece in Welsh while their Welsh competitors insisted on rendering it in English. He saw no contradiction between this stance and a fervent royalism, to the expression of which the death of Queen Victoria allowed him full rein, while his effusive elegy to Edward VII – 'the Peacemaker, the wise and good, one of the ablest monarchs ever to sit on the British throne' – verged on the ludicrous.[14]

In advocating a National Eisteddfod Council to manage its affairs, with a permanent general secretary, he was well in advance of his time. Stage management was a more pressing concern, since its inefficiency permitted a choir to take up to twenty minutes to form up while the conductor wandered through the ranks rearranging some choristers, casually chatting to others, indulging in ego trips of the kind which were rare in England and the occasion for frustration among packed and impatient audiences.[15] He endeavoured to raise the standard of the music performed too. He was a fervent opponent of the narrowness of the choral repertoire, especially the eisteddfod's evening concerts where, he calculated in 1901, *Elijah* had been heard 'twelve or thirteen times in the last twenty years'. It may have felt like that, especially in view of its successive performances in 1897–8–9, but the true figure was eight; the point, however, stood. He bemoaned too the prevalence of 'open' solo competitions where 'soloists are allowed to wander at their own sweet will from "Pop goes the weasel" to a Handel aria'. Such tendencies, typical of the 'debased' popular culture of south Wales, arose from the twin evils of money-making and pot-hunting.

Emlyn Evans's views were nothing if not unpredictable. Take his attitudes to brass bands, whose reputation for mayhem had led them to be branded 'a new eisteddfodic terror' after the police had to be called to a competition at Newport.[16] Emlyn Evans never composed for them, and his puritanism ought naturally to have ill-disposed him towards them. But he preferred to see them as instruments of moral reform. This was certainly his view of the Ferndale Band, founded in 1898, who had established their own Institute, comprising a practice room, seating for 300, a music library, rooms for billiards, cards and smoking and a refreshment bar. On this evidence he was bound to observe that 'the bandsmen of today, taken as a class, are not only looked upon as respectable members of society but are also recognised as agencies which contribute towards the improvement as well as the entertainment of the people'.[17]

He neither sought nor granted favours and had the organic intellectual's conviction of the rightness of his opinion. David Jenkins, his co-editorial colleague for a quarter of a century, thought him merciless and fearless, not least in risking life and limb when after delivering an unpopular adjudication he would descend from the platform and defiantly walk out through an excitable and seething audience.[18] He was not intimidated by the humbug of the more formally qualified, even of *y doctor mawr* himself. Constantly irked by Joseph Parry's self-regard and showmanship, he took pains on more than one occasion to use *Y Cerddor* to repudiate Parry's oft-repeated claim to be the only doctor of music in Wales by pointedly referring to the Greenish brothers of Haverfordwest, one of whom had taken the Oxford D.Mus., the other the Cambridge Mus.Doc., in 1885 and 1895 respectively. It also suited Cyril Jenkins's iconoclastic purposes to point out that 'in England a doctor of music was a doctor of music, but in Wales was frequently mistaken for a great composer'. Was Bach, he demanded, a doctor of music? Was Beethoven? Was Wagner?[19] But Emlyn Evans never enlisted under Cyril Jenkins's anti-Parry banner.

2. 'Pale Melancholy Stalks from Hell'

It was another Jenkins, and one of Dr Parry's pupils to boot, who co-edited *Y Cerddor* with Emlyn Evans. Born like Emlyn into poverty, in Trecastell, Breconshire, in 1848, and, again like him, apprenticed in his youth to a tailor, David Jenkins[20] was never in Emlyn's or indeed Ieuan

14. Professor David Jenkins (1848–1915), the 'Kaiser of the cymanfa', stern critic, strenuous composer, Joseph Parry's eventual successor at Aberystwyth, and founder-editor with D. Emlyn Evans of Y Cerddor *(The Musician) in 1889.*

Gwyllt's class as a writer. Caught up in the sol-fa movement (as Emlyn born five years earlier was not) he had gone to Aberystwyth at the age of twenty-five to study with Parry and become well versed in the complexities of counterpoint and the more abstruse rules of musical syntax. His purely literary effusions however were littered with grammatical errors, and in the editorial respect *Y Cerddor* was fortunate in his death (in 1915) so soon after Emlyn's.[21]

He, too, shared much of Ieuan Gwyllt's purism and determination to reform congregational singing and re-establish Welsh hymnody on firmer foundations, and he became Gwyllt's natural successor on the death of that unbending puritan in 1877, the year of Jenkins's first major composition. Curiously, although renowned for his ability to exercise an

autocratic influence over a congregation of many hundreds in singing
festivals – he earned a reputation as 'the Kaiser of the *cymanfa*' – and
could electrify a congregation with his resonant voice, and, even more
important, read the verse with the appropriate solemnity and sufficient
depth of understanding to satisfy the *sêt fawr* (diaconate)[22] – he was
apparently a most ineffective and unenthusiastic lecturer. Music at
Aberystwyth declined during his tenure (1899–1912), and of his many
pupils R. Maldwyn Price and David de Lloyd were the only ones to make
their mark.

After his initial period of study at Aberystwyth, David Jenkins took his
Mus.Bac. at Cambridge the same year as Parry received his doctorate
there. When the music department at Aberystwyth, after the great
doctor's messy departure in 1880, was reformed in 1893, Jenkins was
appointed first as an instructor, then in 1899 as lecturer, becoming
Parry's successor as professor of music, after a lapse of thirty years, in
1910.

In August 1888 he presented to the Merthyr conference of the newly
formed Welsh National Society of Musicians a paper on 'The Present
State of Musical Composition in Wales', railing against the stranglehold
of competitive, at the expense of non-competitive, festivals with their
limited and therefore limiting repertoire. He frequently berated the
suffocating money-making ethos of the chapel eisteddfod and what he
called *teganau eisteddfodol* (eisteddfodic baubles):[23] were the various
denominations so incapable of paying for their buildings and
schoolrooms without resorting to eisteddfodau to do it for them?, he
protested after a rash of Whitsun competitions seemed only further to
confirm the deficiencies of Welsh choralism exposed so mercilessly by the
Liverpool 'massacre' of 1900 and the subsequent years' results.[24]

Denominationalism and an unthinking congregationalism were David
Jenkins's two bugbears. He regularly attacked the convention that a
denominational *cymanfa* would sing an anthem only by a composer from
that denomination, or be conducted only by one of its 'own' musicians; it
was a matter of historical fact, for instance, that John Thomas (Llanwrtyd
Wells), like Ieuan Gwyllt before him, conducted only at the singing
festivals of his own Presbyterians, M. O. Jones (Treherbert) the
Independents, and Dan Davies (Merthyr) the Baptists. David Jenkins
considered it a matter for comment, and congratulation, that a
Methodist festival he conducted in Caernarfonshire in 1904 deigned to
sing an anthem by Joseph Parry, an Independent.[25] Much in demand as a
conductor himself, he cared deeply about congregational singing, whose

future he viewed pessimistically. Already by 1899, when Welsh congregational singing is thought to have been at its peak of numbers and enthusiasm, he considered it to have been in decline for twenty years and in the grip of a fatal complacency. It was not a decline of popularity; that was the point: like Emlyn Evans he viewed with an ascetic distaste the fact that every session had become a social occasion.[26] Like Emlyn again, while he composed a great deal from the smaller vocal forms to large-scale choral works, it is only by his hymn-tunes that he is still known: 'Builth' in particular ('Rhagluniaeth Fawr y Nef') has the firm clear lines of a tune by Ieuan Gwyllt with added emotion and a declamatory ending for the tenors of f' r' m' (taken from the sub-Handelian 'Teyrnasoedd y Ddaear', in the same C major key) which has led one authority to the opinion that it is a little too easy-going for the noise that it makes.[27]

While claiming to be alarmed by the growing attractions of football and cricket, whose devotees could be numbered in their thousands while those of choral singing were counted 'only in their scores',[28] his concern was not an imagined declining popularity of singing festivals or choral competitions – by 1900 these were recognized, to the displeasure of some, to have eclipsed the bardic ceremonies as the high points of the eisteddfod – but rather the personal lack of application to practice and rehearsal, especially among female members (there is a misogynistic element in the insistence on standards). Jenkins attributed this not to any religious indifference but to its reverse, an excessive piety, the choking proliferation of weekly meetings based on or around the chapel itself which interfered with the rigorous discipline involved in learning new and substantial works; and nowhere was this more true than 'in the populous districts' – a by then familiar complaint. When the religiosity of those districts spilled over into Revival in 1904–5 it found little support from David Jenkins who believed it to be musically counter-productive, arresting and deflecting the progress of Welsh devotional music. Under its influence, eisteddfodau were postponed and the number of sol-fa certificates issued in Wales (a reliable indicator of musical activity) plummeted. Jenkins's quarrel was of a more qualitative nature with the cheap, vulgar tunes that it popularized, and the neglect of the anthem, chant and anything at all musically challenging.[29] David Jenkins's standpoint here is the musical equivalent of that of the staider, formally qualified, authoritarian clerics like the Revd Peter Price of Dowlais and others who adopted a censorious stance towards the popular, anti-intellectualist, anti-authoritarian element in revivalism.[30] Just as Peter

Price decried its theological poverty and doctrinal superficiality, David Jenkins condemned it for its musical ignorance.

From the first David Jenkins was anxious to bring musical provision within reach of the ordinary Welsh man and woman, for Welsh choirs were 'almost entirely formed of the working classes' whereas in England it was only 'a higher class' that subjected itself to this influence. As early as 1882 he was urging the establishment of a Welsh Board of Music to organize classes and appoint lecturers who would give instruction 'on the various branches of music', forty years before such a scheme was established under the aegis of the Welsh Council of Music. There was so much musical talent among the Welsh working class, he told the National Eisteddfod Association, 'it is a pity that . . . in the cry for "Higher Education in Wales" no one as yet has lifted his voice on behalf of the musical education of the people'.[31] It was another twenty-five years before a secondary school system was put in place in Wales with the role of music recognized within it.

In any case, as Jenkins acknowledged, musical education took different forms. Welsh music needed critical journalism, and 'able musicians' were required to write on its various aspects. He went some way to meeting these requirements himself by establishing, with Emlyn Evans, Y Cerddor, whose joint-editorship he retained until his death in December 1915 and which survived him. He saw also the need to educate the working classes in instrumental music, though arguably there was more being accomplished in this direction in many parts of south Wales – in Swansea, Cardiff and the Valleys – than he was aware of, and reflecting in 1913 on the previous twenty-five years he was able to identify the slow but steady rise of instrumental music as one of the more positive aspects of the Welsh musical scene.[32]

David Jenkins never lived to see the Welsh National Council of Music established in 1920, but he had known of Walford Davies. Fifteen years earlier he had reviewed Walford's cantata Everyman, and complimented him on having freed himself from the influence of the organ loft which had shackled several leading figures of the English musical renaissance like Hubert Parry, whom Jenkins accurately described as technically sure but lacking both imagination and invention.[33] In critical terms, clearly, Jenkins was very much his own man. Reluctant, in one issue, to agree with that section of English opinion that elevated Bach above Handel and Mendelssohn, he included in the next number a biography of Johann Sebastian, promptly followed by a four-part life of Handel, Wales's favourite composer. If the country had orchestras, no doubt Beethoven,

Schubert, Wagner and Dvorak would be better appreciated, but as things were, Handel was more accessible because he could be sung, that priceless democratic activity.[34] One of the works that Welsh choirs were singing with increasing gusto was César Franck's *Beatitudes*, but Jenkins dismissed it as monotonous and doleful for a composition devoted to the principles of serenity and blessedness.[35] Franck's compatriot Gounod was also well known through frequent performances of his *Mors et Vita* and *Redemption* – too frequently, thought Jenkins, at the expense of Joseph Parry, who had written far better pieces.[36] Here was Jenkins of Aberystwyth defending his teacher Parry against the censure of Cyril Jenkins, who was attacked by his namesake for running down Welsh composers – 'and this is a man who has failed his ARCO, let alone FRCO, despite being coached by a D.Mus. . . . should he ever write better music than Dr Joseph Parry, or Emlyn Evans, we will listen to him then.'[37]

David Jenkins's views, however, were ambivalent and often contradictory. He could make nothing of Delius, whose *Sea Drift* he heard on its first performance at the 1908 Sheffield Festival: 'drifting somewhere but where exactly he couldn't tell', it was one of the most thankless pieces he could recall singers having to deal with, while *Brigg Fair* he found to be similarly 'ugly and uninteresting'.[38] On the other hand he warmed to Debussy on his first hearing, commending his rich harmonies and flowing melodies as 'exceedingly skilful'. In 1911 he analysed *Pelléas et Mélisande* at length, but on hearing it again his enthusiasm had perceptibly cooled; by now he found Debussy tedious, over-long and so devoid of melody that he thought he, like some other recent composers, must suffer from mental illness.[39]

If, however, on the occasion of this particular London visit he had on the Monday heard the composition of a musical dwarf, the following evening he was in the presence of a giant. On Tuesday this icon of the classical *cymanfa ganu* was seduced by *Salomé*. The Kaiser, he told his readers, had refused permission for the work to be performed in Germany until changes were made and the same restriction applied in England. Jenkins regretted there had not been more drastic changes on account of the blasphemous treatment of John the Baptist, and though this was only to be expected from an author as depraved as Wilde, Salomé's necrophiliac embrace of the dead John the Baptist disgusted him. He confessed he had forced himself to attend against his better judgement, as if he needed confirmation that he would indeed find it shocking. But despite his intense loathing of the opera's content, he confesses that Richard Strauss's music was the most glorious ever written, superior even to that given by Mendelssohn to *Elijah*. Throughout he had been captivated by music that was luscious, melodic and spellbinding. Jenkins had already provided readers of *Y Cerddor* with a synopsis of *Das Rheingold* (he visited Bayreuth, and heard two performances of *Parsifal*, in 1894), an article on Hugo Wolf, and reviewed a production of *Elektra* at Covent Garden. Now this *Salomé* had totally overwhelmed him; his deeply entrenched Wagnerism left him in no doubt who was Richard I; now he knew who was Richard II.[40]

As a critic David Jenkins knew and appreciated the modern idiom; as a composer he ignored it. With the possible exception of his mentor Parry, no Welsh composer wrote so many complete gigantic works. He first attracted attention when he won at the Caernarfon National Eisteddfod in 1877, for his cantata *Arch y Cyfamod* (Ark of the Covenant) and its vehement opening chorus 'Cyfoded Duw' (Arise O Lord) became immediately popular. It was hailed at the time as 'a superior effusion of genius' and it remained a work for which its composer retained an affection to the extent that not long before his death he revised and extended it for publication. Apart from his oratorio *David and Saul* published by Novello in 1891, he was the publisher of his own music, the most felicitous of his works being one of his many glees, 'The Balloon', and his operetta for schools festivals *The Village Children* (1889). Their aesthetic and musical vocabularies have dated disastrously, but it is still difficult to be unimpressed by the ambition of works like his dramatic oratorio *Dewi Sant* first performed at the Caernarfon Eisteddfod of 1894; *The Psalm of Life*, a cantata for chorus and orchestra composed for the Cardiff Triennial Festival of 1895; *The Enchanted Isle* (1902), an opera based on *The Tempest* (hopeless as an opera but with some redeeming music), first performed in the examination hall at Aberystwyth; *Jôb*, an oratorio written for the Rhyl eisteddfod of 1904; *Llyn y Morwynion* (The Maidens' Lake), a dramatic cantata given its première at the 1908 Llangollen eisteddfod; and in his last years *The Storm* (1912), *Scenes from the Life of Moses* (1915) and *The Galley Slave* (1915), a choral work for male voices as yet unperformed and likely to stay that way.[41]

These were all freighted with heavy significance and conceived on the grand scale for soloists, chorus and full orchestra, on whom they imposed weighty demands, for his music was virile, dramatic, thickly textured and sonorous, often indeed giving the impression of straining for sonority's sake and, by resorting to unnatural harmonic progressions and startling but artificial changes of key, of striving too hard to avoid the commonplace.

What is remarkable is that in his formative years David Jenkins can never have heard the works of the major composers performed, and could rarely have heard any orchestral accompaniment to the anthems and choruses he grew up with: he only read them. This later prolific composer of choruses for male choirs had never heard, nor heard of, a male-voice choir either, nor had any member of the Trecastell choir to which he belonged, until they heard one at an eisteddfod in Llanddeusant (Carmarthenshire) in 1858.[42] Nor did he ever learn the piano as a young man, which may go some way to explaining why compositionally he was more original than his teacher Joseph Parry: knowing little about instrumental music, however, his choral works, though large-scale, contain little in the way of orchestral accompaniment, the inner parts being particularly neglected. His originality, unfortunately, was compromised by a trademark excessive fondness for figures like triplets which result in the accompaniments in too many of his works sounding – certainly looking – laboured and over-elaborate.

With an unremitting outpouring of anthems, glees, part-songs and hymn-tunes, as well as the larger-scale works which themselves made unrelenting demands on his singers, David Jenkins, for all his limitations and shortcomings, can be seen to have made heroic efforts single-handedly to alleviate the dearth of Welsh choral music. With his grasp of conveying the fearful and dramatic he wrote particularly effectively for the male choirs which multiplied from the 1870s but were reliant mostly on English and French compositions. With Joseph Parry, Emlyn Evans and Gwilym Gwent he set about remedying this situation too, by providing Welsh male choristers with muscular choruses they could get their teeth into.

As a result, teeth were sunk with competitive relish into such male choral red meat as 'The War Horse', 'Gyrrwch Wyntoedd' (Storm Winds Driving, from *Dewi Sant*), 'Wŷr Philistia' (Men of Philistia), 'Cytgan y Chwarelwyr' (The Quarrymen's Chorus), 'Cytgan y Medelwyr' (The Reapers' Chorus), and 'Meibion Gwalia' (Sons of Gwalia), less demandingly difficult than his large-scale choral works and all concert and competition favourites down to, but rarely beyond, the First World War.

In similar fashion, while Jenkins's large-scale compositions seem rarely to have succeeded as entire works, choruses within them gave him scope for his preferred dramatic breadth and grandeur. Those which became individually popular, as well as providing a stern challenge to the vocal forces required by the chief choral competitions' stipulation of 150 to

200 voices were 'Now the Impetuous Torrents Rise', 'Ye Sons of God', and 'Vengeance Arise', all from *David and Saul* and guaranteed to test the mettle of Wales's finest in the three decades before 1914.

The dramatic, highly charged Welsh choral style that 'tore passions to threads' came in for a good deal of adverse comment during the debate on the crisis of choral singing in Wales. Jenkins himself was foremost in decrying the excessive ardour and emotional overstretch that led to the 'fighting choirs' and 'choral prize fights' that were characteristic of the period.[43] Yet in what other way could his own virile, highly charged works be approached? If the first chorus of his 'dramatic cantata' *David and Saul* is 'Vengeance Arise', the second movement is the blood-curdling 'Pale Melancholy Stalks from Hell'.

No vocal ensemble was more adept at curdling blood and threatening revenge, death and destruction than the Welsh male choir. To this emblematic institution and its distinctive repertoire we now turn.

9

Violence and the Big Male Voice[1]

ඊට

1. Rough Music

Late in 1913 the apocryphal report that the concert pianist and later first prime minister of the Polish Republic, Paderewski, had been chased by nihilists out of Denver prompted the editor of the equally apocryphal *Musical Mirror* to circularize a number of prominent musicians 'with a view to ascertaining the most dangerous experiences they had ever undergone'. Thus the organist Sir Frederick Bridge wrote to say that his worst moment occurred when he was deep-sea fishing off the coast of Florida and a gigantic 400-lb tarpon leaped into the boat with its mouth wide open. With great presence of mind, however, 'the famous organist thrust into the monster's gaping jaws a full score of Strauss's *Elektra* which he was studying between the casts', whereupon the tarpon at once leaped back out of the boat and was never seen again. In the same vein Madame Nellie Melba reported that her most perilous experience was to be caught by a tidal wave which hurled the liner in which she was travelling towards the rocky coast of Sumatra. Noticing that a large whale was following the vessel, Madame Melba, with a presence of mind comparable to the famous organist's, remembered the peculiar susceptibility of these giant mammals to musical sounds and sang the scena 'Ocean, thou Mighty Monster' with such compelling force that the whale allowed itself to be made fast with a hawser and then towed the liner back safely into the open sea.[2]

Significantly, the composer and conductor Sir Frederic Cowen stated in his reply that the closest call he ever had was when adjudicating at a Welsh eisteddfod when 'in consequence of an unpopular award he was besieged in his hotel by an infuriated crowd and only escaped by changing clothes with a policeman'. Apocryphal as it may be, the incident was entirely plausible, for choral rivalries, the dramatic test pieces and the intense interest generated among a large popular following induced behaviour that proponents of music as a civilizing and refining force could hardly have commended, or even anticipated. 'Thousands crowded into the pavilion and excitement ran high, for next after a football match Welshmen enjoy a choral fight', observed a correspondent at the Newport National Eisteddfod of 1897, while the *Manchester Guardian*'s reporter noted that the 10,000 audience at the following year's event displayed all the partisanship 'of the race-meeting class as a whole'.[3]

The intensity of that partisanship was a genuine attraction to the black composer Samuel Coleridge-Taylor, the son of an English mother and a west African doctor, who, on informing Dr Turpin, principal of the Trinity College of Music, that he had been invited to adjudicate at the National Eisteddfod, was told in no uncertain terms not to accept at any price. 'You have no idea what adjudicating in that place is like. Why, I had my hat knocked in and only got safely away with great difficulty.' It was advice that Coleridge-Taylor, after initial reservations, ignored, 'and I have never regretted it'. As a result of his Welsh experiences at national and local eisteddfodau he was able to assure an American agent arranging a visit to the United States on his behalf:

> Please don't make any arrangements to wrap me in cotton wool . . . I do a great deal of adjudicating in Wales among a very rough class of people, [where] most adjudicators have had eggs and boots thrown at them . . . I mention this so that you may know my life is not spent entirely in drawing rooms and concert halls but among some of the roughest people in the world who tell you what they think very plainly. Yet I have four more engagements there for next January.[4]

Not all visitors were as prepared as Coleridge-Taylor to take the rough with the smooth, and Sir Alexander Mackenzie, for one, had good reason to remember being escorted to safety at Newport in 1897.[5] That year too a Bristol choir who accepted an invitation to compete at Brynmawr ('a very isolated place') on the north-eastern rim of the coalfield, arrived to make the (surely unsurprising) discovery that all the other competing choirs were Welsh,

> and their behaviour was most disorderly. We all felt that if the prize was awarded to us there would be a disturbance. The Ebbw Vale choir got it. Several of our members were grossly insulted and pushed about by the Welsh . . . and the language used was anything but decent. Such was our first experience at a Welsh eisteddfod and it will certainly be our last.[6]

The evidence of the Welsh musical press of the period, however, suggests that the 'disgraceful scenes' which greeted the award of the choral prize at a Cwmaman eisteddfod in 1881, and the 'mob law' that prevailed at Merthyr that year when M. O. Jones's established Treherbert choir were shouted down and prevented from singing,[7] were in fact the norm rather than aberrations from it. And as we have seen, the propensity to disorderliness was not confined to south Wales. At Corwen in 1904 an adjudicator was forced to flee coatless from an angry crowd.[8] This occurred only a few years after a concert at the Caernarfon Pavilion, featuring Ben Davies among the soloists, was punctuated by whistling and the striking of matches, a preliminary to uproar when hundreds leapt over the barriers from the 1s. seats into the 2s. reserved places, the blame for which was placed squarely on 'the residents of the quarry districts' rather than the refined citizens of Caernarfon and genteel Bangor. For tumultuous rowdyism in the competitive sphere, however, south Wales took the palm. At a Boxing Day eisteddfod in Neath in 1892 choristers and soloists had to fight their way on to the stage, and face a constant barrage of whistling and hooting once they had reached it.[9]

Adjudicators, and not only English ones, irrespective of any status they enjoyed, were the frequent recipients of disgruntled supporters' protestations. The respected musician J. T. Rees and the conductor William Thomas of Treorchy discovered this in 1897 when they inadvisedly withheld the prize in the male-choir competition at Llandybïe, and were hooted and harried all the way to the station by the disappointed choristers and their frustrated supporters.[10] The adjudicators had been similarly 'menaced, hustled and pushed' at Abergavenny at Easter the previous year,[11] while accusations of mob law (mobyddiaeth) were made by an observer of something akin to a shaming ritual at Cardigan in 1898 when abuse was heaped on the head of the male conductor of a ladies' choir.[12] Contemporary prejudice would have attributed this behaviour to mainly migrant 'Cardis' returning from the high-wage coalfield on a visit to their native county, bringing some of the less welcome habits of their adopted heath with them. At an August Bank Holiday eisteddfod in Swansea in 1904, chagrined choristers invaded the platform and barred the eminent Signor Randegger who was adjudicating from leaving it. So serious was the demonstration that the police had to be called to protect him from physical assault, 'and the veteran musician's trouble did not end there', according to one eye witness, '. . . he was mobbed in the street and must have deemed himself fortunate at getting out of the town whole in body.'[13]

While it is difficult to ignore cases of wanton lawlessness, we can still identify occasions where remonstration was rooted in popular notions of legitimacy. Such occasions arose when, for example, competitors were believed to be securing an unfair advantage by defying either the stipulation as to age (a frequent occurrence involving juveniles) or numbers: a 'stormy scene' at Pontypridd in 1899 led to a local choir being disqualified for exceeding the number allowed.[14] Another source of grievance was the hiring of professional singers for solo roles in choral works. Such an instance occurred when the well-known Ffrangcon Davies appeared on stage with the Treorchy male choir to sing the solo part in Joseph Parry's 'Pilgrims' at the annual Porth eisteddfod in 1894, whereupon the audience registered its disapproval by drowning out the choir's performance; only after repeated threats by the chairman to abandon the competition was the event allowed to proceed.[15]

Mass enthusiasm could on occasion be channelled into smoother grooves. The stentorian voice of Mabon (William Abraham, miners' leader, MP and eisteddfod stage manager) was often sufficient to head off a potentially disruptive challenge to his idea of good order by breaking into 'Hen Wlad fy Nhadau' or leading impromptu community singing at obstreperous public meetings. The Welsh capacity for involuntarily responding to appeals of this kind lends some support to the notion of music as a social tranquillizer. An impressive example occurred at the Treorchy National Eisteddfod in 1928 when a visit by the prime minister threatened to be soured by the strains of 'The Red Flag' emanating from a dissident quarter of the packed pavilion, until an appeal was made from the stage to 'let Mr Baldwin hear "Cwm Rhondda"' and immediately the huge audience responded. 'No man, not even the coldest and most indifferent Saxon could fail to be moved by the sound of that strangely thrilling hymn almost barbaric in the splendour of its harmonies', according to a *Western Mail* relieved that the PM had seen that Wales was 'a great family, happy in the unity of song and in complete oblivion of political dissensions'.[16]

Visitors had never failed to be stirred by these powerful collective renditions. At the turn of the century Dr McNaught was impressed by the methods adopted to manage excited and sometimes inflamed crowds at eisteddfodau, their frustrations caused as much by woefully inept stage management that held up the start of the main choral event on which all attention was focused, as by the dislocated expectations of the defeated afterwards. There were times when unbridled chaos threatened to engulf the entire proceedings, instanced by the pandemonium at Llanelli in 1903 when strenuous exhortation and gesticulation from the platform were all in vain in the deafening clamour. Then someone would start a well-known hymn or national air and in a few moments the angry muttering cloud disappeared and as the sun of glorious four-part harmony poured forth from all corners of the building, the audience forgot its angry strife and became a magnificent resonant choir. Some of us were thrilled to tears and at the end we were all better men in a new and exalted mood. Where else than in Wales could such an incident happen?[17]

This was an indication too of the emergence of overtly popular culture and the role of populist modes of congregational and choral singing in the last quarter of the nineteenth century. At Carmarthen in 1867 mismanagement and atrocious weather were even then eisteddfodic headaches though the festival was not yet the popular institution it was to become. London artists brought down especially for the occasion found themselves at the sharp end of all kinds of elements with the tent-roof leaking and the piano having at intervals to be wheeled about the platform in search of a dry place. Madame Patey-Whytock sang under an umbrella and was shouted down as the audience demanded the popular Welsh buffo Llew Llwyfo, who had a genius for singing popular songs very badly and an enormous following among the common people, though the more cultivated viewed him as little more than a street bawler. 'When it seemed the only thing to do', wrote the critic Joseph Bennett years later, 'the eisteddfod managers sent up a white flag, engaged Llew and appealed for quiet.' Such action appears to have been par for the course for a festival which was perceived in the 1860s as being the victim of the effete ambitions of Brinley Richards and others to drive an Anglicizing wedge between the eisteddfod and its popular base.[18]

Within less than twenty years, the pace of social and economic change had brought about a transformation in popular cultural practices. One of them was the massive following and interest generated by the major choral competitions. An English visitor had commented most favourably on this 'consummation for which social reformers sigh' at Merthyr in 1881, and noted too how 'the intensity of the singers excites the audience by force of sympathy'.[19] It was the increasingly uninhibited behaviour of emotionally involved working-class audiences that purveyors of the ideals of respectable behaviour and other moral reformers could hardly commend. From cussedness based on an ancestral reluctance to conform to the social prescriptions of their superiors, the lower classes were reluctant to become carbon copies of their betters, preferring instead to interpret and appropriate shared cultural forms for themselves and to cultivate their own artistic and behavioural styles.[20] This perceived bloody-mindedness created as many problems for the guardian of public morality as for the educated musician. Civic projectors in the new industrial communities of south Wales saw their programmes for instilling communal pride become vehicles for the rumbustious expression of local patriotism as rivalries were articulated as keenly on the eisteddfod platform as on the football field.

The division between rough and respectable working-class recreation familiar to social historians[21] collapses under the weight of evidence to the contrary in the context of the competitive choral culture of late-nineteenth-century Wales. It did not instil in the unruly proletarian crowds of industrial Wales acceptable standards of collective behaviour. The local rivalries and madding crowds, the fierce partisanship and rapturous home-comings, the gleeful mourning cards distributed to crestfallen losers, the sense of corporate endeavour and harmonious synchronizing of abilities were common characteristics of both the sporting and the eisteddfod scene. The meshing of different vocal parts in an intricate fugal passage was not dissimilar to the realization of an elaborately planned three-quarter move, painstakingly rehearsed and finally executed in front of crowds of fifteen to twenty thousand. The integrative and aesthetic roles of the sport-ing and musical expression of a people's culture testify to the same affirma-tion of solidarities: they provided identical opportunities for theatricality and self-expression, and for geographical and social mobility from the colliery and quarry to Carl Rosa and the Crystal Palace (site both of music festivals and Cup Finals from 1895 to 1914), from anonymity to celebrity.

'The eisteddfod', lamented a Rhondda commentator, 'will soon vie with football and the prize ring for disorderly scenes and rowdyism.'[22] There was creeping professionalism, and there was also gambling. 'Why this feverish hurry? Is there money in it?' asked one enquirer, staggered to discover that 500 private telegrams were dispatched from the post office when the chief choral prize was awarded to Dowlais at the 1903 Llanelli eisteddfod.[23] There was in any case a historically sanctioned tradition in the older iron-making settlements of upland Glamorgan of money payments and of laying wagers on the result. If a man could run naked through a wedding procession in Merthyr High Street for sixpence, he would gamble on anything.[24] What were 'musical prize-fights' and 'choral bullfighting' to a man from Merthyr?[25]

The 'sudden rise of Welsh choralism'[26] was, essentially, a musical manifestation of the sudden growth of industry. Most of the Welsh choirs of this period, and for another half-century, were the artistic products of a specific social and economic context, and we have situated them in some of Wales's best-known once-industrial locations. The most familiar collective voice to emerge from those locations, the male choir, now demands the stage.

2. Martyrs of the Arena

In the course of reporting that £40 was the prize awarded the male-voice choir that rode David Jenkins's 'The War Horse' to victory at the 1892 Whitsun eisteddfod at Porth in the Rhondda, Y Cerddor, of which Jenkins was the joint editor, remarked: 'In the last twenty years no branch of music has seen greater advance in Wales as male voice choirs.'[27] His co-editor, D. Emlyn Evans, recognized in 1904 that 'in the large populous centres of South Wales . . . it is a well understood axiom that "the crowds follow the choirs"', but the fact that these more often than not were male choirs was, he thought, 'not entirely to our gain as a musical people'.[28]

Groups of men in Wales could be found singing pieces written or adapted for male parties from the 1860s. Very often these were not auto-nomous musical organizations but the tenors and basses of existing mixed choirs, like the male-voice party from the Swansea Valley awarded the prize at the 1863 National Eisteddfod, who were the men's section of Ivander's Côr Dyffryn Tawe (Swansea Valley Choral Union), and the Aberdare party of twenty-four, who sang the 'Soldiers' Chorus' from Faust at Pontypridd three years later, an off-cut from the town's Choral Union.[29] This was how the men of the Dowlais Temperance No. 2 Choir came to sing 'Comrades in Arms' in July 1867, and how Caradog conducted a glee party drawn from the Aberdare Choral Union in 'Comrades' at Swansea in 1869.[30] There is elusive evidence, however, that some independent formations were emerging in their own right, like the Blaenau Ffestiniog Glee Party, whose varied programme embraced Rossini and Henry Bishop as well as Joseph Parry and Alaw Ddu in a concert with and for Megan Watts in August 1867, like the Engedi (Caernarfon) choir who performed another French favourite, 'Martyrs of the Arena' as well as the already established 'Comrades' at the annual festival of the Eryri Musical Union in 1869, and like the Ystalyfera Orpheus Glee Society that came to the fore in the 1870s.[31]

By the end of that decade the breakthrough towards self-standing male choirs had occurred: eight of them competed in the category at the south Wales eisteddfod at Cardiff in 1879, twelve in 1884 at the National

Eisteddfod held in Liverpool, and ten at the London National in 1887, when Tom Stephens's Rhondda Glee Society shared the prize with John North's renowned Huddersfield choir. A trawl through the first year's issues of *Y Cerddor*, on its appearance in 1889, reveals male choirs in Gilfach Goch, Kenfig Hill, Tongwynlais, Ferndale, Brynaman, Cwmafan, Dowlais, Pontycymmer, Tylorstown, Treorchy and Treherbert. All these were in Glamorgan (and Brynaman just outside its western border with Carmarthenshire) and the last four named in the Rhondda, evidence of the growth of the coalfield and of the high ratio within it of men to women: in the Rhondda in the 1880s for every 1,000 men aged fifteen to thirty there were 600 women, a proportion mirrored in all age groups except the very old. Many of these were single men attracted by the high wages of the coalfield; if married, they had often left their families behind in rural west or mid-Wales, to whom they regularly sent money and returned at busy times in the agricultural year and at slack times in the coal trade. As lodgers they were often given the room nearest the door: the male choir was a source of companionship and recreation, and an alternative to the less salubrious attractions of the public house. For want of other premises, small groups sometimes met in the local inn: William Thomas, a precentor in his Treorchy chapel, agreed to take on the conductorship of a group of local songsters if they quit the Red Cow for the schoolroom.[32] Within a decade the 'Treorchy boys' were sufficiently respectable, musically accomplished and competitively successful to sing before royalty at Windsor Castle. Their programme on that auspicious occasion – including as it did Joseph Parry's 'Pilgrims' Chorus' and 'Druids' Chorus'; Ambroise Thomas's 'The Tyrol', Laurent de Rille's 'Destruction of Gaza', and, as a no doubt welcome break to the royal listeners from the punishing catalogue of blood and thunder, some part-songs and hymns[33] – is a good indicator of the characteristic repertoire of the Welsh male choir of the period, its susceptibility to Continental influences and its cultivation of a specific style.

The male choir has in fact a longer history than the popular perception of it as originating with a late-nineteenth-century industrial work-force. Today's secular male choral singing, as opposed to ecclesiastical music, has its origins in the upper- and middle-class glee clubs that combined singing and sociability in equal measure – though even medieval monastic life was not alcohol-free, as we may infer from the 'in taberna quando sumus' ('when we are in the tavern') section of *Carmina Burana*. Its immediate forebear was the glee, a characteristic English form that flourished between 1750 and 1850, itself the offspring of the round and the catch, successors in turn to the madrigal, which had died out with the restoration of the Stuart monarchy. The English catch, in which each part appears to be chasing the other but never catching up, though deriving from the Italian *caccia* (the chase), had no actual European equivalent, and although its canonic structure hints at a form strictly adhered to, this was invested with considerable flexibility by the prevailing context of rivalry, inebriation, and jocularity of the lavatorial kind, and the institutional setting was the clubs which provided the opportunity and location for wining, dining and male conviviality.[34]

There could be a serious side to the catch clubs. Most of London's professional musicians, including Thomas Arne, Jonathan Battishill, Samuel Webbe and John Wall Callcott, belonged to the city's 1761 club, and as catch clubs spread to the provinces in the late eighteenth century a professional singer might be employed to take lessons for a couple of hours before the club opened. From the mid-nineteenth century the bawdy element came increasingly to the fore and the catch tradition degenerated into song-and-supper occasions, the forebears of the music-hall. As the catches became lewder, the equally venerable glee acquired greater prominence as the defender of modesty and morality. Its pedigree was even longer, allegedly extending back to the Anglo-Saxon 'gligg' and the medieval sense of a gleeman as both a musician and a general entertainer (a juggler). The glee was a distinct form of musical composition which, having made an initial but short-lived appearance during the Civil War period, resurfaced permanently in the mid-eighteenth century and benefited from the same revival of interest shown in madrigals. Since it included female voices, the more salacious subject matter of the catch was rejected and with its greater independence of parts it developed greater sophistication in composition as well as content.[35] Glee clubs and glee competitions sprang up in London and the provinces, and the hundred years from the accession of George III in 1760 have been dubbed 'the glee century' when a whole raft of composers, including Henry Bishop, Henry Hiles, William Horsley, John Goss and, most prolific of all, Samuel Webbe (d. 1816) wrote for SATB, ATTB (a male-voice formation) and other combinations. Henry Hiles's 'Hushed in Death', which became popular in competitive circles in Wales as well as England, was the prizewinner in a competition sponsored by the Manchester Gentlemen's Glee Club in 1857. In practice the Victorian glee clubs blurred the distinction between the glee, the earlier madrigal and the later part-song: 'if it moved in parts, they sang it.'[36] It was the emergence of the part-song, particularly, that undermined the spirit of the glee, since now the top part predominated at the expense of the independence of the different voices, by the writing – by composers like Bishop – of piano accompaniment, and by tonic sol-fa classes, which encouraged collective singing where the glee required each part to be sung by solo voices.

Few English glees were written after the 1830s, when they were already becoming virtually indistinguishable from the TTBB part-song. But it was another thirty years before they reached their full flowering in Wales, where Joseph Parry, Gwilym Gwent and John Thomas (of Blaen-annerch and Llanwrtyd, not Pencerdd Gwalia) wrote extensively in this medium in the 1860s, with D. Emlyn Evans and D. W. Lewis continuing to do so in the 1870s. However, the glee in its pure form never proved too congenial to Welsh tastes, partly because of its reliance on the male alto, a voice prominent in the English court and cathedral tradition but one distinctly uncommon in a population 80 per cent of whom by 1880 were Nonconformists. What Mendelssohn dubbed 'the bearded alto'[37] noticeably declined in the second half of the nineteenth century, a tendency accelerated by that composer's own encouragement of the use of the female contralto in his *Elijah* in 1847. The popularity of this work in Wales overcame the national preference for boy altos, which in any case created problems of pitch and intonation, and by the 1880s female contraltos had replaced boy altos virtually throughout the Principality.

Glees were intricate, with one voice to a part and each part with an importance of its own, each flowing and melodious. Emerging Welsh choirs found more than adequate nourishment in oratorio choruses written for SATB, in which the contralto line, as in *Elijah*, was written too high for 'bearded altos' and was therefore best sung by women, and in the four-part harmonized hymnody that originated in Germany and was canvassed so enthusiastically by Ieuan Gwyllt. In addition the Welsh sang in large numbers that were too unwieldy for the glee, a tendency implicit within Nonconformity, especially Methodism's encouragement of lusty singing, driven forward from the 1840s by the tonic sol-fa revolution. While the movable doh permitted more flexible reading and a certain amount of chromaticism with a basic tonality, the sol-fa system overall worked against harmonic enterprise, even that of the early Schubert who in his late teens wrote over a hundred part-songs for male voices.

It was not Vienna but Prussia and Paris that decisively influenced the male-choir repertoire: the Franco-German choral tradition of the *orphéonistes* and *Männerchöre* was, given the recent history of both countries, militaristic and aggressive. The glee tradition which tempered it in England hardly existed in Wales, whose choirs and audiences savoured to the full martial numbers like 'Comrades in Arms', a setting by Adolphe Adam, professor of composition at the Paris Conservatoire from 1849 to 1856, of the radical poem 'Les Enfants de Paris'.[38] Other favourites from the French school, written originally for the *orphéoniste* movement which had 2,000 societies affiliated to it between 1815 and 1900, included Gounod's 'By Babylon's Wave' (Gounod was himself director of the Paris Orphéon, 1852–60), De Saintis's 'On the Ramparts', Ambroise Thomas's 'The Tyrol', Boulanger's 'Cyrus in Babylon', Saint-Saëns's 'Soldiers of Gideon' and Dard-Janin's 'King of Worlds'. But nothing could match for popularity or excitement Laurent de Rille's 'Martyrs of the Arena'[39] with its rising diminished chords that announce the bloody saga of the dying Christians as they submit to Great Caesar, Lord of Life and Death.[40]

To the writer and broadcaster Wynford Vaughan Thomas, born in 1908, it was 'a musical folk ritual' of his boyhood, when

> at the small eisteddfodau [which] were one of the joys of our lives . . . we waited breathlessly for the inevitable Battle of the Parties. The Party, outside South Wales, conjures up pictures of grim-faced, padded-shouldered Iron Curtain massmen, automatically obeying orders from above. But in the South Wales of my youth, the Party was simply the male voice choir. Like the local rugby team they symbolised our pride of defiance against the rows of slate-roofed cottages, the un-paid-for welfare halls and the coal tips perched on rain-sodden mountains which were the background of our lives. We gave the Party a fierce loyalty and the Party, in return, attacked the music as if they were exacting revenge at last for the defeat of Owain Glyndwr. In the battles that formed the male voice competitions there were no holds barred . . .

especially when the test piece was the ubiquitous 'Martyrs' as it was at one small eisteddfod in rural Carmarthenshire in the 1920s, when such eisteddfodau and the 'Martyrs' were still in their prime, and where the competing choirs warmed up beforehand in the clearings in the surrounding woodland.

> But our local choirs were facing those formidable songsters the Penybont Gleemen and everyone realised that the battle was going to turn on that vital phrase just before the end 'and when their life-blood is pouring'. Should the choir pour its life-blood *mezzo-forte* or *double forte*? The adjudicator was known to have strong views on this point.

Martyrs of the Arena.

15. M. Laurent de Rille, composer of 'Martyrs of the Arena' and adjudicator of the Cardiff International Male Voice Choir Competition at Christmas 1903, presents the laurels of victory to the Manchester Orpheus Choir, with Cardiff second and Mountain Ash third.

It was to resolve the agonizing problem that the young Thomas and his chum were asked whether they were 'prepared to take a risk for the honour of the choir'.

'Oh of course, Mr Rees', we hurried to declare.

'Then will you crawl through the undergrowth and find out what Penybont are doing about the *forte* in bar eight after the *Tutti* before the end? Our fate depends upon it!'

Like Red Indians we slipped from the tent. We crawled through the brambles, slid on our stomachs amongst the heather and became spies for the cause of art. We came back dirty but triumphant. 'Mr Rees, it's a *double forte*.' Mr Rees raised two eyes to the hills in the mood of Cromwell before Dunbar, 'Pouring out their life-blood *double-forte*! The Lord hath delivered them into our hands!' Indeed he had.[41]

Despite, probably even because of its doggerel verse by the improbably named J. C. Stallybrass, the fruity harmonies, in-your-face dynamics and full-blooded climax of the choral epic that was 'Martyrs of the Arena' endeared it to generations of choristers and audiences alike. Welsh male choirs, traditionally well endowed with short, stockily built tenors and compressed but powerful necks have been drawn as much by physique as by temperament to the distinctive and dramatic Gallic style, and Welsh composers were not slow to follow suit: David Jenkins's 'The War Horse', D. C. Williams's 'Charge of the Light Brigade' and 'Destruction of Pompeii', Daniel Protheroe's 'Spartan Heroes', 'Invictus', 'Nidaros' and 'The Crusaders', Cyril Jenkins's 'Fallen Heroes' and 'The Assyrians Came Down', T. Maldwyn Price's 'Crossing the Plain' and T. Osborne Roberts's 'The Battle of the Baltic' were all composed in the thirty years before 1914 and were all test pieces at the National Eisteddfod for which many of them were specifically written.

They were also, as their titles suggest, exactly the bellicose kind of 'pieces of vocal artillery . . . that headlined menace and ruin and reconciled thousands to the Social Insurance as an option' which Gwyn Thomas, born in 1913, remembered hearing during his Rhondda boyhood,[42] all providing rich opportunities for choristers to show off their capacity for intense dramatic expression, and almost all reliant on that technique found so commonly in the Victorian ballad from which it may have been derived, of the pause on the penultimate dominant chord, a sure signal for premature rapturous applause.

Prominent choral figures in England, by contrast, were openly scornful of this musical fare: J. C. Clarke, the eminent conductor of the Southport choir, took a dim view of the selection of a typical representative of this genre, Joseph Parry's 'Caractacus' for the 1903 National Eisteddfod, dismissing it as 'tawdry, unclassical, unworthy of the effort put into learning it, and being of a tendency to diminish instead of to improve the taste',[43] an opinion endorsed by another English critic the following year who noted that 'the fondness of Welsh male choirs for realistic and picturesque music of a rather low art-value is remarkable'.[44] But insofar as 'music has actually no existence until it has become a shared experience between the composer-performer and the audience',[45] composers like Joseph Parry and Daniel Protheroe knew exactly how to involve singers and auditors in a musical mutuality.

The modern male-voice choir – a phrase unknown until the *Musical Times* used it in 1882, though the Welsh *côr meibion* had been already current for twenty years – 'had its roots in working-class conditions, attitudes and values',[46] and emerged where large numbers of men worked at the same premises, generally in manual heavy industry. The well-drilled, disciplined choir was as much a pleasurable extension of the work-place as an escape from it: choristers were told what to do and they did it (even if their supporters were less easily regimented). Choirs were products of their society in other ways too. The Rhondda Gleemen were formed during the lock-out of 1893, and the hundred-strong Williamstown male choir during the Cambrian strike of 1910–11. On the other hand, J. Turner Thomas's Ebenezer Mission which defeated seventeen other choirs at the Abergavenny National in 1913 was formed during the 1904–5 religious Revival.[47] While the Swansea mission invited boys off the streets, the Revival was not always so accommodating: at the London Welsh Royal Albert Hall eisteddfod in February 1905 only four Welsh choirs presented themselves, many other choirs having intended competing 'but the Revival in Wales prevented proper rehearsal.'[48] Indissolubly bound to their communities, which they often represented on a national stage, male choirs sought to alleviate hardship at times of industrial stoppage by money-raising concert tours. The Penrhyn choir raised £50 one Sunday night in 1901 from a sympathetic congregation in the coal-mining choral nursery of Rhosllannerchrugog, a large sum compared with the £58 which a striking colliery choir from the Garw Valley took twelve days to raise in Bradford in 1905. The Porth and Cymmer choir toured major towns in England in 1898. English towns would see a great deal more of singing Welsh miners during the inter-war years.

3. Comrades in Arms

The signal success of English choirs in a demoralizing sequence of victories from 1900 in the mixed and male choir categories triggered, as we have seen, a bout of anguished musical self-appraisal in Wales. It became fashionable to point to the more challenging, ambitious test pieces set for male choirs at the newly founded festivals of Morecambe, New Brighton and Blackpool – festivals established by Welshmen like Llew Wynne (brother of Edith Wynne) who moulded the one at New Brighton on the eisteddfod format, and where accomplished Welsh musicians like Harry Evans frequently adjudicated. In 1907 the *Musical Times* invited its readers to compare the test pieces for that year's Blackpool Festival with those selected for the National Eisteddfod at Llangollen the following year.[49] They were as follows:

16. The hundred-strong Williamstown (Rhondda) Male Voice Choir, conducted by Ted Lewis, formed during the prolonged miners' strike of 1910–11.

Blackpool Tests 1907

Female voices	Ricerari	Scarlatti
	Slumber Song	Arensky
Male voices	The Patriot's Vow	Cornelius
	A War Song	Granville Bantock
	Sorrow's Tears	Cornelius
	The Crusaders	E. A. Macdowell
Mixed voices	Footsteps of Angels	J. Holbrooke
	Fest und Gedenkspruche	Brahms
	O Fly Not, Love	Thos. Bateson
	Throne of Mercy	Cornelius
	My Dearest Love	Sweeting
	Angel Spirits	Tchaikovsky

Llangollen Tests 1908

Female voices	Bring we Blossoms	Schubert
	Blodau Mai (Flowers of May)	J. Owen Jones
Male voices	Trysorau'r Dyfnder (Treasures of the Deep)	J. H. Roberts
	Meibion Gwalia (Sons of Gwalia)	D. Jenkins
Mixed voices	Dan Wawd yn Gaeth (Insulted, Chained)	D. Emlyn Evans
	Ye nations	Mendelssohn
	Bryn Calfaria (The Hill of Calvary)	J. H. Roberts
	Y lefndeg afon lithra'n mlaen (The Gliding River)	
		J. Price (Beulah)
	Cydgan yr Angelion (The Angels' Chorus)	
		Miss A. J. Williams (Eurgain)

This list is somewhat misleading in that it included the three choral categories of mixed, male and ladies' choirs. Of the four Blackpool pieces for male voices, two were by Peter Cornelius, who had only recently become known in Britain as more of his output, recognizably 'glee' in style, became available. A pupil of Liszt in Weimar in the 1850s, then of Wagner, Cornelius acquired sudden prominence in Britain in 1905 when Novello published fifteen of his voice compositions for male choir, a situation eventually realized by the National Eisteddfod when two of them, 'The Rider's Song' and 'Sorrow's Tears', were chosen as the set pieces at Colwyn Bay in 1910 and Nesbitt's Manchester Orpheus won it, finding these were more congenial than the third piece, Osborne Roberts's stormy 'Battle of the Baltic' which better suited their Welsh opponents.

English choirs had long sung a repertoire unrecognizable to a contemporary Welsh chorister. In 1890, the Bristol Orpheus Glee

Society, a male choir of eighty-seven voices (including twenty-one altos, inconceivable in Wales) sang 'Strike the Lyre' (Cooke), 'Haste ye Soft Gales' (Martin). 'I Wish to Tune my Quivering Lyre' (Wesley), Brahms's 'Lullaby' and music by Bexfield, Goss, Holton and Venuti. Only three of their pieces would have been familiar to Welsh choirs: Henry Hiles's 'Hushed in Death', Sullivan's 'The Long Day Closes' and Richard Genée's 'Italian Salad'. The male-voice repertoire in the West Riding was similarly distinctive, certainly different from the Welsh: Samuel Webbe's 'Wanton Gales', Yarwood's 'Gently Sighs the Evening Breeze' and Battye's 'Child of the Sun', with Hiles's 'Hushed in Death' once again the only common denominator, and the early twentieth century saw 'a considerable degree of change' as Palestrina motets and new works by Elgar, Bantock and Delius were tackled for the English festival competitions.[50]

The National Eisteddfod began biting on the bullet of the tough test piece. None was tougher for amateur working-class choirs than Elgar's 1907 setting of Bret Harte's poem 'The Reveille', the challenge posed to the eight male choirs at Carmarthen in 1909, won by Dowlais under Harry Evans's successor W. J. Watkins, in a competition for seventy-five to a hundred voices, an indication of the inflation in male choir size and popularity. Elgar, with his range of harmonic colour, wide dynamic span, and quasi-orchestral detail to interpretative markings on individual parts, allied to carefully chosen words, saw vocal writing as an aspect of his symphonic art, and he made stern demands of amateur choristers. In 'The Reveille' he dispatches the bass to bottom B flat, and obliges the tenors in 'Feasting I Watch' (published in 1903) to start on top A. 'Feasting', 'Zut! Zut!' and 'The Wanderer' (1923) made a prompt entry into eisteddfod schedules in the inter-war period.

Granville Bantock was another whose unaccompanied part-songs required textured singing of a symphonic kind. His lurid 'Glories of our Blood and State', with a piece by Cyril Jenkins and D. Vaughan Thomas's setting of Wordsworth's 'The Lost Love' – three contemporary pieces, therefore – was the test when Bantock himself adjudicated at Wrexham in 1912 and sensibly awarded the prize to Llew Bowen's Swansea and District choir, pushing the reputable Colne Orpheus into fourth place out of seven. His 'Ballade' was the test piece at Barry in 1920, and he retained a greater popularity among the Welsh than he did in England: his setting of Robert Browning's 'Paracelsus' featured as late as 1964 in Swansea, alongside William Mathias and de Victoria, in a competition reminiscent of the mighty struggles of previous years, won by the

Treorchy Male Choir to confirm the post-war success they had enjoyed under John Haydn Davies and the celebrity they had first won for themselves under William Thomas in the 1890s.[51]

Crowds certainly did follow the choirs, especially when these choirs strenuously applied themselves to numbers specializing in revenge, death and destruction. In 1902 a packed marquee of 10,000 heard fifteen male choirs in a competition lasting two and three-quarter hours; the chief choral for mixed choirs lasted twice as long. Twenty-two choirs competed on 'Comrades in Arms' at the Abergavenny semi-national in 1906, won by Beaufort,[52] and ten embraced 'The Nun of Nidaros', Protheroe's splendid setting of Longfellow at the Swansea National in 1907, an unlikely theme for Glyndwr Richards's winning hundred-strong Resolven male choir. At Abergavenny in 1913, 12,000 sat on unrelenting benches for four and a half hours listening to eighteen male choirs competing on Cyril Jenkins's clamorous 'Fallen Heroes'.[53]

The twin challenge of Boulanger's 'Cyrus in Babylon' and T. Maldwyn Price's 'Crossing the Plain' drew eleven choirs and 19,000 listeners to the 1900 Liverpool National, a tandem rough ride representing the French dramatic school and a widespread *fin de siècle* fascination with an American West whose frontier was now rapidly closing, and therefore no longer quite so Wild, to which the arrival in south Wales of the flickering cinematograph and spectacular visits by Buffalo Bill Cody's Wild West Show gave vivid immediacy.[54]

The professional, detached view that this was sumptuous sound but musically questionable was nicely expressed by the *Musical Times* in 1903:

> The hurly burly of a battle with its moans and gasps of the wounded, the roaring of the lions – if not the wagging of their tails – earthquakes, hurricanes, catastrophes are the subject matter on which the Welsh chorister loves to vent his tense emotionalism and tear his passions to shreds. It is often magnificent . . . but is it music?

Surely it is. Music that followed the line of least resistance it may indeed have been, much of it responding with unerring accuracy to facile emotionalism and written to formula by composers content merely to supply fodder for the voracious appetites of rapidly proliferating Welsh choirs. Yet we dismiss these popular examples of cultural production at our peril. Some of these compositions, for all their apparent dreadfulness to our sophisticated post-modern ears, are minor masterpieces that have retained a popular appeal for over a hundred years and any account of music or society that fails to accommodate them is deaf to a crucial aspect of Welsh musical and social history.

Such a history must also take account of the immense debt owed by the vigorous popular cultural life of eisteddfodic, industrial south Wales to the influence of the Welsh-language rural heartlands of mid- and west Wales. By 1901 there were nearly 16,000 Cardiganshire-born people living in Glamorgan, more than a third of them in the Rhondda.[55] At holiday times the exiles and prodigal sons returned to infuse local events like the Newcastle Emlyn eisteddfod with a new and vigorous lease of life.

Other factors contributed to the galvanization of one particular area in southern Cardiganshire, the consequence of the small industrial revolution that turned the picturesque vale of the River Teifi into an important centre of woollen manufacture. The expansion of the rail network which reached Newcastle Emlyn in 1895 brought coal for fulling mills in and took flannels out, chiefly to meet the insatiable demands of the extensive south Wales market, demands that brought technological and social change to the hitherto sleepy rural hamlets of Drefach-Felindre, Henllan and Llandysul. Mills and factories employing up to a hundred people at a time sprang up, power-driven equipment was installed, and hand-loom weavers were converted into factory operatives. At the turn of the century the Teifi Valley had the appearance, appurtenances and social characteristics of an industrial community: a billiard hall, football and cricket teams, thriving chapels, brass bands and choirs.[56] This could have been the Rhymney Valley in south-east Wales, or Rhosllannerchrugog in the north-east, Blaina (Monmouthshire) or Blaenau (Ffestiniog). It could have been Bargoed. It *was* Bargoed: Bargoed Teifi, Cardiganshire.

In the early years of the twentieth century the Bargoed Teifi male choir moved with confident assurance up the competitive ladder from the lower rungs of local and county level to pose a major challenge to the choirs from the more populous, industrial areas of the country. They posted a warning by coming hard on the heels of the champion Manchester Orpheus choir at the Llangollen National Eisteddfod in 1908, sharing second prize with the slate-quarrying Moelwyn choir. At the Carmarthen National in 1911 the main prizes, initially, went in predictable, or at least expected directions, to areas of proven musicality and established formations. The brass-band prizes went to Gwaun-caegurwen in the Swansea Valley and to the Cory Band from the Rhondda; and the chief choral, tested by Bach and Peter Cornelius (unaccompanied), to Teddy Evans's Brynaman, ahead of Southport and Dowlais. The competition for male choirs of up to eighty voices required, under the professional eyes of Drs Walford Davies, Daniel Protheroe and David Vaughan Thomas and their fellow composers, Coleridge-Taylor and D. Emlyn Evans, the execution of test pieces by the nineteenth-century German Frederick Hegar, whose choral music was then in vogue, and David Jenkins. Conducted by Daniel Jenkins, no relation, of Henllan, Llandysul, the Bargoed Teifi choir beat nine other choirs, were awarded a full one hundred marks on one of the pieces, and snatched the winning prize of £50 from under the noses of seasoned veterans from Glamorganshire. This eisteddfod was a notable one for the Teifi Valley, for both the Newcastle Emlyn Mixed Choir and the Cardigan Ladies' Choir won their respective sections too, thus contributing to a triple triumph made possible by its sudden, unhistorical and short-lived spasm of industrial growth on the borders of Carmarthenshire and Cardiganshire.

To the east, where Carmarthenshire met Glamorgan, a similar pattern had emerged. The rapid industrialization of the Aman Valley, with the development of the anthracite coalfield from the 1890s, brought in its wake a thriving religious and popular literary activity, democratic labour politics, and a musical excellence in choralism and banding that came to fruition in the several national victories of concurrent Brynaman and Ammanford choirs in the years each side of the First World War, reaching a remarkable twin peak at Neath in 1918 when they occupied three of the first four places in the chief choral competition, and at the Ammanford National Eisteddfod in 1922, when local choirs combined to form a choir of 500 which gave the first amateur performance in Wales of Bach's B minor Mass.[57]

The descent from Bach to Bantock – let alone to Protheroe and Parry – is a downward leap of quantum proportions, but it was one the amateur musicians of Wales took in their stride, just as today they will happily juxtapose 'Myfanwy' and William Mathias. The modern aesthetic frowns on the eclectic male-choir repertoire as one supremely lacking in authenticity, an indiscriminate *mélange* of arrangements, spirituals, medleys, hymn-tunes and operatic choruses wrenched from context. Yet in Wales it draws upon the accumulated capital of an industrially based process of cultural production that contributed to the shaping of the social order between 1880 and 1914. The Welsh male choir survives as a social and musical phenomenon and a remarkable institution of popular culture.

10

Fled is that Music

 ℬ

Unlike Keats's nightingale, the sudden rise of Welsh choralism had not been 'a vision or a waking dream'. In April 1918 Professor David Evans of Cardiff, who had taken up the editorship of *Y Cerddor* in December 1915, wrote to *The Times* to point out that the musical life of Wales, far from 'dying of inanition' as the newly published (1917) Report of the Royal Commission on University Education in Wales had suggested, had been transformed from the situation of thirty years earlier. He also drew attention to the fact that the number of complete works performed in that period had risen tenfold, including, now, Bach, Beethoven, Brahms and Bantock, as well as César Franck and all of Elgar's choral works – in fact, 'practically all the choral masterpieces'. The progress in instrumental music too had been 'phenomenal', to the extent that in the populous districts of Wales 'a creditable orchestra could be organized for choral performances without much difficulty'. He also rejected the claim that the sol-fa was a bar to progress; on the contrary, it was a system which had 'taught the Welsh democracy to sing', and been the means of enlarging the musical knowledge of thousands, including professional musicians (like himself) who had been 'induced to proceed with the study of the universal notation as a result of their previous study of the sol-fa'.[1]

Post-war activity in the Cynon Valley seemed to confirm this picture. The birthplace of the Côr Mawr was still in musical ferment, its amateur instrumentalists now capable of attaining standards of performance that Caradog, the one-time 'Paganini of Wales', could hardly have dreamed of. At the Ammanford National Eisteddfod in 1922 the Aberpennar Orchestra from Mountain Ash, conducted by a local hairdresser and self-taught musician, came first out of thirteen orchestral groups; and another orchestra from the same valley, the Aberdare Philharmonic Society, came fourth. The Aberpennar Orchestra was conducted by Bumford Griffiths, who was later persuaded to pursue a course of formal musical study at Aberystwyth under Walford Davies to whom he became assistant musical organizer for Wales. The director of the Welsh National Council of Music claimed 'that he went to Mountain Ash for a haircut and found a musical genius wielding the scissors', whose orchestra in 1926 gave a series of concerts in the Mountain Ash Pavilion 'for the benefit of the distressed of the area', attended by audiences of eight thousand who bought tickets at 1*d.*, 2*d.* and 3*d.*[2] Bumford Griffiths's concerts became the prototype for the Three Valleys Festival at the same venue, begun in May 1930 and continued for the rest of the decade with Dr Malcolm Sargent as popular guest conductor. Fully a third of the 3,000 Festival singers from the Rhondda, Cynon and Merthyr valleys were reckoned to have been out-of-work miners' families.

Sargent, according to his biographer, 'exulted in the lustre and power of his Welsh voices' as they tackled the standard oratorio repertoire in which *Messiah* predominated (though alongside, now, the Bach B minor Mass and Verdi *Requiem*), and where a regular feature was the massed male-choir concert which Caradog had pioneered in 1895. 'Listen to my tenors . . . every one of them has a good top B flat', crowed Sargent as he set about improving and refining Welsh choralism to 'quell' the native enthusiasm of his choristers and teach them to sing sensitively while losing none of their old fire. Much was made of the improvement in audience behaviour and outlook at Mountain Ash too. During the early festivals the audience would break into enthusiastic applause before the end of all the big *Messiah* choruses, and crack nuts, suck oranges and chatter during the 'Pastoral' Symphony in Part I. As the years went by, good listening manners evolved of their own accord. The Three Valleys Festival was 'a seminal chapter' in Sargent's career. If he taught the Valleys much,

> the valleys taught him something in return. He never forgot the evening when he stopped his motor car to hear the song of thousands come up the mountainside as if in greeting. He pulled up and listened, marvelling. It was as though the very spirit of Wales, the spirit of a people acquainted with beauty and hope and pain was walking the hills.[3]

Not all visitors to Wales were so impressed. *Musical Opinion*'s correspondent came away from the Treorchy National Eisteddfod in 1928 reflecting that

> conceivably an audience elsewhere might break into a performance of the 'Dream of Gerontius' by applauding loudly after the Demons had

sung, and again after Gerontius had heard the angels singing round the throne of God, though the moment is at hand when he must approach his Maker. But where else would a conductor be found who at that solemn moment would turn round to acknowledge the applause? Nowhere else, I imagine.[4]

Clearly, the spirit of Merthyr's Dan Davies was alive and well in the three Valleys; equally clearly, to judge Professor Evans's 'democracy' by metropolitan standards was a pointless exercise, as events at the Swansea National two years earlier had shown. On that occasion people were leaving the pavilion in droves during a performance of Beethoven's Choral Symphony, which came at the end of a long evening that had begun forty minutes late. As the first three movements ran their course the audience became increasingly restive, and the end of the third was the signal for a mass exodus; when the Finale began and the choir still remained seated the stream of departures became a torrent. When at last Horace Stevens stood up to begin the baritone recitative which heralds the chorus, he was greeted with a burst of applause.[5]

Yet this same audience could also show a keen musical knowledge: when, at Swansea, three of the male choirs came to grief in J. Owen Jones's 'Blow, Blow, thou Winter Wind' at the point where the second tenors sing a G on the word 'Blow' and are immediately followed on a syncopated A flat by the first tenors, 'there was a noticeable shudder through large sections of the vast audience indicating that they were possessed by a sense of "something wrong".'[6]

This was a more restrained response than the 'wild shout' that broke out from the audience when Llanelli's sopranos came in early on the last page at the Aberdare National in 1885.[7] Yet it serves as a reminder that post-1918 developments saw nothing that could not have been anticipated before 1914, whether the high standard of orchestral playing that drew genuine admiration from Ralph Vaughan Williams and Sir Hugh Allen at the National Eisteddfodau of Barry (1920) and Ammanford (1922), or the non-competitive festivals of choral and orchestral concerts soon to be established at Newtown, Aberystwyth, Harlech and Gregynog, all modelled on precursors like the pre-war South Wales Festival of 1913, the stuttering and – to its justifiably aggrieved valley hinterland whose immense vocal talents were urbanely snubbed – socially pretentious triennial Cardiff Festival of 1892–1910, and the even earlier Harlech Festival of the 1860s. Even the setting up, following the recommendations of the 1917 Royal Commission into Welsh University

Education, of the National Council of Music for Wales under the proconsulship of Henry Walford Davies was the logical outcome of schemes proposed since at least the 1890s to accelerate Welsh musical, especially orchestral development.[8]

Despite these continuities, the outbreak of the Great War was a watershed in the musical as in so many other aspects of Welsh life. The years around 1914 marked the end of an era: John Thomas (Pencerdd Gwalia), R. C. Jenkins of Llanelli, and D. Emlyn Evans died in 1913, Harry Evans in 1914, David Jenkins in 1915, Rees Evans of Aberdare in 1916, and the sol-fa crusader W. T. Samuel in 1917. It is true that Marie Lloyd had been entertaining the larger coastal towns of south Wales since 1891, and visited Cardiff just prior to her death in 1922, but for all his Welsh connections it must still have discomfited readers of *Y Cerddor* to be told that the most popular song of 1915 was Ivor Novello's 'Till the Boys Come Home'.[9]

A new generation of professionally trained, formally qualified musicians like D. Vaughan Thomas of Swansea, David de Lloyd of Skewen and E. T. Davies of Merthyr in their respective posts at Aberystwyth and Bangor, T. Hopkin Evans and his cousin the *Times* letter-writer David Evans, both of Resolven, would complement – not always harmoniously – the work of Walford Davies in widening the musical horizons of the Welsh, and instilling a much-needed confidence in place of the sensitivity to criticism that fed the paranoia of courageous but educationally insecure conductors of an earlier era like Dan Davies.

The cataclysm of 1914–18 ended Wales's cultural isolation as her people came into contact with the wider world. The arrival of the gramophone and radio brought a new awareness of standards elsewhere. Secularization and the steady, soon accelerating, decline of the Welsh language made further inroads into what had been an identifiable and distinct Welsh choral tradition. While the inter-war years inflicted deep wounds on the valleys of the Rhondda, Cynon and Taf, it was musical activity and industrial inactivity that were now in David Allsobrook's phrase 'antiphonally joined': the celebrated Cwmbach Male Choir, Aberdare, was founded during the coal stoppage of 1921, and that of Pendyrus, in the Rhondda Fach, in 1924. In the 1930s 60 per cent of Pendyrus's 150 choristers were unemployed.[10]

It was the two rival male choirs of Morriston near Swansea, and on the mixed choral front the choirs of Ystalyfera and Pontarddulais in the relatively less ravaged western coalfield that dominated the choral competitions of the decade after 1926, and drew the superlatives of the critics. After hearing the Ystalyfera choir – from Ivander's Swansea Valley stamping-ground of the 1860s – at Neath in 1934, the chairman of the adjudicators, Sir Edward Bairstow, spoke for the audience of 20,000 when he confessed to having 'been through a great experience' which left him feeling 'very much like a wet rag', while another English critic found their performance

> so brilliant, so moving, so perfectly balanced that no praise could be too high. Every word was not only clearly enunciated but given its exact need of musical emphasis; every detail of the score was intelligently phrased and moulded; every subtle inflection of light and shade was eloquently expressed, with great climaxes and exquisitely modulated *pianissimi* arising out of no arbitrary calculated attempts at virtuosity but growing naturally from the shape and content of the music itself. A marvellous and unforgettable experience.[11]

Here surely was an effective antidote to the fanatical bigotry of the arch-iconoclast Cyril Jenkins's ally Gerald Cumberland, for whom

> the Welsh are a musical race only in their emotions. They love the obvious phrase, the insensate high note, the chromatic melody; their deepest (but not so deep) emotions are stirred by luscious harmony . . . sheer but exciting noise, familiar cadences, rich and fruity voices, and all the paraphernalia employed by vulgar exploiters of sound . . . Wales is a cemetery for those who possess a musical talent . . . [inhabited by] a people only half educated, a people of swift but shallow enthusiasms.[12]

The Education Commissioners of 1847 were come again.

If this finest Welsh choir of the inter-war period was guilty, on occasion, of striving for dramatic effects 'instead of for an effect',[13] of excessive colouring in the manner of the choirs of the 1880s and 1890s, it was because it sprang from the same social matrix. The Ystalyfera choir was founded during the 1925 anthracite strike in the western coalfield. 'It is', wrote one admirer seeking to convey something of its character to a mostly non-Welsh audience

> composed almost entirely of miners and tinplate-workers and their women folk. Twenty-five per cent of the men are unemployed . . . The choir has no wealthy backers. Out of its poverty – goodness knows how – Ystalyfera finds the money to keep its choirs and bands alive. It cost

the choir £350 to travel to the last National Eisteddfod to compete for a
prize of £150. Why do they do it? To ask that question is to show an . . .
incapacity to grasp the fact that to these people Music is Life.[14]

Even this formidable phalanx had to yield, in the late thirties, to the
reviving choral juggernauts of the slowly recovering steam-coal valleys
further east. At Cardiff in 1938, when the seven competing choirs,
aggregating well in excess of 1,500 singers, each had to learn the Brahms
Requiem in its entirety, Ystalyfera came fourth behind Merthyr, Dowlais
and Blaenrhondda.

Naturally there were nineteenth-century habits that died hard in the
twentieth. In 1924, the *Musical Opinion* wished to

> direct attention to the following remarkable achievement of a Welsh
> choir on Bank Holiday: Carmarthen Eisteddfod – Male voice party: 1st,
> Treorky and District, 93 marks . . . The test piece was 'The Pilgrims'.
>
> Clynderwen Eisteddfod – Male voice competition: ('The Pilgrims')
> Prize £100. The winners were the Treorky choir.
>
> Burry Port Eisteddfod – Male voice competition ('The Pilgrims')
> £50. First prize was awarded to Treorky Male Voice.[15]

The pilgrims from 'Treorky', amateur songsters spending their summer
Bank Holiday in west Wales, more than cleared their expenses. This was
little advance on the Cymmer (Rhondda) choir who sang 'Worthy is the
Lamb' at four eisteddfodau in two days at Christmas 1899,[16] except that
the pilgrims had made an excursion of it, with Joseph Parry in the van.

The Welsh choral tradition, then, is not above criticism, but it ought
not to be beyond our sympathetic understanding, even if it is by now
beyond our imagination. We need to recognize its significant achievements as well as its severe limitations. In its heyday, in those places, it was
one of the most significant cultural practices by which the artistic
aspirations and social and emotional satisfactions of ordinary people
were met and enriched, one in which women seized the opportunity to
attain something approaching equal status with men, and one through
which thousands of the underprivileged literally found their voice.[17] It
mobilized entire communities and engaged collective, often national,
passions.

Fled is that music now. A changed society has brought changing social
patterns in its wake and new, constantly evolving forms of cultural
production. It would be foolish to regret the passing of the society and

the conditions that made possible the golden age of Welsh choralism. And yet . . . The Welsh, says Wyn Griffith's Englishman, ' "can always sing". To which a Welshman can only reply, "We could".'[18]

Notes

&

Notes to Introduction

1 The English visitor was John Spencer Curwen, son of the tonic sol-fa pioneer John Curwen, who was adjudicating at the Eisteddfod. His remarks are quoted in an unsigned article, 'The Eisteddfod and popular music in Wales', *Y Cymmrodor*, 5 (1882), pp. 286–7.

2 'Choirs', in *The Collected Poems of Glyn Jones*, ed. M. Stephens (Cardiff, 1996), pp. 3, 141.

3 *Musical Times* (September1897), p. 607.

4 See 'English notes: the eisteddfod', *Y Cerddor* (October 1897), For a fuller account, see pp. 101–6 below.

5 At least, not on the evidence of Dave Russell's admirable *Popular Music in England 1840–1914* (Manchester, 1987).

6 *Y Cerddor*, (1903), p. 96.

7 *Merthyr Express*, 5 September 1885; O. M. Edwards, *Tro Trwy'r Gogledd, Tro i'r De* (Wrexham, 1958 edn.), p. 162.

8 *Musical Herald*, (September 1911), p. 264.

9 John Graham, *A Century of Welsh Music* (1923), p. 4.

10 Notably Peter Stead, 'Amateurs and professionals in the cultures of Wales', in G. H. Jenkins and J. B. Smith (eds.), *Politics and Society in Wales 1840–1922: Essays in Honour of Ieuan Gwynedd Jones* (Cardiff, 1988), pp.113–34, and W. D. Jones, *Wales in America: Scranton and the Welsh 1860–1920* (Cardiff, 1993), pp. 132–45.

11 Andrew J. Croll, 'Civilising the urban: popular culture, public space and urban meaning, Merthyr *c.*1870–1914' (University of Wales Ph.D. dissertation, Cardiff, 1997), esp. ch. 2.

12 *Collected Stories of Gwyn Jones* (Cardiff, 1998), p. 2.

13 David Andrews, in J. Nauright and T. J. L. Chandler (eds.), *Making Men: Rugby and Masculine Identity* (London, 1996), p. 66.

14 Richard Holt, *Sport and the British: A Modern History* (Oxford, 1989), p. 357.

15 A historian rather than a musicologist, I am reassured by the words of Dylan Thomas's close friend, the composer Daniel Jones: 'The story of music in Wales can be told in many different ways, but there is only one way, to my mind, in which its inner meaning can be brought out: the story must not be limited to Welsh music; it must include the Welsh people.' Daniel Jones, *Music in Wales: Annual Lecture of the BBC in Wales* (Cardiff, 1961), p. 5.

Notes to Chapter 1

1   *Y Gerddorfa* (1873), p. 42.

2   Quoted in Osian Ellis, *The Story of the Harp in Wales* (Cardiff, 1980), p. 54.

3   Prys Morgan, *The Eighteenth Century Renaissance* (Llandybïe, 1981), p. 132; idem, in E. Hobsbawm and T. O. Ranger (eds.), *The Invention of Tradition* (Cambridge, 1983), pp. 74–9.

4   For John Thomas, see *Dictionary of Welsh Biography* (*DWB*); M. O. Jones, *Bywgraffiaeth Cerddorion Cymreig* (Cardiff, 1890), pp. 128–30; *Y Cerddor* (1913), p. 45; Carys Ann Roberts, 'Pencerdd Gwalia', in Hywel Teifi Edwards (ed.), *Llynfi ac Afan, Garw ac Ogwr* (Llandysul, 1998), pp. 252–73.

5   See A. J. Heward Rees, ' "Songs of Wales": a brief centenary note', *Welsh Music* (Winter 1973/4), pp. 90–2.

6   Brinley Richards, *The Songs of Wales* (1873; 4th edn. 1879), Preface. For a valuable evaluation, and an appraisal of his career overall, see A. J. Heward Rees, 'Henry Brinley Richards (1817–1885): a nineteenth-century propagandist for Welsh music', *Welsh Music History*, 2 (1997), pp. 173–92. See also A. F. Leighton Thomas, 'Random thoughts on Brinley Richards', *Anglo-Welsh Review* (Winter 1967), pp. 102–24.

7   *The Times*, 9 September 1867, quoted in Hywel Teifi Edwards, *Gŵyl Gwalia* (Llandysul, 1980), pp. 212–13.

8   Joseph Bennett, *Forty Years of Music* (London, 1908), p. 132.

9   Heward Rees, *Welsh Music History*, 2, p. 182.

10 *Y Cerddor* (1893), p. 3. Emlyn Evans's caustic appraisal of Brinley Richards is at odds with the more generous assessment of M. O. Jones, op. cit., pp. 102–9.

11 *Y Cerddor Cymreig* (November 1867), p.63. For Ieuan Gwyllt see *DWB*, M. O. Jones, op. cit., pp. 112–17 and see pp. 26–31 below.

12 This debate, which rumbled on until 1913, is discussed in Osian Ellis and Hywel Teifi Edwards, opp. cit., and in Ann Rosser, *Telyn a Thelynor* (Cardiff, 1981), pp. 47–59. For that matter, the classic symbol of Welsh musicality, the male voice choir, had originated elsewhere in the French *orphéonistes* and the *Männerchöre* of Germany. See ch. 9 below.

13 *Y Cerddor Cymreig* (1864), p. 143.

14 Ibid. (1862), p. 143.

15 Hywel Teifi Edwards, op. cit., pp. 249–50.

16 *Y Cerddor Cymreig* (July 1865), pp.12–13.

17 *Y Faner*, 15 October 1873.

18 There had been three short-lived predecessors: *Blodau Cerdd* (Musical Flowers 1852–3, edited by Ieuan Gwyllt in Aberystwyth), *Yr Athraw Cerddorol* (The Music Teacher, 1854, John Mills, Llanidloes), and *Y Cerbyd Cerddorol* (The Music Wagon, 1860–1, Thomas Jones, Holywell). See Rhidian Griffiths, 'Cyhoeddi Cerddoriaeth yng Nghymru yn y cyfnod 1860–1914' (Music publishing in Wales 1860–1914, Ph.D. thesis, University of Wales 1991), pp. 57ff.

19 *Y Cerddor Cymreig* (1861), p. 24.

20 Ibid. (January 1863), p. 177.

21 Ibid. (1861), pp. 23, 32, 54–5.

22 John Haydn Davies, in K. Hopkins (ed.) *Rhondda Past and Future* (Ferndale, 1975), p. 145.

23 *Y Cerddor* (1900), p. 99; Hywel Teifi Edwards, *Eisteddfod Ffair y Byd Chicago 1893* (Llandysul, 1990), pp.137–41.

24 *Y Cerddor Cymreig* (1866), p. 74.

25 On these, see chs. 3 and 4 below.

26 For this account I am indebted to John Hugh Thomas, 'Cerddoriaeth yn Abertawe', in Ieuan M. Williams (ed.), *Abertawe a'r Cylch* (Llandybïe, 1982), pp. 176–97, and *idem*, 'Music', in R. A. Griffiths (ed.), *The City of Swansea: Challenge and Change* (Swansea, 1990), pp. 218–28.

27 C. Price, *The Professional Theatre in Wales* (Swansea, 1984), p. 16.

28 *Herald of Wales*, 8 February 1933.

29 *The Musical Herald* (July 1889), pp.146–8; *Y Cerddor* (1917), p. 40; Ifano Jones, *Bywyd a Gwaith W.T. Samuel* (Llanelli, 1920), pp. 38–9.

30 *Slater's Royal National Directory of North and South Wales 1880:* South Wales, p. 319; John Hugh Thomas, 'Music', pp. 221–3.

31 *Herald of Wales*, 26 April 1933.

32 W. Ivander Griffiths, 'Fy adgofion', *Y Cerddor* (1901), p.108. My account of Ivander's career draws on these memoirs which appeared in eleven instalments in *Y Cerddor* (1901–2), and his *Record of over Fifty Years Music, Temperance, Eisteddfod and other Mission Work in Wales and Cumberland* (Workington, [1903]). See also *Y Cerddor* (1903), p.5; (1910), p. 46.

33 *Y Cerddor Cymreig* (1863), p. 2. A counter-claim from Gwent on behalf of a *Messiah* conducted by Heman Gwent with the Cyfarthfa Band in 1861 has been made by Siân Rhiannon Williams in *Welsh Music* (Summer 1985), pp. 104–5. It is unlikely that, whatever Ieuan Ddu accomplished in Merthyr (see pp. 60–1 below), he supervised a full performance of the entire work. The first known occasion this occurred in Wales was at the North Wales Musical Festival at Rhuddlan Castle, 24–7 September 1850. The names of the chorus, soloists and *ad hoc* orchestra indicate that this was an English and professional affair. Nevertheless, it was an auspicious and historic event: 'On no previous occasion has the "Messiah" been performed in Wales . . .' states the programme for Wednesday evening, 25 September 1850 (NLW, Miscellaneous concert programmes, Wales).

34 H. A. Bruce, *Lectures and Addresses* (1917), p. 209, quoted in H. Cunningham, *Leisure in the Industrial Revolution* (London, 1980), p. 103.

35 There was also a thriving colony of Welsh immigrant ironworkers on the north-east coast of England. The Middlesbrough and Teesside Welsh had a flourishing musical life of choral societies, eisteddfodau and singing festivals of the kind found on a larger scale among the Welsh communities of North America, South Africa and Australia. See R. Lewis and D. Ward, 'Culture, politics and assimilation: the Welsh on Teesside c. 1850–1940', *Welsh History Review* (December 1995), pp. 550–70.

36 For Ivander's later career, see Selwyn Jones, 'Ivander Griffiths and the eisteddfod abroad', *Planet, 2* (October/November 1970), pp. 60–4 and Huw Williams, *Taro Tant* (Denbigh, 1994), pp.74–80. The champion soloist at the 1938 Workington Festival, an institution lineally descended from Ivander's eisteddfod, was a young contralto called Kathleen Wilson, soon to win international acclaim as Kathleen Ferrier (ibid., p. 78).

37   For the luminous choral tradition of the Morriston Tabernacle (Y Tabernacl, Treforys), initiated in the 1870s by David Francis of Merthyr, which extends via Eos Morlais of Dowlais, Penfro Rowlands (composer of the hymn-tune 'Blaenwern'), Edgar Hughson and Alun John to the present day, see T. Lloyd Evans, *Y Cathedral Anghydffurfiol Cymraeg* (Swansea, 1972), pp. 147–74.

38   *Y Cerddor* (1912), p.56. Such an uplifting achievement was motivated by nakedly mercenary considerations: 'thanks to their efforts [i.e. of Ben Hughes and his choir] the chapel cleared several hundred pounds of debt.' *Y Cerddor* (1926), p. 48.

39   The choral achievements of Ivander and Clee are neatly juxtaposed by Rhidian Griffiths, 'Dau gôr', in Hywel Teifi Edwards (ed.), *Cwm Tawe* (Llandysul, 1993), pp.188–210. For Clee's Ystalyfera Choir (340 on stage in the chief choral at the 1926 Swansea National), see Islwyn Williams, *William David Clee a'r Côr Mawr Ystalyfera* (Llandybïe, 1955). See also pp. 197–8 below.

Notes to Chapter 2

1   *Y Cerddor* (1894), p. 7.

2   R. D. Griffith, *Hanes Canu Cynulleidfaol Cymru* (Cardiff, 1948), pp. 68–9.

3   W. R. Lambert, *Drink and Sobriety in Victorian Wales* (Cardiff, 1983), p. 12.

4   Ibid. pp. 12, 14, 105–6.

5   *Y Cerddor Cymreig* (1862), pp. 156–7; (1867), p. 44.

6   Anthony Jones, *Welsh Chapels* (Stroud, 1996), p. 46.

7   *Y Cerddor*, (1904), p. 53.

8   Ibid. 1900, pp. 84–5.

9   V. and S. Gammon, in T. Herbert (ed.), *Bands* (Milton Keynes, 1991), pp. 127–8.

10   *Y Cerddor* (1897), pp. 122–3. For the programme of the Tabernacle Choral Society's Third Concert of Sacred Music at the New Town Hall, Aberystwyth on Good Friday evening, 14 April 1854, see C. F. Lloyd, *Cofiant John Ambrose Lloyd* (Wrexham. 1921), pp. 76–7. For Edward Edwards, see *Y Cerddor* (1897), pp. 122–3 and Tegwyn Jones, *Eisteddfod Aberystwyth 1865* (Llandysul, 1992), pp. 31–4.

11   R. D. Griffith, op.cit., pp. 60–7.

12   Rhidian Griffiths, 'Cyhoeddi cerddoriaeth yng Nghymru yn y cyfnod 1860–1914' (Ph.D. thesis, University of Wales, Aberystwyth, 1991), p. 14.

13   Griffiths, 'Cyhoeddi cerddoriaeth', p. 15. See in general on this topic, Rhidian Griffiths, 'Welsh chapel music: the making of a tradition', *Journal of Welsh Ecclesiastical History* (1989), pp. 35–43.

14   R. D. Griffith, op. cit., pp. 172–5.

15   E. Keri Evans, *Cofiant D. Emlyn Evans* (Carmarthen, 1919), p. 23.

16   Rhidian Griffiths, 'Musical life in the nineteenth century', in P. Morgan (ed.) *Glamorgan County History*, vol. 6 (Cardiff,1988), p. 371.

17   M. O. Jones calculated that the 280 *cymanfaoedd* held in Wales in 1895, averaging 480 per meeting, were attended by 134,550 singers. This was 7.6 per cent of the entire population. *Musical Herald* (February 1896), p. 57.

18   D. Emlyn Evans, 'Music in Wales 1899–1912', NLW MS 8033 D, vol. 1 (22
     June 1901). For Giraldus, see Philip Weller, 'Gerald of Wales's view of music',
     Welsh Music History, 2 (1997), pp. 1–32, and Shari Burstyn, 'Is Gerald of Wales
     a credible musical witness?', *Musical Quarterly*, 72 (1986), pp. 155–69.
19   Rhidian Griffiths, 'Welsh chapel music'.
20   D. Morgans, *Music and Musicians of Merthyr and District* (Merthyr, 1922),
     pp. 20–1.
21   Rhidian Griffiths, 'Y gymanfa ganu: ei gwreiddiau a'i natur', *Bwletin Cymdeithas
     Emynau Cymru*, 2 (1986–7), p. 276.
22   *Y Cerddor* (1912), pp. 52–3.
23   In order to take the sectarian heat out of the argument it became fashionable to
     present this *cymanfa* as non-denominational. David Jenkins, himself of
     Aberystwyth, was anxious to accomplish this so that no one denomination could
     claim priority. *Y Cerddor* (1901), pp. 18, 43–4, 104; (1902), p. 105; (1909), p. 24.
24   My reading of Ieuan Gwyllt is based on *DWB*, M. O. Jones, *Bywgraffiaeth
     Cerddorion Cymreig*, pp. 112–17, a series of articles by David Jenkins in *Y
     Cerddor* (January–May 1909), and W. T. Rees (Alaw Ddu) papers, National
     Library of Wales.
25   His own tune, 'Moab', was famously if extravagantly described as one of the six
     best in the world by Sir Henry Hadow. Ieuan Gwyllt as a composer of hymn-
     tunes is assessed by Alan Luff, *Welsh Hymns and their Tunes* (London, 1990),
     pp. 203–4, and Huw Williams, 'Cofio Ieuan Gwyllt, 1977', *Bwletin Cymdeithas
     Emynau Cymru* (1978), pp. 19–20.
26   R. D. Griffith, *Hanes Canu Cynulleidfaol*, pp. 92–4.
27   Ibid., pp. 100–4. These figures may err on the side of caution. W. T. Samuel, a
     sol-fa partisan, and like all sol-fa partisans obsessed with statistics, claimed that
     the Baptist *Llawlyfr Moliant* had sold 93,900 copies in TSF, and a precise 19,403
     in staff, within five years of its appearance. Samuel, 'Wales and the tonic sol-fa
     system', *Fourteenth Annual Report of the National Eisteddfod, Caernarfon, 1894*
     (Cardiff, 1895), pp. 51–2.
28   Anthony Jones, op. cit., pp. 48–9.
29   *Y Cerddor* (1891), p. 143.
30   N. Temperley (ed.), *Music in Britain: The Romantic Age 1800–1914* (London,
     1981), p. 7.
31   Rhidian Griffiths, 'Cyhoeddi cerddoriaeth' is the authoritative source on this
     topic.
32   See ch. 5 below.
33   *Y Cerddor* (1909), p. 38. For Rosser Beynon, see pp. 62–3 below.
34   *Y Cerddor* (1909), p. 13.
35   Huw Williams, 'Rhai o gymwynasau Ieuan Gwyllt', *Welsh Music* (Spring
     1977–8), pp. 71–5.
36   'Canu nes mynd yn goeg', *Yr Ysgol Gerddorol* (September 1878), p. 65.
37   Quoted in *Y Gerddorfa* (March 1874), p. 76.
38   *Musical Herald* (October 1895), p. 308; 'F.T.S.C.', 'The relation of Wales to the
     Tonic Sol-fa College', *Wales* (October 1911), pp. 273–5; *Y Cerddor* (1911), p. 132.
     These figures, used in support of a call for greater Welsh representation on the
     college Council, were challenged by the TSC's secretary, *Y Cerddor* (1912), p. 40.

39   *Y Cerddor* (1897), p. 1.

40   *Musical Herald* (February 1896), p. 57.

41   See pp. 186–9 below.

42   R. Pearsall, *Victorian Popular Music* (Newton Abbot, 1973), p. 119.

43   D. Russell, 'The popular musical societies of the Yorkshire textile district 1850–1914' (University of York Ph.D. thesis, 1979), pp. 122–30.

44   Ibid., pp. 121–30; B. Rainbow, 'Music in education,' in Temperley, *Music in Britain*, ch. 4.

45   By the mid-1850s, over 6,000 children attended the Sunday schools of Merthyr's 33 chapels (Anthony Jones, op. cit., p. 48). According to the 1905 Royal Commission on the Church of England and other religious bodies in Wales, some Sunday schools had enormous enrolments: 730 children at Bethania, Dowlais, 714 at Capel yr Alltwen, Pontardawe, 835 at Mount Pleasant, Swansea, 762 at the Tabernacle, Morriston, nearly two thousand at the three Rhondda chapels, Noddfa and Bethlehem Treorchy, and Cymmer, Porth. Thirty-seven per cent of the whole population of Glamorgan attended Sunday school in 1906.

46   NLW, W. T. Rees (Alaw Ddu) papers, p. 16.

47   See, for example, Dr McNaught's impression at Llanelli in 1903, *Musical Times* (1903), p. 599.

48   Owain T. Edwards, in R. Brinley Jones (ed.), *Anatomy of Wales* (Cardiff, 1972), p. 224.

49   John Marc Davies, 'Twf a datblygiad y gerddorfa yng Nghymru' (The growth and development of the orchestra in Wales), MA dissertation, University of Wales, Bangor, 1986).

50   H. E. Meller, *Leisure and the Changing City* [Bristol] *1870–1914* (London, 1976), p. 224. For evidence from Merthyr and the Rhondda, see pp. 87–8 and 134–5 below.

Notes to Chapter 3

1   Ieuan Gwynedd Jones, *Communities* (Llandysul, 1987), p. 266.

2   Martin Barclay, 'Aberdare 1880–1914: class and community' (University of Wales MA thesis, Cardiff, 1985), pp. 10–11.

3   Ieuan Gwynedd Jones, op. cit., p. 268.

4   Barclay, op. cit., pp. 109–10; Richard Arnold, 'The pubs, clubs and breweries of Aberdare', *Old Aberdare*, 2 (Aberdare, 1982), pp. 107–21; R. Ivor Parry, *The History of Aberdare* (unpublished, n.d., Aberdare Central Library).

5   Gwilym P. Ambrose, 'The Aberdare background to the South Wales Choral Union', *Glamorgan History*, 9 (Barry, 1980), pp. 191–202; Brynley F. Roberts, 'Argraffu yn Aberdâr', *Journal of the Welsh Bibliographical Society*, 9 (1973–4), pp. 1–53.

6   Ieuan Gwynedd Jones, op. cit., pp. 264–83, 317 n. 67.

7   Ambrose, op. cit., pp. 191–2.

8   K. O. Morgan, *Wales in British Politics 1868–1922* (Cardiff, 1963), p. 206; E. W. Evans, *The Miners of South Wales* (Cardiff, 1961), p. 102; W. W. Price, 'Y gymanfa

ganu gyntaf', *Yr Ymofynnydd* (Mehefin 1957), pp. 85–7; idem, 'Y gymanfa ganu', *Y Tyst*, 7 (Tachwedd, 1957).

9   Ambrose, op. cit., pp. 194–5: *The Morning Star and Dial*, 23 April 1861, quoted in H. T. Edwards (ed.), *Cwm Cynon* (Llandysul, 1997), p. 147.

10   Ambrose, op. cit., pp. 196–7.

11   Ibid.

12   John H. Davies, 'Rhondda choral music in Victorian Times', in K. S. Hopkins (ed.), *Rhondda Past and Present* (Ferndale, 1975), p. 142; *Y Cerddor Cymreig* (1863), 58–9.

13   For Caradog's family tree, constructed by W. W. Price, see W. W. Price Collection, Aberdare Central Library, B 33/1(i).

14   I am grateful to Dr Trevor Herbert for allowing me to see his entry on Caradog for the forthcoming *New Dictionary of National Biography*.

15   Watcyn Wyn, 'Caradog', *Ceninen Gwyl Ddewi* (1898), 46, Twynog Jeffries, in *Côr Mawr Caradog Centenary Festival Brochure* (Aberdare, 1972), p. 15; Harry Evans, in *Wales* (1911), p. 186.

16   For Caradog's 'Farmyard Fantasia', see John H. Davies, op. cit., pp. 145–6 and *Y Cerddor* (1898), p. 30.

17   *Y Cerddor* (1924), p. 84; Philip Jenkins, *A History of Modern Wales 1536–1990* (London, 1992), pp. 225, 244; John Davies, *Hanes Cymru* (London, 1990), p. 395.

18   *Y Cerddor Cymreig* (1867), p. 29.

19   Ibid. (1868), p. 21.

20   Ibid (1870), p. 6.

21   John H. Davies, op. cit., p. 140; 'A brief history of the Treorchy Male Voice Choir 1883–1897', *Excelsior (The Voice of the Treorchy Male Choir)*, (Treorchy, 1987), pp. 42–7.

22   *Y Cerddor Cymreig* (1871), p. 38; *Y Cerddor* (1898), p. 15.

23   Wilfred Mellers in the *Times Literary Supplement*, 29 March 1996; Michael Musgrave, *The Musical Life of the Crystal Palace* (Cambridge, 1995), pp. 190–6.

24   *Y Cerddor Cymreig* (1872), p. 23.

25   *Côr Mawr Centenary Festival Brochure*, pp. 8, 12; *Y Cerddor* (1898), p. 14.

26   *Côr Mawr Centenary Festival Brochure*, p. 12.

27   The sources on which my account of the Côr Mawr's 1872 triumph is based are primarily *Y Cerddor Cymreig* (1872) pp. 57–61, and the *Aberdare Times*, April to July 1872.

28   *Tonic Sol-fa Reporter*, 15 July 1872, p. 213.

29   *Y Gerddorfa* (1872), p. 18; *Y Cerddor* (1904), p. 32.

30   *Y Cerddor Cymreig* (1872), p. 58; *Tonic Sol-fa Reporter*, loc. cit..

31   Watcyn Wyn, op. cit., p. 50.

32   *The Times*, quoted in the *Aberdare Times*, 13 June 1872.

33   *Y Cerddor Cymreig* (1872), p. 59.

34   Ibid.

35   Barclay, op. cit., pp. 21, 28.

36   *Aberdare Times*, 13 July 1872.

37   *Western Mail*, 11 July 1872.

38   From information provided by Dr Trevor Herbert.

39   Despite Willert Beale's attempts to persuade choirs to compete from populous

centres of choral activity like Birmingham, Manchester, Bradford and Leeds, none took up the gauntlet, to the wider disappointment of the music press: 'Where are the Potteries Prize Choirs, and the West Riding Prize Choir? Cannot Edinburgh, or Newcastle, or Manchester, or Bristol, or Sheffield do battle in this choral fight?', *Tonic Sol-fa Reporter* (November 1872), p. 329.

40 *Y Cerddor Cymreig* (1873), p. 6.

41 According to *Y Cerddor* (1898), p. 126.

42 For the second assault on the Crystal Palace see T. Alun Davies 'The Crystal Palace Challenge Trophy', *Welsh Music*, 4, (Spring 1972), pp. 24–37, and the report in *Cerddor y Tonic Sol-ffa*, 5 (1873), pp. 30–1. Brinley Richards (ed.), *The South Wales Choral Union at the Crystal Palace . . . July 1873: Reports and Criticisms* (London, n.d.) and Morien's 'The March of Cambria's Five Hundred', in his *Sketches of Wales* (Pontypridd, 1875) are remarkable only for their sycophantic accounts of the reception given to the choir by the Prince of Wales at Marlborough House the day after the competition.

43 T. Alun Davies, op. cit., p. 27.

44 *Musical Herald* (April 1892), p. 100.

45 *Cerddor y Tonic Sol-ffa* (1873), p. 11.

46 *Y Gerddorfa* (1873), p. 86; *Western Mail*, 28 June 1873; *Y Cerddor Cymreig* (1873), p. 38; T. Alun Davies, op. cit., pp. 30–1.

47 *Cerddor y Tonic Sol-ffa* (1873), p. 31; *Y Cerddor* (1904), p. 32; *Cerddor y Tonic Sol-ffa* (1874), p. 43. The 'effect' Barnby referred to owed something to the vocal balance, or imbalance, of the choir in 1873: there were about 105 sopranos, 92 altos, 126 tenors and 124 basses, so the women needed to be at full throttle to match the thunderous 250 male voices.

48 *Tonic Sol-fa Reporter*, 15 July 1873, p. 213; *Cerddor y Tonic Sol-ffa* (1873), p. 31; *Y Cerddor Cymreig* (1872), p. 60. For Rivière, see Henry Wood, *My Life of Music* (London, 1938), p. 84.

49 D. Emlyn Evans, 'Music in Wales 1899–1912', NLW MSS 8033D–8036D, vol. 4 (24 September 1910).

50 *Cerddor y Tonic Sol-ffa* (1874), p. 1.

51 *Aberdare Times*, 19 July 1873, quoted in T. Alun Davies, op. cit., p. 32.

52 *Y Gerddorfa* (1874), p. 113; *Western Mail*, 23 October 1873.

53 NLW, W. J. Parry Papers, p. 108. Since the Challenge Cup was not competed for in 1874, the Crystal Palace Company reclaimed it. In 1900 Sir Arthur Sullivan, a director of the company, suggested it should be offered to the National Brass Band Championships, and the bands competed for it until 1939. Thereafter it was placed in storage in County Hall, London, until the early 1970s when Merthyr-born Illtyd Harrington, deputy leader of the LCC at the time, led a campaign to return it to Wales. Since 1974 it has been a central showpiece in the music section of the Museum of Welsh Life, St Fagan's, Cardiff. 'This is like one of the great scrolls of Egypt going home', declared Harrington. *Western Mail*, 27 and 28 June 1974.

54 This paragraph is based on the *Western Mail*, 16 and 21 October 1885, 27 February and 11 July 1886; H. T. Edwards, *Eisteddfod Ffair y Byd Chicago 1893* (Llandysul, 1990), pp. 104, 134–6; *Y Cerddor* (1895), p. 139.

55 *Cerddor y Cymry*, 2 (1884–5), p. 106.

56   *Y Cerddor* (1905), pp. 86–7. Cf. Harry Evans, 'There can be no doubt now that the victory...at the Crystal Palace some thirty years ago did much to disturb the equilibrium of Welsh people, inasmuch as they held the belief from that time forth that they had conquered the world, and that nothing more was necessary', in T. Stephens (ed.), *Wales, Today and Tomorrow* (Cardiff, 1908), p. 323. For Rees Evans's career, see *Aberdare Almanack* (1893), pp. 23–7, in W. W. Price Collection (Aberdare Central Library), B33/6.

57   *Y Gerddorfa* (1878), p. 70; John H. Davies, op. cit., p. 136.

58   *Y Gerddorfa* (1875), pp. 18–19; *Merthyr Express*, 30 December 1893.

59   *Aberdare Times*, 30 March, 6 and 13 April 1878; *Merthyr Express*, 2 December 1893.

60   I owe this felicitous expression to Dave Russell, *Popular Music in England 1840–1914* (Manchester 1987), p. 155.

61   R. Nettel, *Music in the Five Towns 1840–1914* (London, 1944), p. 26.

62   *Aberdare Times*, 8 June 1878.

63   *Merthyr Express*, 23 April 1892; *Aberdare Times*, 27 April 1897; *Aberdare Almanack* (1893), pp. 27–9.

64   *Aberdare Times*, 4 January, 1913.

65   This was not the first time for the *Christmas Oratorio* to be heard in Wales, but it was its first performance by a chapel choir (*Y Cerddor* (1914), p. 18, cf. ibid. (1904), p. 58). In the 1920s the Cwmaman Choral Society would exceed even this remarkable achievement with performances of Bach's B minor Mass and the *St. Matthew Passion*. Their conductor was a Cwmaman collier, Edward Lewis (1879–1941).   D. L. Davies, *A History of Cwmaman Institute 1866–1993* (Aberdare, 1995), pp. 62–3. W. J. Evans's son, and therefore Rees Evans's grandson, was Ifor L. Evans, principal of the University College of Wales, Aberystwyth, 1934–52.

66   John H. Davies, op. cit., p. 145.

Notes to Chapter 4

1   *Merthyr Express*, 10 August 1901.

2   Ibid., 27 August 1904.

3   NLW, D. Rhys Phillips MSS, no. 127, p. 36.

4   David Morgans, *Music and Musicians of Merthyr and District* (Merthyr, 1922), p. 12.

5   D. Rhys Phillips MSS, p. 37; Huw Williams, 'Brass bands, jazz bands, choirs: aspects of music in Merthyr Tydfil', *Merthyr Historian*, 3 (1980), pp. 98–111.

6   Morgans, op. cit., p. 28.

7   NLW MS 4381B, M. O. Jones MSS, no. 11, 'Choral singing in Wales', p.5. The account of Ieuan Ddu's career which follows is based on M. O. Jones MSS, 4381B; M. O. Jones, *Bywgraffiaeth Cerddorion Cymreig* (Cardiff, 1890), pp. 131–3; and Morgans, op. cit., pp. 28–33.

8   Gwyn A. Williams, *The Merthyr Rising* (London, 1978), pp. 86–7; NLW MSS 4381B, pp. 5–6.

 9 NLW MS 21457D, 'Life of Megan Watts Hughes', p. 27. For the provenance of
    this manuscript memoir of his sister by John Watts, see Huw Williams, *Taro Tant*
    (Denbigh, 1994), pp. 65–8.
10 D. Morgans, op. cit., pp. 50–2; NLW MS 4318 B, pp. 6–7.
11 *Y Cerddor* (1893), p. 52.
12 For Moses Davies, see Morgans, op. cit., pp. 19–27; M. O. Jones, *Bywgraffiaeth*,
    pp. 12–13.
13 NLW MS 4318 B, p. 13.
14 Morgans, op. cit., p. 24.
15 Ibid., p. 24.
16 For Rosser Beynon see M. O. Jones, *Bywgraffiaeth*, pp. 2–4; Morgans, op. cit.,
    pp. 38–40.
17 Morgans, op. cit., p. 48.
18 Ibid., pp. 13–14.
19 *Merthyr Express*, 22 June 1901; Morgans, op. cit., pp. 12–13.
20 Morgans, op. cit., pp. 214–17.
21 Ibid., p. 219.
22 *Y Cerddor Cymreig* (1872), p. 54.
23 W. R. Lambert, *Drink and Sobriety in Victorian Wales* (Cardiff, 1983), p. 26.
24 NLW MS 21457D, Megan Watts Hughes, p. 16.
25 Andrew J. Croll, 'Civilising the urban: popular culture, public space and urban
    meaning, Merthyr c.1870–1914' (University of Wales Ph.D. diss., Cardiff,
    1997), p. 105.
26 NLW MS 21457D, 'Megan Watts Hughes', p. 23.
27 *Rhondda Leader,* 12 November 1910.
28 NLW MS 21457D, 'Megan Watts Hughes', pp. 49–50.
29 *Y Cerddor Cymreig* (1864), pp. 87, 95.
30 Ibid. (1867), p. 39.
31 NLW MS 21457D, 'Megan Watts Hughes', p. 43.
32 *Merthyr Express*, 13 July 1901; NLW, D. Rhys Phillips MSS, p. 38; Morgans, op. cit.,
    p. 221.
33 NLW, D. Rhys Phillips MSS, pp. 13–14; NLW 8661D 'Joseph Parry: A Draft
    Autobiography', p. 3 (holograph).
34 *Y Cerddor Cymreig* (1862), p. 95.
35 *Merthyr Express*, 27 July 1901.
36 D. Emlyn Evans, 'Music in Wales', NLW MS 8034D, vol. 2 (2 April 1904).
37 NLW, Alaw Ddu MSS, p. 114, letter of June 1880 (in Welsh).
38 For a vivid evocation of the pestilential living conditions of Merthyr in the
    1840s, when the average age at death of colliers, miners and ironworkers was
    seventeen years, see Ieuan Gwynedd Jones, in Glanmor Williams (ed.), *Merthyr
    Politics* (Cardiff, 1966), pp. 35–8; idem, *Communities* (Llandysul, 1987),
    pp. 239–62; idem, *Mid-Victorian Wales* (Cardiff, 1992), ch. 2, pp. 24–53.
39 T. Herbert, 'The Virtuosi of Merthyr', *Llafur*, 5 (1988), pp. 60–7.
40 Idem, 'A softening influence: R. T. Crawshay and the Cyfarthfa Band', *Merthyr
    Historian*, 5 (1992), pp. 35–42.
41 E. Keri Evans, *Cofiant Joseph Parry* (Cardiff, 1921). Parry acknowledged and
    repaid the debt by becoming the first composer of any status to write for the

brass band with 'Tydfyl', his arrangement for brass of the overture to his oratorio *Emmanuel*.

42   Ieuan Gwynedd Jones, in *Merthyr Politics*, p. 36.

43   Joseph Parry in a letter to Moses Davies's son Mynorydd, *Y Cerddor Cymreig* (1869), p. 30.

44   *Y Cerddor Cymreig* (1865), p. 77.

45   Ibid. (1864), pp. 87–8.

46   Quoted in E. Keri Evans, op. cit., p. 104.

47   For instance in Parry's counterpoint, Dulais Rhys points to the over-long and ultimately uninteresting choral fugue that concludes his winning 1863 motet at Swansea. D. Rhys 'Joseph Parry: ei fywyd a'i waith' (University of Wales Ph.D. thesis, Bangor, 1986), pp. 316–17. Much of this section draws on Dr Rhys's thesis, E. Keri Evans, op. cit., and Owain T. Edwards, *Joseph Parry 1841–1903* (Cardiff, 1970).

48   Morgans, op. cit., pp.101–2.

49   *Y Gerddorfa* 1 (1878), p. 43.

50   Ibid. (1914), p. 6.

51   Rhys, op. cit., p. 338.

52   *Musical Herald* (October 1892), p. 297; *Musical Times* (1892), p. 611.

53   *The Times*, 13 May 1880. 'Dr Parry . . . a musician who esteems his art . . . possesses more than a common degree of learning . . . If we add that Dr Parry's melodies are as yet dependent on his memory at least as much as on spontaneous production, and that he writes judiciously for the voices, we have said enough . . .'

54   E. Keri Evans, op. cit., pp. 93–106.

55   As an example of Parry's erratic impulses as an adjudicator, when he discovered the identity of 'Corelli', the composer to whom he had awarded the prize at the Merthyr National Eisteddfod in 1881, he tried to get the decision changed. The notoriety of W. Jarrett Roberts ('Corelli') for 'getting at' adjudicators earned him the nickname 'Jarring' Roberts among eisteddfod secretaries.

56   For the first and subsequent performances of *Blodwen* see Huw Williams, 'Canmlwyddiant Blodwen', in *Taro Tant*, pp. 84–89; idem, '*Canu'r Bobol*' (Denbigh, 1978), pp. 50–1; D. Rhys, 'Joseph Parry: ei fywyd a'i waith', pp. 125–6.

57   Quoted in O. T. Edwards, op. cit., p. 65.

58   *Yr Ysgol Gerddorol*, 7 (July 1878), p. 50.

59   *Y Cerddor* (1913), p. 133.

60   An ally of Cyril Jenkins (1889–1978) in attacking 'this fatuous countryman of his' was the critic Gerald Cumberland, to whom 'Joseph Parry in the strangle-hold of Gioacchino Rossini is a ludicrous and repellent sight'. G. Cumberland, *Written in Friendship* (1923), pp. 173–80.

61   Cyril Jenkins, 'Dr Joseph Parry', *The Sackbut* (November 1921), pp. 19–22; G. Cumberland, 'Cyril Jenkins: Musician and Composer', *Wales*, 1 (1913), pp. 34–8. Cyril Jenkins's antagonistic attitude to Joseph Parry gained most publicity after the chapter he contributed to E. Keri Evans, *Cofiant Dr Joseph Parry* (1921), pp. 239–44. It won him few friends in Wales, as the organist T. D. Edwards discovered when, on arriving at Sardis Chapel, Pontypridd, to give a

recital, he found 'a strong feeling of indignation among certain members of the audience' because of his inclusion of a piece by Cyril Jenkins in the programme, which had been printed before Jenkins's attack on Parry. The chairman's announcement that the piece would not be performed was received with cries of 'Hear, hear'. 'Cyril Jenkins and Joseph Parry', undated (1921?), loose press cutting in *The Provincial Musical Agency and Concert Directory*, NLW shelf mark ML3790, p. 96.

62 For a dramatic account see Emrys Pride, *Rhondda My Valley Brave* (Risca, 1975), pp. 40–51.

63 *Cerddor y Cymry* (October 1883), pp. 37–8. For a warts-and-all portrait of Joseph Parry by one who knew him well, see the four-part assessment of David Jenkins in *Y Cerddor* (November 1913–February 1914).

64 D. Morgans, op. cit., pp. 102–3.

Notes to Chapter 5

1 *Merthyr Express* (*ME*), 13 March 1880.

2 *ME*, 10 April 1880.

3 *ME*, 26 March 1881.

4 *ME*, 24 July 1889.

5 *ME*, 10 August 1889

6 *ME*, 30 May 1896.

7 *ME*, 10 August 1901.

8 *ME*, 22 May 1880.

9 *Western Mail*, 7 April 1874.

10 *ME*, 29 August 1891.

11 *South Wales Daily News*, 31 August 1880.

12 *ME*, 25 June 1887.

13 *ME*, 29 August, 1885.

14 *ME*, 29 August, 5 September 1885.

15 *ME*, 15 November 1884.

16 *ME*, 22 November 1884.

17 Lest it be thought such behaviour was peculiar only to Dowlais, we can note a comparable incident at an Ebbw Vale eisteddfod in aid of a chapel renovation fund. When the chief choral prize was withheld, a large number of disappointed choristers ascended the platform and commenced a heated argument with the adjudicator, who came in for a further hostile reception outside the hall. *ME*, 7 March 1896.

18 *ME*, 29 December 1888, 29 June 1895.

19 *ME*, 30 May 1896.

20 *ME*, 16 May 1891.

21 This identification did not extend to more dubious forms of musical expression like lewd ballads, as a defendant discovered on being prevented from singing an indecent Welsh song in Market Square in front of women and children. His defence that he had sung the same song at Aberdare, Aberaman, Pontypridd and Maesteg without any complaints failed to impress the magistrate. *ME*,

20 October 1894. I owe this reference to Dr Andy Croll.

22   *ME*, 29 August 1891, *Merthyr and Dowlais Times*, 15 January 1892.

23   *ME*, 11 November 1891.

24   *ME*, 8 April 1893.

25   *ME*, 2 February 1895.

26   Ieuan Gwynedd Jones, in Glanmor Williams (ed.), *Merthyr Politics* (Cardiff, 1966), p. 39.

27   G. Crossick and H. G. Haupt, *The Petite Bourgeoisie in Europe 1780–1914* (London, 1995), pp. 202–15.

28   Andrew J. Croll, 'Civilising the urban: popular culture, public space and urban meaning, Merthyr *c.*1870–1914' (University of Wales Ph.D. diss., Cardiff, 1997), p. 116.

29   *ME*, 16 June 1886.

30   D. Morgans, *Music and Musicians of Merthyr and District* (Merthyr, 1922), p. 161; *ME*, 30 January 1892. 'All grades of the community' were represented at her funeral, noted the *Merthyr and Dowlais Times* 29 January 1892. I owe this reference to Andy Croll. For Meta Scott, see also Morgans, op. cit., p. 161.

31   *ME*, 31 August 1889.

32   *ME*, 8 September 1888.

33   *ME* 12 January 1895.

34   *ME*, 15 December 1906.

35   Cecil Price, *The Professional Theatre in Wales* (Swansea, 1984), p. 18.

36   *ME*, 12 March 1881.

37   *ME*, 3 January 1885.

38   *ME*, 4 June 1887.

39   *ME*, 27 April 1901.

40   *ME*, 23 April 1892.

41   *ME*, 2 September 1893.

42   *ME*, 26 January 1895.

43   *ME*, 10 January 1903. The three Dowlais FRCOs – Harry Evans and his pupils E. T. Davies and W. J. Watkins – occupied the house called Cartrefle between the old County School and Merthyr General Hospital. Sydney Northcote called them 'the Cartrefle Dynasty'. See Glynne Jones, 'The end of the "Cartrefle dynasty"', *Welsh Music*, 3, no. 6 (Spring 1970), pp. 11–15.

44   Morgans, op. cit., pp. 155–8; *ME*, 30 May 1896, 30 July 1897.

45   *ME*, 19 February 1881.

46   *Y Cerddor* (1896), pp. 74–5.

47   Huw Williams, *Canu'r Bobol* (Denbigh, 1978), p. 86.

48   *ME*, 11 and 18 April 1885.

49   *ME*, 19 September 1885.

50   *ME*, 23 April 1887.

51   P. Scholes (ed.), *The Mirror of Music 1844–1944* (London, 1947), vol. 2, p. 644.

52   *ME*, 29 December 1888.

53   *ME*, 7 May, 22 October 1892; *Merthyr and Dowlais Times*, 10 March 1893.

54   J. Bennett, *Forty Years of Music* (London, 1908), p. 398.

55   *Y Cerddor* (1896), p. 74.

56   *ME*, 27 May 1893.

57 *ME*, 8 July 1895, 30 May 1896.
58 *ME*, 3 August 1895.
59 *ME*, 30 May 1896.
60 *ME*, 25 September 1895.
61 *ME*, 10 August 1895.
62 On their dissolution, R. C. Jenkins's Llanelli choir divided their accumulated monies between the conductor (£50), secretary (£25), accompanist (£30) and 11*s*. 1*d*. (56p) for each chorister, *Y Cerddor* (1892), p. 18.
63 *ME*, 6 June 1896.
64 Ibid.
65 *Y Cerddor* (1896), p. 4; *ME*, 20 June 1896.
66 *ME*, 30 May 1896.
67 In May 1892 the Dowlais Harmonic Society was addressed at rehearsal by the Revd Rowe Evans (Protestant) *and* Father Bruno (Roman Catholic). For the representative aspects of Merthyr choralism, see Croll, op. cit., pp. 107–8.
68 *ME*, 4 July 1896.
69 Bennett, op. cit., p. 399.
70 F. Cowen, *My Art and My Friends* (1913), p. 307. Cowen (1852–1935) was an orchestral conductor and composer, and permanent conductor of the Cardiff Festival, 1902–10.
71 *South Wales Daily News*, 5 August 1897.
72 *ME*, 31 July 1897.
73 *ME*, 7 August 1897.
74 Bennett, op. cit., p. 400.
75 *ME*, 14 August 1897; *Musical Herald* (September 1897), p. 288.
76 *ME*, 14 August 1897.
77 Alexander Mackenzie (1847–1935) was a conductor and composer, and principal of the Royal Academy of Music from 1888.
78 *Musical Times* (September 1893), quoted in Scholes, *Mirror of Music,* p. 643.
79 Bennett, op. cit., p. 400.
80 *Y Cerddor* (1893), p. 33.
81 *Y Cerddor* (1897), p. 115; *ME*, 21 August 1897.
82 The following section follows the rumpus through the eyes of the *Merthyr Express* during August 1897.
83 *ME*, 13 August 1897.
84 Quoted in *Y Cerddor* (1897), p. 124.
85 *ME*, 21 and 14 August 1897.
86 *Musical Herald* (April 1899), p. 113.
87 *ME*, 4 April 1903.
88 *ME*, 27 August 1904.
89 *ME*, 10 September 1904.
90 *Y Cerddor* (1896), pp. 134–5.
91 *Musical Herald* (August 1901), pp. 227–9.
92 *ME*, 5 August 1893.
93 *ME*, 22 October (1892).
94 *Y Cerddor* (1895), p. 18.
95 Croll, op. cit., p. 109.

96 *Musical Herald* (August 1901), p. 228.

97 *Y Cerddor* (1900), p. 117.

98 *Musical Herald* (September 1903), pp. 262–3; *Merthyr Express,* 16 May 1903.

99 *Musical Herald* (September1903), pp. 262–3.

100 *Musical Times* (1903), p. 598.

101 [R. Gwylfa Roberts], 'Trêf y gân – Dowlais', *Y Dysgedydd* (1932), pp. 113–22.

102 *Musical Herald* (August 1901), p. 228.

103 For Harry Evans's enlightened and constructive ideas on the then current state, future prospects and necessary reform of music in Wales, see *Musical Herald* (August 1901), pp. 227–9, Harry Evans, 'Music in Wales', *Young Wales,* 7 (1901), pp. 214–15, and idem, 'Welsh choral singing', in T. Stephens (ed.), *Wales Today and Tomorrow* (Cardiff, 1908), pp. 323–5.

104 *Y Cerddor* (1909), p. 131.

105 Ibid. (1912), p. 139; (1914), p. 29.

106 Ibid. (1914), p. 91. See obituary in *Western Mail,* 24 July 1914. For Harry Evans, whose son was the noted royal physician Horace (Lord) Evans (1903–63), see also Glynne Jones, 'Harry Evans (1873–1914)' in *Welsh Music,* 4, no. 5 (Winter 1973/4), pp. 39–48.

107 See tributes by Bantock, McNaught and others in *Musical Times* Competition Festival Record Supplement (August 1914).

Notes to Chapter 6

1 *Rhondda Leader,* 5 January 1907.

2 Ibid., 19 January 1907.

3 These paragraphs are based on the *Rhondda Leader* 12 and 26 January, 9, 16 and 23 February, 2 and 9 March 1907 and 18 January, 23 February and 9 March 1908.

4 Ibid., 9 and 30 November 1907. When Mary King Sarah won the soprano solo at Caernarfon in 1906, the second place went to Master Ivor Novello Davies.

5 Ibid., 26 October 1907.

6 What follows is based on *Rhondda Leader,* 4 January 1908.

7 *Merthyr Express,* 27 May 1893.

8 *Rhondda Leader,* 9 December 1899.

9 Ibid., 14 July 1900.

10 Ibid., 12 May 1900. In point of detail, *Messiah* was not unknown in the Rhondda. Its first Rhondda performance was given by M. O. Jones's United Choir in September 1876, and repeated the following year: individual choruses from it were familiar to Rhondda choirs even fifteen years before that. John Haydn Davies, 'Rhondda choral music in Victorian times', in K. S. Hopkins (ed.), *Rhondda Past and Future* (Ferndale, 1975), pp. 144, 152.

11 *Rhondda Leader,* 4 August 1900.

12 Rhys Davies, *Print of a Hare's Foot* (London, 1969), p. 87. He added, 'Our concerts stifled me.'

13 *Rhondda Leader,* 29 December 1900, 5 January 1901.

14 Ibid., 26 January 1901.

15 Ibid., 9 March, 11 May 1901.

16 John Haydn Davies, op. cit., p. 129.

17 E. D. Lewis, *The Rhondda Valleys* (London, 1959), pp. 235, 239; idem, 'Population changes and social life 1860 to 1914', in K. S. Hopkins, op. cit., pp. 110–28.

18 *Y Cerddor Cymreig* (1861), p. 46.

19 Ibid. (1867), p. 44.

20 I owe this point to Dr Rhidian Griffiths

21 John Haydn Davies, op. cit., p. 132.

22 *Y Cerddor Cymreig* (1862), p. 159.

23 *Y Gerddorfa* (1872), p. 6.

24 *Cerddor y Tonic Sol-fa* (1874), p. 43.

25 *Cerddor y Cymry* (1884), p. 105.

26 NLW MS 4383E (M. O. Jones MSS no. 13), 'History of Ystradyfodwg', p. 190.

27 *Y Cerddor Cymreig* (1871), p. 38; *Cronicl y Cerddor*, 3 (1882–3).

28 *Cerddor y Cymry* (September 1883), p. 29.

29 *Y Cerddor Cymreig* (1878), p. 65; *Y Gerddorfa* (1878), p. 70.

30 *Y Cerddor* (1898), p. 15; John Haydn Davies, op. cit., pp. 135–6.

31 For Taliesin Hopkins, *Y Cerddor* (1896), p. 110.

32 For M. O. Jones, *Y Cerddor* (July 1897, September and November 1908); *Rhondda Leader*, 1 August 1908.

33 NLW MSS 4381B, pp. 12–13.

34 NLW MSS 4371–84

35 C. Williams, *Democratic Rhondda* (Cardiff, 1996), p. 17; E. D. Lewis, op. cit., p. 239.

36 For Tom Stephens, *Y Cerddor* (1897), pp. 26–7; *Rhondda Leader*, 27 January 1906.

37 *Excelsior: The Voice of the Treorchy Male Choir* (Treorchy, 1993), p. 36.

38 A colourful account of the events at the 1893 World's Fair Eisteddfod at Chicago is to be found in Hywel Teifi Edwards, *Eisteddfod Ffair y Byd Chicago 1893* (Llandysul, 1990), esp. pp. 137–41.

39 *Musical Herald* (August 1898), p. 104.

40 John Haydn Davies, op. cit., pp. 137–40; for William Thomas, *Y Cerddor* (1896), p. 62.

41 'The Treorchy boys at Windsor', *Musical Herald* (January 1896), p. 21.

42 *Rhondda Leader*, 27 July 1901.

43 *Y Cerddor* (1895), p. 95.

44 The account that follows is based on: *Musical Herald* (January 1896) 'The Treorchy boys at Windsor', p. 21; *Western Mail*, 30 November 1895; the report in the *Pontypridd Chronicle*, published separately as *An Account of the Appearance of the Treorky Male Voice Choir before Her Majesty at Windsor Castle, on November 29th 1895* (Pontypridd, 1895); 'Respectable Welsh colliers', in *Excelsior* (op. cit.), pp. 6–12; Rhidian Griffiths 'Y gân orchfygol', in Hywel Teifi Edwards (ed.), *Cwm Rhondda* (Llandysul, 1996), pp. 184–93; NLW, William Thomas Collection, ex 1075.

45 Museum of Welsh Life, St Fagans, Cardiff: W. P. Thomas papers 1823/1–27; C. Williams, op. cit., pp. 51, 54. As a contribution to the public good, and to

keep restless Rhondda minds occupied, W. P. Thomas was instrumental in establishing an annual eisteddfod at Noddfa in the tense year of 1910. In 1912 male-voice choirs competed on Joseph Parry's 'Myfanwy' for £5 and an umbrella, as much a comment on the local climate as on W. P.'s machiavellian propensities, *Rhondda Leader*, 6 August 1912.

46   For William Jenkins, 'the Squire of Ystradfechan', see C. Williams, op. cit., pp. 37, 51; W. P. Thomas was Jenkins's protégé, ibid., p. 61.

47   *Y Cerddor* (1900), p.3.

48   NLW, D. Emlyn Evans papers 8033D, vol. 1 (9 December 1899); *Musical Herald* (January 1900), p. 23.

49   *An Account of the Appearance of the Treorky Male Voice Choir*, op. cit., p. 10.

50   *Baner ac Amserau Cymru*, 4 December 1894, p. 4 (quoted in the original Welsh in Rhidian Griffiths, 'Y gân orchfygol', p. 19). In similar vein, *Y Cerddor* (1896, p. 7) was proud 'the "boys" have brought honour on themselves, their conductor and the land of their birth, not only by their performance but by their respectable and gentlemanly behaviour'.

51   Reported in the *Rhondda Leader* 26 January, 23 February and 9 March 1907.

52   Ibid., 25 September 1907; NLW, William Thomas collection, 'A Few Press Notes, Brochure from their Recent Successful Around the World Tour'.

53   John Haydn Davies, op. cit., p. 137.

54   *Rhondda Leader*, 1 August 1903.

55   Ibid., 30 December 1899. One of the reasons for this was the increasing dominance in eisteddfodau of music: 'poets and poems, englyn and such like effusions will soon be elbowed out of the way in eisteddfodau. Music and musicians seem to monopolize the whole proceedings' (ibid., 4 April 1903). Accessible, non-language-specific, the role increasingly allocated to music in late-nineteenth-century Wales involved a transformation in the character of cultural institutions like the eisteddfod, the concomitant functional displacement of the bards and literary activities being a price Victorian Wales was prepared to pay in order to forge a distinctive but inclusive national identity that could embrace all its residents. The adoption of amateur rugby football fulfilled the same role for similar ideological reasons; in each case a further price was 'disorderly scenes and rowdyism'. See 'Sporting success and social function in Wales 1880–1914', in Gareth Williams, *1905 and All That* (Llandysul, 1991), pp. 68–89.

56   *Rhondda Leader*, 27 January 1906.

57   Ibid., 27 September 1906.

58   William Thomas quoted in the *Musical Herald* (July 1902), p. 201. See also *Rhondda Leader*, 2 January 1904 on this openly acknowledged system among all Welsh competing choirs of hiring paid singers.

59   For the assertion, in the context of rugby football, that 'professionalism is rampant in the Rhondda Valley', see G. Williams, op. cit., p. 155.

60   *Rhondda Leader*, 22 December 1906.

61   I owe this expressive phrase to Dr Bill Jones's splendid evocation of the choral rivalries of the American Welsh: W. D. Jones, *Wales in America: Scranton and the Welsh 1860–1920* (Cardiff, 1993), p. 139.

62   *Rhondda Leader*, 5 March 1904.

63   Ibid., 21 April 1900.

64 *Rhondda Leader*, 5 January 1907. For J. T. Jones, *Y Cerddor* (1910), p. 15.

65 Ibid., 2 December 1899.

66 Ibid., 4 May 1901.

67 Ibid., 25 May 1901.

68 Ibid., 17 September 1904, 24 November 1906.

69 Ibid., 17 September 1904.

70 D. Russell, *Popular Music in England 1840–1914*, pp. 196–7.

71 *Rhondda Leader*, 18 February 1911.

72 Ibid., 15 June, 1901, 9 December 1911.

73 Ibid., 8 August 1903, 23 June 1906.

74 Ibid., 21 May 1904.

75 Ibid., 20 April 1912.

76 Ibid., 23 March 1912.

77 Ibid., 31 October 1908.

78 C. Williams, op. cit., p. 18.

79 *Rhondda Leader*, 22 January 1901.

80 Ibid., 25 January 1902.

81 Ibid., 14 March 1903.

82 Ibid., 4 April 1903.

83 Ibid., 14 April 1900, 22 April 1911.

84 Ibid., 30 December 1899.

85 Ibid., 14 January 1905, 5 January 1907, 13 June 1908.

86 Ibid., 4 February 1911, 18 January 1902.

87 Ibid., 1 and 8 May 1909.

88 Ibid., 26 June 1909.

89 Ibid., 27 January 1900, 5 April 1902.

90 Ibid., 1 June 1907, 18 September 1909.

91 Ibid., 6 and 13 May 1911; D. Russell, op. cit., p. 238.

92 NLW MS 8034D, D. Emlyn Evans papers, 'Music in Wales 1899–1912', vol. 2 (12 July 1902).

93 *Rhondda Leader*, 18 January 1908.

94 Ibid., 30 December 1905.

95 Ibid., 1 January 1910.

96 John Hughes, a Rhosllannerchrugog collier, former student of Walford Davies at Aberystwyth and brother of Arwel Hughes, became conductor in 1924, remaining until 1942. He was responsible for the evening concerts at the Treorchy National Eisteddfod 1928, conducting the Bach B minor Mass, *Elijah*, *The Dream of Gerontius* and a Christmas concert at Noddfa in 1934 consisting entirely of Bach motets and chorales. See H. J. Hughes (ed.) *Gŵr wrth Gerdd: John Hughes 1896–1968* (Llandysul, 1973).

97 *Rhondda Leader*, 30 December 1911.

98 Ibid., 7 January 1911.

99 H. C. Colles, *Walford Davies* (Oxford, 1944), pp. 121–2; D. I. Allsobrook, *Music for Wales* (Cardiff, 1992), p. 92.

100 D. Smith, 'Tonypandy 1910: definitions of community', *Past and Present*, 87 (May 1980), p. 171. For the Rhondda's changing cultural climate at the turn of the century, see E. D. Lewis in K. S. Hopkins, op. cit., pp. 123–7.

Notes to Chapter 7

1   Anthony Jones, *Welsh Chapels* (Stroud, 1996), p. 118.
2   *Musical Herald* (October 1892), p. 296.
3   H. C. Banister, *George Alexander Macfarren* (London, 1890), p. 368.
4   Joseph Bennett, in *Transactions of the Royal National Eisteddfod of Wales 1883* (Cardiff, 1884), pp. 432–3.
5   Harry Evans, in *Musical Herald* (July 1902), p. 201; Barnby, quoted in John Graham, *A Century of Welsh Music* (London, 1923), p. 43; *Musical Herald* (May 1898), p. 139.
6   *Musical Herald* (May 1898), p. 139, quoting the *South Wales Argus* (Newport).
7   John Spencer Curwen, quoted in 'The eisteddfod and popular music in Wales', *Y Cymmrodor*, 5 (1882), p. 287; Macfarren, in *Transactions of the Royal National Eisteddfod 1883*, p. 450; Harry Evans, 'Music in Wales', *Young Wales*, 7 (1901), p. 204.
8   *Y Cerddor* (1901), pp. 105–7.
9   NLW, D. Emlyn Evans papers, Press Cuttings, 'Music in Wales 1899–1912', 4 vols. (NLW MSS 8033D–8036D), vol. 1 (20 October 1900).
10 D. Emlyn Evans, 'Music in Wales', vol. 3 (10 August 1907), reacting to an article in *Musical Times* (August 1907), p. 526. For the list in full, see p. 188 below.
11 *Y Cerddor* (1902), p. 128.
12 Ibid., (1901), p. 109.
13 D. Emlyn Evans, 'Music in Wales', vol. 2 (4 October 1902).
14 Ibid., vol. 4 (24 September 1910); *Musical Herald* (September 1901), p. 264.
15 *Y Cerddor* (1901), pp. 105–7.
16 Ibid. (1901), p. 111.
17 D. Emlyn Evans, 'Music in Wales', vol. 1 (5 October 1901); *Y Cerddor* (1902), p. 118
18 Elfed Jones, *Côr Meibion y Penrhyn: Ddoe a Heddiw* (Denbigh, 1984); *Y Cerddor* (1904), p. 57.
19 R. Nettel, *Music in the Five Towns 1840–1914* (London, 1944), pp. 57–8.
20 For Whewell see *Musical Herald* (January 1910); Nettel, op. cit., pp. 56ff.
21 Partisans of the Five Towns like Reginald Nettel believed that as a result of a sequence of English victories, 'the Welsh changed the date of their Festivals and the new dates never seemed to suit the Potteries, so the Welsh recovered the choral prestige they enjoy to this day' (op. cit., p. 59).
22 *Western Mail*, 24 December 1903.
23 The International Male Voice Contest, Cardiff, Boxing Day 1903, was fully reported in the *Western Mail*, *South Wales Daily News*, and *Musical Herald* (January 1904), pp. 19–23.
24 *Western Mail*, 28 December 1903.
25 For Nesbitt's Manchester Orpheus, see *Musical Herald* (January and March 1904).
26 *Y Cerddor* (1908), p. 113.
27 Graham, op. cit., p. 39; *Y Cerddor* (1902), p. 47.
28 R. Rogers, 'Choral training in Wales', *6th Annual Report of the National Eisteddfod* (Cardiff, 1887), pp. 76–82; Graham, op. cit., pp. 46–7.

29 Rogers, op. cit., p. 79.

30 *Cerddor y Cymry* (September 1994), p. 105, quoting Bennett in the *Musical Times*.

31 Quoted in *Y Cerddor* (1892), pp. 126–8. For the view of south Wales choirs as vulgar (*canu claptrap*) see *Y Cerddor* (1900), p. 114; (1903), pp. 1–2; (1904), p. 75.

Notes to Chapter 8

1 N. Temperley (ed.), *Music in Britain: The Romantic Age 1800–1914* (London, 1981), p. 7.

2 Rhidian Griffiths, 'Cyhoeddi cerddoriaeth yng Nghymru yn y cyfnod 1860–1914' (Ph.D. diss., University of Wales, Aberystwyth, 1991), p. 50.

3 D. Emlyn Evans papers, NLW MSS 8033D–8036D, 'Music in Wales 1895–1912', 4 vols., vol. 2 (23 April 1904).

4 These and other biographical facts are drawn from the memoir written by his brother, E. Keri Evans, *Cofiant D. Emlyn Evans* (Carmarthen, 1919), and *Musical Herald* (April 1892).

5 E. Keri Evans, op. cit., p. 28.

6 *Y Cerddor* (1896), p. 15; (1895), p. 72.

7 Ibid. (1904), pp. 121–2.

8 Ibid. (1905), pp. 8, 21.

9 *Musical Herald* (April 1892), p. 101.

10 'The repetition of the same rhythmic pattern throughout, which could be merely boring in some hands . . . gives the tune a hypnotic power. The problem in using this tune outside Wales is in finding words strong enough to sing it.' Alan Luff, *Welsh Hymns and their Tunes* (1990), p. 208.

11 English-language 'Notes and opinions' appeared in *Y Cerddor* for the first time in 1892.

12 D. Emlyn Evans, 'Music in Wales', vol. 1 (20 October 1900).

13 *Y Cerddor* (1889), pp. 29, 54; (1890), pp. 16–17.

14 Ibid. (1901), p. 26; (1910), p. 66.

15 D. Emlyn Evans, 'Music in Wales', vol. 1 (15 March 1902).

16 *Western Mail*, quoted in *Y Cerddor* (1896), p. 54.

17 D. Emlyn Evans, 'Music in Wales', vol. 1 (20 January 1900); vol. 2 (12 July 1902).

18 E. Keri Evans in *Y Dysgedydd* (1919), p. 241.

19 Cyril Jenkins, 'Music in Wales', *Welsh Outlook* (March 1913), pp. 133–4. In fairness, this was never claimed by, or on behalf of, the brothers Greenish.

20 His early life in Trecastell is recalled by D. B. Evans, *Y Cerddor* (1916), pp. 22–3.

21 The assessment of David Jenkins that follows is based on J. Herbert Jones, *Er Cof am yr Athro David Jenkins gan naw o'i Gydnabod* (Liverpool, 1935); a series of articles by J. Lloyd Williams in *Y Wawr*, 4 (1916–17); *Welsh Outlook*, 3 (1916), pp. 6–7; *Young Wales*, 1, pp. 65–7; D. H. Lewis, in *Y Traethodydd*, 3rd series (1957), pp. 168–73; the tribute by David de Lloyd in *The Dragon*, 38 (1915–16); and Jenkins's own contributions to *Y Cerddor* (1889–1915).

22   *Y Traethodydd* (1957), pp. 171–2; *Y Wawr*, 4 (1917), p. 73; *Welsh Outlook*, 3 (1916), pp. 6–7.

23   *Y Cerddor* (1904), p. 75.

24   Ibid. (1900), p. 117; (1901), p. 71.

25   Ibid. (1898), p. 33; (1904), pp. 85–6.

26   Ibid. (1889), p. 63; (1901), p. 74.

27   Luff, *Welsh Hymns and their Tunes*, pp. 210–11. Jenkins's tune 'Bod Alwyn', like Joseph Parry's 'Sirioldeb', is uncomfortably close to the mellifluous style of J. B. Dykes. 'Penlan' mediates between this and the Welsh rhetorical.

28   *Y Cerddor* (1901), p. 71.

29   Ibid. (1905), pp. 22–3, 29, 77. The revival caused the cancellation of many eisteddfodau at Christmas 1904, e.g. at Aberdare, Merthyr, Dowlais, Aberystwyth. *Y Cerddor* (1905), p. 15.

30   At least the 1904–5 revival. The Revd Peter Price wrote a notorious letter published in the *Western Mail*, 31 January 1905, hostile to the 'uncultured' Evan Roberts and the superficiality of his campaign, drawing attention to the fact that he himself was 'B.A. (Hons.) Mental and Moral Sciences Tripos, Cambridge'.

31   D. Jenkins, 'The working class and music in Wales', *National Eisteddfod Association Reports, 1882* (Wrexham, 1883), pp. 76–81. Joseph Parry, who set up his own music colleges in Aberystwyth, Swansea and Cardiff in the 1880s, echoes Jenkins's proposals in his paper 'A musical college for Wales', ibid., pp. 82–7.

32   *Y Cerddor* (1913), pp. 1–2.

33   Ibid. (1905), pp. 17–18; (1908), p. 123.

34   Ibid. (1908), p. 57.

35   Ibid. (1908), p. 123.

36   Ibid. (1916), p. 5.

37   Ibid. (1913), p. 34.

38   Ibid. (1908), p. 122; (1911), p. 9.

39   Ibid. (1911), p. 9.

40   Ibid., pp. 9–10; (1909), p. 9; (1910), p. 31.

41   Aberystwyth College Choral Society also performed *Jôb* and as Professor David de Lloyd drily observed, 'The vivid rendering of the chorus "The Sabeans fell upon their oxen" would readily be recalled by the students of those days for many years afterwards' (*The Dragon*, 38, p. 114). *Yr Ystorm* (The Storm) has long blown over, but as if in anticipation of the dire events about to unfold, it was performed by the Neath Choral Society under T. Hopkin Evans in December 1913 and at the Denbigh National Eisteddfod in 1939, where the patience of the *Musical Opinion*'s critic was sorely tried by 'this interminable and regrettable work' on which 'some fine singing by the choir and the soloist (David Lloyd) was wasted'. Norman Cameron, in *Musical Opinion* (September 1939), p. 1051. Professor Jenkins regarded his *Scenes in the Life of Moses* as his supreme achievement, but only the first movement was ever performed, at the Aberystwyth National Eisteddfod in 1916, conducted by J. T. Rees.

42   *Y Cerddor* (1906), p. 12.

43   Ibid. (1897), p. 33.

Notes to Chapter 9

1 Title of short story by Gwyn Thomas, *Selected Short Stories* (Bridgend, 1988), pp. 84–97.
2 *Punch*, 7 January 1914.
3 *Musical Times* (1897), p. 607; *Manchester Guardian,* quoted in *Musical Herald* (August 1898), p. 250.
4 W. C. Berwick Sayers, *Samuel Coleridge-Taylor: Musician* (London, 1915), pp. 119, 154–5.
5 See p. 102 above.
6 *Musical Herald* (June 1897), p. 189. The editor felt obliged to reply that 'we have never before heard a complaint of hustling and unfriendly remarks; the Welsh being, in our experience, singularly polite to visitors' (ibid.).
7 *Cronicl y Cerddor*, 2 (1881–2), p. 213; 1 (1880–1), pp. 127–8.
8 D. Emlyn Evans papers, NLW MSS 8033D–8036D, 'Music in Wales', vol. 2 (23 August 1904).
9 *Y Cerddor* (1896), p. 137; (1893), p. 21.
10 Ibid. (1897), p. 103.
11 Ibid. (1896), p. 54.
12 Ibid. (1898), pp. 113–14.
13 D. Emlyn Evans, 'Music in Wales', vol. 2 (10 September 1904).
14 *Rhondda Leader*, 2 December 1899.
15 *Y Cerddor* (1894), p. 79.
16 *Western Mail*, 9 August 1928. See also Hywel Teifi Edwards (ed.), *Cwm Rhondda* (Llandysul, 1996), pp. 200–1. The correspondent of the *Musical Times*, noting that 'it would be difficult to imagine anything less supportive of industrial unrest' than the sight – and sound, for three and a half hours – of the eighteen male choirs competing at the Corwen National Eisteddfod in 1919, was inclined to wonder 'why our none too economical government does not spend a few thousand pounds on male voice choralism as an antidote to Bolshevism', *Musical Times*, September 1919, p. 475.
17 *Musical Times* (September 1903), p. 599.
18 Hywel Teifi Edwards, *Gŵyl Gwalia* (Llandysul, 1980), pp. 291–9.
19 John Spencer Curwen, quoted in (anon), 'The eisteddfod and popular music in Wales', *Y Cymmrodor*, 5 (1882), pp. 286–7.
20 On the appropriation of cultural practices see Roger Chartier, *Cultural History: Between Practices and Representations* (Cambridge, 1988).
21 'An extraordinarily crude tool for the description of social reality', according to Hugh Cunningham in F. M. L. Thompson (ed.), *The Cambridge Social History of Britain 1750–1950* (Cambridge, 1980), vol. 2, pp. 289–90.
22 *Rhondda Leader*, 30 December, 1899.
23 *Musical Herald* (September, 1903), p. 263.
24 Gwyn A. Williams, *When was Wales?* (Harmondsworth, 1985), p. 187.
25 *Y Cerddor* (1897), pp. 33, 115.
26 J. Graham, *A Century of Welsh Music* (London, 1923), p. 4.
27 *Y Cerddor* (1891), p. 127.
28 D. Emlyn Evans, 'Music in Wales', vol. 2 (12 March 1904).

29   *Y Cerddor Cymreig* (1863), p. 59; (1867), p. 4.

30   Ibid., (1867), p. 44; (1869), p. 59.

31   Ibid. (1867), p. 59; (1869), p. 55; *Y Cerddor* (1894), p. 11. These parties may
     have owed something too to the mid-century popularity of the Christy
     Minstrels, imitators of Edwin P. Christy's troupe of 'nigger minstrels', with their
     blacked-up faces and cleverly composed songs (by Stephen Foster and others)
     laced with snatches of bogus African-American harmony. S. Sadie (ed.), *The
     New Grove Dictionary of Music and Musicians* (London, 1980), vol. 4, p. 377.

32   See ch. 6, pp. 125–6 above.

33   'The Treorchy boys at Windsor', *Musical Herald* (January 1896), p. 21.

34   C. R. Wiltshire, 'The British male voice choir: a history and contemporary
     assessment' (Ph.D. thesis, University of London, Goldsmith's College, 2 vols., 1993),
     ch. 1.

35   Wiltshire, op. cit., ch. 2.

36   Michael Hurd in N. Temperley (ed.), *Music in Britain: The Romantic Age
     1800–1914* (London, 1981), p. 243.

37   The phrase is attributed to Mendelssohn in the *Musical Times* (1900), p. 730.
     See also Wiltshire, op. cit., pp. 70–80; P. Scholes (ed.), *The Mirror of Music
     1844–1944*, vol. 1, pp. 57–8.

38   D. Emlyn Evans thought that not only 'Comrades' but even Protheroe's 'The
     Crusaders' (1891) were hackneyed *by 1901*, 'Music in Wales', vol. 1 (11 May 1901).

39   Twelve choirs competed on 'Martyrs' at the Liverpool National Eisteddfod in
     1884, the only time it has ever appeared as a National test piece. With Gounod's
     'Soldiers' Chorus', Parry's 'Pilgrims' Chorus' and Protheroe's 'The Crusaders'
     it was sung at the first concert of 500 male voices, a popular genre in late-
     twentieth-century Wales, held in November 1895 at Swansea's Albert Hall,
     when choirs from Neath to Carmarthen were conducted by Caradog. *Y Cerddor*
     (1895), p. 139.

40   M. de Rille appeared as adjudicator of his own 'Song of the Crusaders', and as
     conductor of a massed performance of 'Martyrs of the Arena', at the Cardiff
     International Competition at Christmas 1903. The test piece was considered to
     be particularly well suited to Welsh choirs' fervent style of singing; but it was
     Manchester Orpheus who won. See pp. 152–3 above.

41   Wynford Vaughan Thomas, *Madly in All Directions* (1967; 2nd edn, Carmarthen,
     1988), pp. 177–9.

42   Gwyn Thomas, in Gwyn Jones and Michael Quinn (eds.), *Fountains of Praise:
     University College of Wales, Cardiff 1883–1982* (Cardiff, 1983), p. 32.

43   *Musical Times* (1903), pp. 482, 453.

44   De Rille's 'Martyrs of the Arena' has lasted better than his other one-time
     favourite 'Destruction of Gaza', described by one English newspaper
     correspondent as 'the sort you need to hear if you are in search of evidence to
     disprove the assertion . . . that the singing male is an intelligent animal', after
     hearing twenty-eight choirs singing it at the 1927 Leicester Festival. *Birmingham
     Post*, 10 October 1927, quoted in Wiltshire, op. cit., p. 294.

45   E. Mackerness, *A Social History of English Music* (London, 1964), p. 9.

46   Wiltshire, op. cit., p. 240.

47   *Y Cerddor* (1913), p. 134.

48 *Musical Herald* (March 1905).

49 *Musical Times*, (August 1907), p. 526. The comparison was not lost on D. Emlyn Evans, 'Music in Wales', vol. 3 (8 October 1907).

50 *Musical Herald* (1890), p. 423; D. Russell, 'The popular musical societies of the Yorkshire textile district 1850–1914'(D.Phil. thesis, University of York, 1979), p. 202.

51 This memorable contest (8 August, 1964) was fought in front of 9,000 in the eisteddfod pavilion with another 20,000 listening outside. The competing choirs were arguably the finest in Wales at that time: Rhosllannerchrugog, Treorchy, Pontarddulais, Pendyrus, Morriston Orpheus and Manselton (Swansea). The adjudicators (the orchestral conductor Meredith Davies, Peter Gellhorn, chorus-master at Sadler's Wells, and Elfed Morgan) placed Treorchy first, one mark superior in each of the three pieces to Pontarddulais, with Pendyrus third and Morriston fourth.

52 *Y Cerddor* (1906), p. 55.

53 *South Wales Daily News*, 9 August 1913.

54 This fascination with the West, enhanced by the inherent attractiveness of the music, made Coleridge-Taylor's *Hiawatha* highly popular, and the composer himself a welcome adjudicator at Welsh eisteddfodau, a delight clearly reciprocated. See Sayers, op cit., pp. 119–20, 154–5; T. J. Morgan, *Diwylliant Gwerin* (Llandysul, 1972), p. 47. On the popularity of *Hiawatha's Wedding Feast* (1899), memorably described by the *Amman Valley Chronicle* as 'the stirring North American Mabinogi', see R. Stradling and M. Hughes, *The English Musical Renaissance 1860–1940* (London, 1993), pp. 197–8.

55 E. D. Lewis, *The Rhondda Valleys* (London, 1959), p. 286.

56 J. Geraint Jenkins, *Dre-fach Felindre and the Woollen Industry* (Llandysul, 1976), pp. 5–6.

57 On the musical, literary and political culture of the Aman Valley, see the chapters by Lyn Davies, Rhianydd Morgan, Huw Walters and Ioan Matthews in Hywel Teifi Edwards (ed.), *Cwm Aman* (Llandysul, 1996); articles by Huw Walters in the *South Wales Guardian*, 13 and 27 October 1977; and NLW, Gwilym R. Jones papers.

Notes to Chapter 10

1 Unpublished letter from Professor David Evans to *The Times*, sent 26 April 1918. Quoted in full in *Y Cerddor* (June 1918), p. 64.

2 David Ian Allsobrook, *Music for Wales* (Cardiff, 1992), pp. 86, 137.

3 Charles Reid, *Malcolm Sargent* (London, 1968), pp. 234–7.

4 *Musical Opinion* (September 1928), p. 1158.

5 Ibid. (September 1926), p. 1184.

6 William H. Howe in *Y Cerddor Newydd* (1926), p. 90.

7 *Merthyr Express*, 29 August 1885. See p. 84 above.

8 On these developments see Allsobrook, op. cit., *passim*.

9 Richard A. Baker, *Marie Lloyd: Queen of the Music Halls* (London, 1990), pp. 39–53; *Y Cerddor* (1915), p. 121.

10 Allsobrook, op. cit., p. 137; Gwilym Williams, *Cwmbach Male Choir: Half a Century of Song 1921–71* (Aberdare, 1971); Aldo Bacchetta and Glyn Rudd (compilers), *Porth and Rhondda Fach* (Stroud, 1996), pp. 101–3.

11 Quoted by Rhidian Griffiths, 'Dau gôr', in Hywel Teifi Edwards (ed.), *Cwm Tawe* (Llandysul, 1993), p. 204.

12 Gerald Cumberland, *Written in Friendship* (London, 1923), pp. 173–80.

13 This observation was made about the singing of Hubert Parry's 'Blest Pair of Sirens' in the chief choral competition at Treorchy in 1928, when 'the prevailing tendency was to sing Parry's suave polyphony in the manner of a martial chorus from *Judas Maccabaeus*'. *Musical Opinion* (September 1928), p. 1164.

14 H. S. Gordon, 'Song from a Welsh valley', *Radio Times*, 25 November 1933 quoted by Rhidian Griffiths, op. cit., p. 207.

15 *Musical Opinion* (September 1924), p. 1174.

16 John H. Davies, 'Rhondda choral music in Victorian times', in K. S. Hopkins (ed.), *Rhondda Past and Future*, p. 137.

17 There was more than a kernel of truth in the defiant words delivered by the actress Rachel Thomas in the film *Valley of Song* (1953): 'None of you could ever know what it means to me to sing that part. All the year it's cooking and washing and mending I am. But when "Messiah" came around I stopped being Mrs Lloyd undertaker. I was Mair Lloyd – contralto.' For this and other filmic representations of 'the land of song', see David Berry, *Wales and Cinema* (Cardiff, 1994), pp. 234–5.

18 Wyn Griffith, *The Welsh* (Harmondsworth, 1950), p. 130.

Select Bibliography

℘

A. Primary Sources

1. Manuscripts

National Library of Wales Aberystwyth:

Personal Papers
D. Emlyn Evans
David Jenkins
Gwilym R. Jones
M. O. Jones
Selwyn Jones
D. W. Lewis
W. J. Parry
D. Rhys Phillips
Daniel Protheroe and Rhys Morgan
J. T. Rees
W. T. Rees (Alaw Ddu)
John Thomas (Pencerdd Gwalia)
D. Vaughan Thomas
William Thomas

Manuscripts
Cwrtmawr Music MSS

4381 B	M. O. Jones, MS 11, 'Choral Singing in Wales'
4383 E	M. O. Jones, MS 13, 'History of Ystradyfodwg'
8033D–8036	D. Emlyn Evans, 'Music in Wales 1899–1912'
8840C	W. J. Parry, MS 108, 'The North Wales Choral Union'
9661D	Draft Autobiography of Joseph Parry
11116E	Cambrian Society MSS
21457D	'Life of Megan Watts Hughes', by her brother John Watts

Aberdare Central Library:
R. Ivor Parry, 'The history of Aberdare ' (unpublished, n.d.)

W. W. Price Collection:
  Aberdare Almanack (1893) (B33)
  Biography and genealogy (B33)
  Music (M3)

Museum of Welsh Life, Cardiff
W. P. Thomas Papers 1823/1–115.

2. Periodicals

Musical Herald
Musical Opinion
Musical Times
Tonic Sol-fa Reporter

Blodau Cerdd, 1852–3 (Aberystwyth)
Cerddor y Cymry, 1883–94 (Llanelli)
Cerddor y Tonic Sol-ffa, 1869–74 (Wrexham)
Cronicl y Cerddor, 1880–83 (Treherbert)
Greal y Corau, 1861–3 (Denbigh)
Perl Cerddorol, 1880 (Merthyr)
Y Cerbyd Cerddorol, 1860–1 (Holywell)
Y Cerddor, 1889–1921 (Wrexham)
Y Cerddor Cymreig, 1861–73 (Merthyr, Wrexham)
Y Cerddor Newydd, 1922–29 (Wrexham)
Y Cerddor, third series, 1930–39 (Wrexham)
Y Gerddorfa, 1872–81 (Pontypridd)
Y Solffaydd, 1891–2 (Pontarddulais)
Yr Ysgol Gerddorol, 1878–80 (Llanelli)

3. Books

(Place of publication London unless otherwise stated)
Banister, H. C., *George Alexander Macfarren* (1908).
Before the Queen: An Account of the Appearance of the Treorky Male Voice Choir . . . at Windsor Castle . . . November 29th, 1895 (Pontypridd, 1895).
Bennett, J., *Forty Years of Music* (1908).
Coward, H., *Reminiscences* (1911).
Cowen, F. H., *My Art and My Friends* (1913).
Davies, Clara Novello, *The Life I have Loved* (1940).
Edwards, O. M., *Tro i'r Gogledd, Tro i'r De* (Wrexham, 1958 edn).
Evans, E. Keri, *Cofiant Dr Joseph Parry* (Cardiff, 1921).
Griffith, F., *Notable Welsh Musicians of Today* (1896).
Griffiths, W. Ivander, *Record of over 50 Years Music, Temperance, Eisteddfod and Other Mission Work in Wales and Cumberland 1850–1903* (Workington, [1903]) .
Macfarren, W. C., *Memoirs: An Autobiography* (1905).
Parry, W. J., *Cofiant Tanymarian*, 2nd edn (Dolgellau, 1906).

Protheroe, Daniel, *Nodau Damweiniol a D'rawyd o Dro i Dro* (Liverpool, 1924).

Protheroe, W. R., *Griffith Rhys Jones* (Aberdare, 1911).

Richards, Brinley, *The Songs of Wales* (1873).

Richards, Brinley (ed.), *The South Wales Choral Union at the Crystal Palace . . . July 1873: Reports and Criticisms* (n.d.).

Rivière, J., *My Musical Life and Recollections* (1893).

Scholes, P. (ed.), *The Mirror of Music 1844–1944*, 2 vols. (1947).

Sonley Johnstone, W. H., *History of the First Cardiff Festival 1892* (London and Cardiff, n.d.).

Transactions of the Royal National Eisteddfod 1883 (Cardiff, 1884)

4. Articles

Anon., 'The Eisteddfod and popular music in Wales', *Y Cymmrodor*, 5 (1882).

Bennett, J., 'Music in Wales', *Trans. Cymmrodorion*, 1896–7.

Bennett, J., 'Music in Wales', *Young Wales*, 7 (1901).

Cumberland, G., 'Cyril Jenkins: musician and composer', *Wales*, 5 (Nov. 1913).

Evans, Harry, 'Music in Wales', *Young Wales*, 7 (1901).

Evans, Harry, 'Welsh choral singing', in T. Stephens (ed.), *Wales Today and Tomorrow* (Cardiff, 1908).

Griffiths, W. Ivander, 'Fy atgofion', *Y Cerddor* (1902).

Guion, D. M., 'Eisteddfod Gydgenedlaethol: a Welsh festival at the world's Columbian exposition', *Welsh Music*, 9, no. 2 (Winter 1989–90).

Jenkins, Cyril, 'Music in Wales', *Wales*, 3 (March 1913).

Jenkins, Cyril, 'Welsh music and modern life: breaking the shackles of Handel and Mendelssohn', *Wales*, 4 (May 1913).

Jenkins, Cyril, 'Dr Joseph Parry', *The Sackbut* (November 1921).

Jenkins, Cyril, 'Some aspects of Welsh music', *Y Cerddor Newydd* (August 1922).

Jenkins, D., 'The working class and music in Wales', *National Eisteddfod Association Reports 1882* (Wrexham, 1883).

Jones, M. O., 'Choral singing in Wales', *Fifteenth Report of the National Eisteddfod Association Llanelly 1895* (Cardiff, 1896).

Jones, M. O., 'The culture of music amongst the masses in Wales', in T. Stephens (ed.), *Wales Today and Tomorrow* (1908).

Lloyd, C. F., 'The present state of music in Wales', *Trans. Liverpool Welsh National Society*, 8 (1892–3).

Parry, Joseph, 'A musical college for Wales', *National Eisteddfod Association Reports 1882* (Wrexham, 1883).

Rees, J. T., 'Music in the Land of Song', in T. Stephens (ed.), *Wales Today and Tomorrow* (1908).

Rogers, R., 'Choral training in Wales', *Sixth Annual Report of the National Eisteddfod Caernarfon 1886* (Cardiff, 1887).

Samuel, W. T., 'Wales and the tonic sol-fa system', *Fourteenth Report of the National Eisteddfod Caernarfon 1894* (Cardiff, 1895).

Thomas, John, 'The national music of Wales', *Y Cymmrodorion*, 2 (1878).

Thomas, John, 'Music and musicians as relating to Wales', *Trans. Liverpool Welsh National Society*, 1 (1885–6).

B. Secondary Sources

1. Books

(Place of publication London unless otherwise stated)

Allsobrook, D. I., *Music for Wales: Walford Davies and the National Council of Music 1918–41* (Cardiff, 1992).

Bailey, C., *Hugh Percy Allen* (Oxford, 1948).

Baker, R. A., *Marie Lloyd: Queen of the Music Halls* (1990).

Bantock, M., *Granville Bantock: A Personal Portrait* (1972)

Berry, D., *Wales and Cinema: The First Hundred Years* (Cardiff, 1994).

Bradley, I., *Abide with Me: The World of Victorian Hymns* (1997).

Charlton, P., *John Stainer and the Musical Life of Victorian Britain* (Newton Abbot, 1984).

Cleaver, E., *Musicians of Wales*, trans. Eirian Lloyd Jones (Cardiff, 1968).

Colles, H. C., *Walford Davies* (Oxford, 1944).

Côr Mawr Caradog Centenary Festival Brochure (Aberdare, 1972).

Crossick, G. and Haupt, H. G., *The Petite-Bourgeoisie in Europe 1780–1914* (1995).

Crossley-Holland, P. (ed.), *Music in Wales* (1948).

Cumberland, G., *Written in Friendship* (1923).

Davies, D. L., *A History of Cwmaman Institute 1866–1993* (Aberdare, 1995).

Davies, M. Ffrangcon, *David Ffrangcon Davies: His Life and Work* (1938).

Edwards, E. E., *Echoes of Rhymney* (Risca, 1974).

Edwards, H. T., *Gŵyl Gwalia* (Llandysul, 1980).

Edwards, H. T., *Eisteddfod Ffair y Byd Chicago 1893* (Llandysul, 1990).

Edwards, O. T., *Joseph Parry 1841–1903* (Cardiff, 1970).

Ehrlich, C., *The Music Profession in Britain since the Eighteenth Century* (Oxford, 1985).

Ellis, E. L., *The University College of Wales, Aberystwyth 1872–1972* (Cardiff, 1972).

Evans, E., *Cofiant John Thomas, Llanwrtyd* (Caernarfon, 1926).

Evans, E. K., *Cofiant David Emlyn Evans* (Carmarthen, 1919).

Evans, T. L., *Y Cathedral Anghydffurfiol Cymraeg* (Swansea, 1972).

Evans, W. L. and Bodger, W., *Pontnewydd Male Choir: A History 1904–79* (Cwmbrân, 1979).

Foreman, L., *Music in England 1885–1920* (1994).

Graham, J., *A Century of Welsh Music* (1923).

Griffith, R. D., *Hanes Canu Cynulleidfaol Cymru* (Cardiff, 1948).

Griffith, W., *The Welsh* (Harmondsworth, 1950).

Herbert, T. (ed.), *Bands: The Brass Band Movement in the Nineteenth and Twentieth Centuries* (Milton Keynes, 1992).

Hughes, H. J. (ed.), *Gŵr wrth Gerdd: John Hughes 1896–1968,* (Llandysul, 1973).

Jacobs, A. (ed.), *Choral Music* (Harmondsworth, 1963).

Jones, A., *Welsh Chapels* (Stroud, 1996).

Jones, Daniel, *Music in Wales: Annual Lecture of the BBC in Wales 1961* (Cardiff, 1961).

Jones, E., *Côr Meibion y Penrhyn: Ddoe a Heddiw* (Denbigh, 1984).

Jones, Ifano, *Bywyd a Gwaith W.T. Samuel* (Llanuwchllyn, 1920).

Jones, I. G., *Communities* (Llandysul, 1987).

Jones, I. Wynne, *Llandudno, Queen of the Welsh Resorts* (Cardiff, 1975).

Jones, J. H. (ed.), *Er Côf am yr Athro David Jenkins gan naw o'i Gydnabod* (Liverpool, 1935).

Kennedy, M., *Portrait of Elgar*, 2nd edn (Oxford, 1982).

Lambert, W., *Drink and Sobriety in Victorian Wales c. 1820-c. 1895* (Cardiff, 1983).

Lewis, D. H., *Cofiant J. T. Rees* (Llandysul, 1955).

Lewis, E. D., *The Rhondda Valleys* (1959).

Lewis, Idris, *Cerddoriaeth yng Nghymru* (Cardiff, 1948).

Lidtke, V. L., *The Alternative Culture: Socialist Labour in Imperial Germany* (Oxford, 1985).

Lloyd, C. F., *Cofiant John Ambrose Lloyd* (Wrexham, 1921).

Luff, A., *Welsh Hymns and Their Tunes* (1990).

Mackerness, E., *A Social History of English Music* (1964).

Mellers, W., *Music and Society* (1946).

Moore, J. N., *Edward Elgar: A Creative Life* (Oxford, 1984).

Morgan, P., *The Eighteenth-Century Renaissance* (Swansea, 1981).

Morgan, T. J., *Diwylliant Gwerin ac Ysgrifau Eraill* (Llandysul, 1972).

Morgans, D., *Music and Musicians of Merthyr and District* (Merthyr, 1922).

Musgrave, M., *The Musical Life of the Crystal Palace* (Cambridge, 1995).

Nettel, R., *Music in the Five Towns 1840–1914* (Oxford, 1944).

Pearsall, R., *Victorian Popular Music* (Newton Abbot, 1973).

Pearsall, R., *Edwardian Popular Music* (Newton Abbot, 1975).

Price, C., *The Professional Theatre in Wales* (Swansea, 1984).

Rainbow, B., *The Choral Revival in the Anglican Church* (1970).

Raynor, H., *Music and Society since 1815* (1976).

Reid, C., *Malcolm Sargent* (1968).

Rhys, D., *Joseph Parry: Bachgen Bach o Ferthyr* (Cardiff, 1998).

Russell, D., *Popular Music in England 1840–1914: A Social History* (Manchester, 1987).

Russell, J. F. and Elliott, J. H., *The Brass Band Movement* (1936).

Sayers, W. C. Berwick, *Samuel Coleridge-Taylor: Musician*, 2nd edn (1927).

Stradling, R. and Hughes, M., *The English Musical Renaissance, 1860–1940* (1993).

Taylor, A. R., *Brass Bands* (1979).

Temperley, N. (ed.), *The Athlone History of Music in Britain: vol. 5, The Romantic Age 1800–1914* (1981).

Thomas, W. Vaughan, *Madly in All Directions*, 2nd edn (Carmarthen, 1988).

Walvin, J., *Leisure and Society 1830–1950* (1978).

Weber, W., *Music and the Middle Class: The Social Structure of Concert Life in London, Paris and Vienna* (1975).

Williams, A. Tudno, *E. T. Davies* (Denbigh, 1981).

Williams, C., *Democratic Rhondda: Politics and Society, 1885–1951* (Cardiff, 1996).

Williams, G. A., *The Merthyr Rising* (1978).

Williams, H., *Taro Tant* (Denbigh, 1994).

Williams, Islwyn, *William David Clee a'r Côr Mawr Ystalyfera* (Llandybïe, 1955).

Wood, H., *My Life of Music* (1938).

Young, P. M., *A History of British Music* (1967).

Young, P. M., *The Choral Tradition* (1962).

Young, P. M., *The Oratorios of Handel* (1959).

2. Articles

Allsobrook, D., 'The Cardiff Festival one hundred years ago', *Welsh Music*, 9, no. 4, (Winter 1991–2).

Ambrose, G. P., 'The Aberdare background to the South Wales Choral Union', *Glamorgan Historian*, 9 (1980).

Arnold, R., 'The pubs, clubs and breweries of Aberdare', *Old Aberdare*, 2 (1982).

Bradley, Ian, 'Changing the Tune', *History Today* (July 1992).

Croll, A., 'From bar-stool to choir-stall: music and morality in late-nineteenth-century Merthyr', *Llafur*, 6, no. 1 (1992).

Cunningham, H., 'Leisure', in Benson, J. (ed.), *The Working Class in England, 1875–1914* (1985).

Davies, John H., 'Rhondda choral music in Victorian times', in Hopkins, K. (ed.), *Rhondda Past and Future* (Ferndale, 1975).

Davies, L., 'Towards an authentic Celtic voice in music: the life and work of David Vaughan Thomas (1873–1934)', *Welsh Music History*, 2 (1997).

Davies, L., 'Golwg ar ddiwylliant cerddorol Dyffryn Aman, 1910–1922', in Edwards, H. T. (ed.), *Cwm Aman* (Llandysul, 1996).

Davies, T. Alun, 'The Crystal Palace Challenge Trophy', *Welsh Music*, 4, no. 1 (Spring 1972).

Dowe, D., 'The workingmen's choral movement in Germany before the First World War', *Journal of Contemporary History*, 13 (April 1978).

Ellis, O., 'Welsh music: history and fancy', *Trans. Cymmrodorion*, 1974.

Edwards, H. Teifi, 'Y gân a ganai Morlais', in Edwards, *Codi'r Hen Wlad yn ei Hôl* (Llandysul, 1989).

Edwards, O. T., 'Music in Wales', in Jones, R. Brinley (ed.), *Anatomy of Wales* (Peterston-super-Ely, 1972).

Griffiths, R., 'Alaw Ddu: o'r pwll i'r gân', *Y Casglwr*, August 1988.

Griffiths, R., 'Musical life in the nineteenth century', in P. Morgan (ed.), *Glamorgan County History*, vol. 6 (Cardiff, 1988).

Griffiths, R., 'Gwlad y gân: y traddodiad cerddorol yn oes Victoria', *Côf Cenedl*, 8 (1993).

Griffiths, R., 'Dau gôr', in Edwards, H. T. (ed.), *Cwm Tawe* (Llandysul, 1993).

Griffiths, R., 'John Hughes (1896–1968), Dolgellau: trem ar ei fywyd a'i waith', *Journal of the Merioneth Historical Society*, 13 (1996).

Griffiths, R., 'Y gymanfa ganu: ei gwreiddiau a'i natur', *Bwletin Cymdeithas Emynau Cymru*, 2, 9 (1986–7).

Griffiths, R., 'Welsh chapel music: the making of a tradition', *Journal of Welsh Ecclesiastical History*, 6 (1989).

Griffiths, R., 'Y gân orchfygol', in Edwards, H. T. (ed.), *Cwm Rhondda* (Llandysul, 1995).

Harrison, B., 'Religion and recreation in nineteenth-century England', *Past and Present*, 38 (1967).

Herbert, T., ' "A softening influence": R. T. Crawshay and the Cyfarthfa Band', *Merthyr Historian*, 5 (1992).

Jones, B., 'Daniel Protheroe, Haydn Evans and Welsh choral rivalry in late-nineteenth century Scranton, Pennsylvania', *Welsh Music*, 9, no. 3 (Spring 1991).

Jones, Glynne, 'The end of the "Cartrefle Dynasty" ', *Welsh Music*, 3, no. 6 (Spring 1970).

Jones, Glynne, 'Harry Evans (1873–1914)', *Welsh Music*, 4, no. 5 (Winter 1973/4).

[Jones, Revd. R], 'A musical scholarship for Wales', *Y Cymmrodor*, 1 (1877).

Lewis, D. H., 'Cerddoriaeth yng Nghymru yn y bedwaredd ganrif ar bymtheg', *Y Genhinen* (Spring 1951).

Lewis, E. D. and Jones, I. G., 'Capel y Cymer', *Morgannwg*, 25 (1981).

Lewis, G. H., 'The Welsh choral tradition: fact and myth', *Welsh Music*, 5, no. 4 (Winter 1976–7).

Morgan, Rh., 'Sain, cerdd a chân ym Mrynaman', in Edwards, H. T. (ed.), *Cwm Aman* (Llandysul, 1995).

Morgan, T. J., 'Peasant culture in the Swansea Valley', *Glamorgan Historian*, 9 (1980).

Nettel, R., 'The influence of the Industrial Revolution on English music', *Proceedings of the Royal Musical Association*, 72 (1946).

P[owell], D., 'A brief history of the Treorky Male Voice Choir 1883–1897', *Excelsior: The Voice of the Treorchy Male Choir 1994* (Treorchy, 1994)

Price, W. W., 'Y gymanfa ganu gyntaf', *Yr Ymofynnydd* (June 1957).

Rainbow, B., 'The rise of popular music education in nineteenth-century England', *Victorian Studies*, 30, 1 (Autumn 1986).

Rees, A. J. Heward, 'Henry Brinley Richards (1817–1885): a nineteenth-century propagandist for Welsh music', *Welsh Music History*, 2 (1997).

Rees, A. J. Heward, ' "Songs of Wales": a brief centenary note', *Welsh Music*, 4, no. 5 (Winter 1973–4).

Roberts, C. A., 'Pencerdd Gwalia', in Edwards, H. T. (ed.), *Llynfi ac Afan, Garw ac Ogwr* (Llandysul, 1998).

Roberts, L. J., 'The outlook for music in Wales', *Welsh Outlook* (March 1920).

[Roberts, R. Gwylfa], 'Tref y Gân - Dowlais', *Y Dysgedydd* (April 1932).

Russell, D., 'Provincial concerts in England 1865–1914: a case-study of Bradford', *Journal of the Royal Musical Association* (Spring 1989).

Russell, D., 'The "social history" of popular music: a label without a cause?', *Popular Music*, 12 (1993).

Smith, D., 'Tonypandy 1910: definitions of community', *Past and Present*, 87 (1980).

Stead, P., 'Amateurs and professionals in the cultures of Wales', in Jenkins, G. H. and Smith, J. B. (eds), *Politics and Society in Wales, 1840–1922: Essays in Honour of Ieuan Gwynedd Jones* (Cardiff, 1988).

Temperley, N., 'The Lost Chord', *Victorian Studies*, 30, 1 (Autumn 1986).

Thomas, A. F. Leighton, 'Random thoughts on Brinley Richards', *Anglo-Welsh Review* (Winter 1967).

Thomas, J. Hugh, 'Cerddoriaeth yn Abertawe', in Williams, I. M. (ed.), *Abertawe a'r Cylch* (Llandybïe, 1982).

Thomas, J. Hugh, 'Music', in Griffiths, R. A. (ed.), *The City of Swansea: Challenge and Change* (Swansea, 1992).

Tusler, A. L., 'The Three Valleys Festival', *Welsh Music*, 7, no. 6 (Spring 1984).

Weber, W., 'Artisans in [the] concert life of mid-nineteenth-century London and Paris', *Journal of Contemporary History*, 13 (April 1978).

Williams, H., 'Brass bands, jazz bands, choirs: aspects of music in Merthyr', *Merthyr Historian*, 3 (1980).

Williams, Huw, 'Canmlwyddiant "Blodwen" ', *Welsh Music*, 5, no. 10 (Winter 1978–9).

Williams, Huw, 'Cofio Ieuan Gwyllt', *Bwletin Cymdeithas Emynau Cymru* (1978).

Williams, Huw, 'Rhai o gymwynasau Ieuan Gwyllt', *Welsh Music*, 5, no. 7 (Winter 1977–8).

Williams, Huw, 'William Griffiths (Ivander) 1830–1910', *Welsh Music*, 7, no. 8 (Autumn/ Winter 1984–5).

'Work and leisure in industrial society: conference report', *Past and Present*, 30 (1965).

3. Works of Reference

Dictionary of Welsh Biography (1959).

Y Bywgraffiadur Cymreig 1941–1950 (1970).

Y Bywgraffiadur Cymreig 1951–1970 (1997).

Jones, M. O., *Bywgraffiaeth Cerddorion Cymreig* (Cardiff, 1890).

Price, W. W. (ed.), *Biographical Index*, 30 vols. (NLW, Aberystwyth).

Sadie, S. (ed.), *The New Grove Dictionary of Music and Musicians*, 20 vols. (1980).

Stephens, M. (ed.), *Companion to the Literature of Wales*, 2nd edn (Cardiff, 1998).

Williams, Huw, *Tonau a'u Hawduron* (Caernarfon, 1967).

Williams, Huw, *Rhagor am Donau a'u Hawduron* (Caernarfon, 1969).

Williams, Huw, *Canu'r Bobol* (Denbigh, 1978).

4. Theses

Barclay, M., 'Aberdare 1880–1914: class and community'. MA, University of Wales, Cardiff, 1985.

Croll, A. J., 'Civilising the urban: popular culture, public space, and urban meaning, Merthyr *c.*1870–1914'. Ph.D., University of Wales, Cardiff, 1997.

Davies, J. M., 'Twf a datblygiad y gerddorfa yng Nghymru'. MA, University of Wales, Bangor, 1987.

Evans, P. A., 'D. Christmas Williams'. MA, University of Wales, Aberystwyth, 1981.

Griffiths, W. R. M., 'Cyhoeddi cerddoriaeth yng Nghymru yn y cyfnod 1860–1914'. Ph.D., University of Wales, Aberystwyth, 1991.

Pritchard, B. W., 'The music festival and the choral society in England in the eighteenth and nineteenth centuries: a social history'. Ph.D., University of Birmingham, 1967–8.

Rhys, D., 'Joseph Parry: ei fywyd a'i waith'. Ph.D., University of Wales, Bangor, 1986.

Russell, D., 'The popular musical societies of the Yorkshire textile district 1850–1914'. D.Phil., University of York, 1979.

Wiltshire, C. R., 'The British male voice choir: a history and contemporary assessment'. Ph.D., University of London (Goldsmith's College), 1993.

Index

&